By Stephanie

VIRTUAL
LAW PRACTICE
How to Deliver Legal Services Online

ABA **LawPracticeManagementSection**
MARKETING · MANAGEMENT · TECHNOLOGY · FINANCE

Commitment to Quality: The Law Practice Management Section is committed to quality in our publications. Our authors are experienced practitioners in their fields. Prior to publication, the contents of all our books are rigorously reviewed by experts to ensure the highest quality product and presentation. Because we are committed to serving our readers' needs, we welcome your feedback on how we can improve future editions of this book.

Cover design by RIPE Creative, Inc.

Nothing contained in this book is to be considered as the rendering of legal advice for specific cases, and readers are responsible for obtaining such advice from their own legal counsel. This book and any forms and agreements herein are intended for educational and informational purposes only.

The products and services mentioned in this publication are under or may be under trademark or service mark protection. Product and service names and terms are used throughout only in an editorial fashion, to the benefit of the product manufacturer or service provider, with no intention of infringement. Use of a product or service name or term in this publication should not be regarded as affecting the validity of any trademark or service mark.

The Law Practice Management Section, American Bar Association, offers an educational program for lawyers in practice. Books and other materials are published in furtherance of that program. Authors and editors of publications may express their own legal interpretations and opinions, which are not necessarily those of either the American Bar Association or the Law Practice Management Section unless adopted pursuant to the bylaws of the Association. The opinions expressed do not reflect in any way a position of the Section or the American Bar Association.

Printed in the United States of America.

12 11 10   5 4 3 2 1

Library of Congress Cataloging-in-Publication Data

Kimbro, Stephanie L.
    Virtual law practice : how to deliver legal services online / by Stephanie L. Kimbro.
        p. cm.
    Includes index.
    ISBN 978-1-60442-828-5
  1. Law offices—United States—Automation. 2. Internet in legal services—United States. 3. Legal services—Internet marketing—United States. 4. Practice of law—United States. I. Title.
    KF320.A9K56 2010
    347.73002854678—dc22

                                                                        2010035985

Discounts are available for books ordered in bulk. Special consideration is given to state bars, CLE programs, and other bar-related organizations. Inquire at Book Publishing, American Bar Association, 321 N. Clark Street, Chicago, Illinois 60654.

Dedication

To BEN, THE MASTERMIND who programmed my virtual law office and encourages my academic endeavors. To my children, Madeleine and William, for motivating me to think creatively. To my parents, for putting a computer in my hands at a young age, supporting my education, and teaching me to use my imagination. To my brother, for hours spent together in front of the computer when we were kids and for his encouragement today.

Contents

About the Author

Stephanie Kimbro

Stephanie Kimbro, Esq., MA, JD, has operated a Web-based virtual law office in North Carolina since 2006 and delivers estate planning and small-business legal services to clients online. She is the recipient of the 2009 ABA Keane Award for Excellence in eLawyering and has won the *Wilmington Parent Magazine* Family Favorite Attorney Award four years in a row for her virtual law office. She is the cofounder of Virtual Law Office Technology, LLC (VLOTech), which was acquired by Total Attorneys in the fall of 2009. In addition to her virtual law practice, Ms. Kimbro is a consultant and technology evangelist providing assistance to other legal professionals interested in the online delivery of legal services. Ms. Kimbro writes about the ethics and technology issues of delivering legal services online on her blog, VirtualLawPractice.org. She has presented continuing legal education (CLE) courses on virtual law practice for the American Bar Association (ABA) and the North Carolina and South Carolina Bar Associations, and she teaches a course on virtual law practice as a faculty member of Solo Practice University, a Web-based legal education community. Ms. Kimbro serves on the board of the Legal Services National Technology Assistance Project (LSNTAP) and is a member of the ABA eLawyering Task Force, the North Carolina Bar Association (NCBA) Law Practice Management (LPM) Council and NCBA Technology Advisory Committee. She lives in Wilmington, NC, by the beach with her husband and two children.

Acknowledgments

I WOULD LIKE TO thank the Publishing Board of the ABA Law Practice Management Section, especially Timothy Johnson, Executive Editor, Denise Constantine, Book Production Manager, and Trish Cleary, Marketing Director, of the ABA LPM Publications staff for guiding me through the publication process. I would also like to thank the individuals who took the time to review the manuscript. Burgess Allison, Project Manager for the book, Sharon Nelson, Richard Granat, and Art Garwin all provided helpful feedback and guidance. Thank you also to Kathryn Thompson, research counsel for EthicSearch, a service of the ABA Center for Professional Responsibility, for sending me down the right path in my search of the rules and regulations pertaining to virtual law practice.

There are many attorneys who over the years have pioneered in elawyering and virtual law practice. I am grateful for the risks they took in taking the path less traveled and for the insights of their collective experiences. Thank you to the following individuals for providing guidance, whether by responding to my interview questions for the book or through their work on the advancement of innovation in technology to deliver legal services online: Denise Annunciata, Nicole Black, Dawn Elaine Bowie, Blair Janis, Susan Cartier Liebel, Jared D. Correia, Carolyn Elefant, Richard Furguson, Jordan Furlong, Robert Grossbart, Bernardo Granwehr, Tina Marie Hilton, Laurie Mapp, Erik Mazzone, Darryl Mountain, Sharon Nelson, Meaghan Olson, Larry Port, Charlene Quincey, Ellyn Rosen, Dave Ryan, Kathryn Sheehan, Ronald Staudt, Camille Stell, and Mark Williams.

I am also grateful to the members of the ABA eLawyering Task Force, in particular the co-chairs, Marc Lauritsen and Richard Granat, for their encouragement and for sharing their knowledge and enthusiasm about future innovations in law practice management.

CHAPTER ONE

Virtual Law
Practice Basics

Introduction

The goal of this book is to provide detailed information on how to responsibly deliver legal services online to your clients and how to successfully operate a virtual law office. In addition to operating my own virtual law office, I have the privilege to work with innovators in the field of eLawyering and with other lawyers enjoying their own virtual law practices. I've combined my experience with state-by-state research of the different rules of professional responsibility and ethics and advisory opinions related to this topic. Also included are tips and guidance from experts in the legal and IT professions along with case studies from other lawyers delivering legal services online.

ELawyering and using technology to practice law are not new concepts. Many lawyers and law firms have been using technology to provide legal services to clients and communicate with other legal professionals since it was feasible to do so. What has changed is the growing demand by the general public for the use of technology to receive legal services specifically through the use of the Internet. The continued push toward the delivery of legal services online affects the legal profession across the board, from solos to large law firms, and affects our clients' expectations. Mainstream legal professionals who have preferred to stick with more traditional law practice methods can no longer turn a blind eye to this change if they wish to remain competitive.

Our clients are going online to seek out legal professionals and to find ways to solve their legal needs through the Internet. The continuing trend is toward e-commerce transactions as consumers shop, bank, conduct business, and pay their credit cards and taxes online.[1] While it is not clear how many prospective clients are choosing online legal services over traditional law firms, we do know that Legal Zoom, Inc. has been serving thousands across the nation over the past few years and has generated millions in revenue from the sale of form-generated legal documents.[2] Online demand for legal services and the number of people using the Internet to transact business is surging.[3]

Online companies such as Legal Zoom, Inc., Nolo, Inc., and USLegal, when available for specific areas of law, are being turned to by the public and individuals who may otherwise have consulted with a lawyer in person. The problem with these online legal services is that they are not reviewed by a lawyer and therefore may not provide the best legal guidance even though they are more affordable and easy to access online.[4] Members of the public are also turning to "do it yourself" legal kits or forms purchased online or in bookstores. In some cases, they are searching for legal documents online and then cutting and pasting together their own versions, attempting to solve their own legal needs. The motivation for using these methods is clearly an issue of access and affordability.

---

[1] According to Forrester, e-commerce will continue to grow as factors including ease of accessibility and changing demographics of online users will help support this growth. By 2013, the estimated US online retail sales will reach $299 billion at a compound annual growth rate (CAGR) of 10% over a five-year forecast period. *US Online Retail Forecast, 2008-2013*, Evans, Patti Freeman, updated March 4, 2009, Forrester Research, Inc. See also, *US Ecommerce Growth to Pick up In 2010, But Hit Mature Stride, Bloomberg BusinessWeek* Blog (February 2, 2009). **http://www.businessweek .com/the_thread/the_thread/blogspotting/archives/2009/02/us_ecommerce_gr.html** (accessed May 27, 2010) providing a summary of the Forrester predictions for ecommerce over a five-year period.

[2] For example, in a petition to have a case removed from a court in Missouri to federal court, Legal Zoom states that it has served over 14,000 Missouri residents over five years which generated over $5,000.000 in sales. See IPWatchdog.com blog for links to the legal documents related to *Janson v. Legal Zoom, Inc.*, Western District of Missouri, December 18, 2009, **http://www.ipwatchdog .com/2010/02/09/legalzoom-sued-in-class-action-for-unauthorized-law-practice/id=8816/** (accessed May 27, 2010).

[3] During March, 2010—one month alone—an estimated 535,000 people in the US searched online seeking legal solutions through the Legal Zoom website and an estimated 164,000 people in the US searched for legal services through the USLegal website. See Quantcast audience statistics related to websites providing online legal services. The number of duplicate people searching is not quantified. **http://www.quantcast.com**. (accessed May 27, 2010).

[4] Nolo, Inc., sells blank legal forms to individuals online, whereas LegalZoom prepares the documents for the clients through a document-assembly program online. USLegal provides both legal documents for sale and online document preparation. With both types of services, the customers do not communicate directly with a licensed lawyer and the product being sold does not go through individual lawyer review. See **www.legalzoom.com, www.nolo.com**, and **www.uslegal.com**.

Nonprofit form services created by legal aid organizations and some state court systems have begun to provide online solutions to the public's demand for access to affordable legal services.[5] For example, Law Help Interactive (**www.lawhelpinteractive.com**), powered by ProBono.net (**www.probono.net**), assists members of the public online with filling out legal forms.[6] A2J (Access to Justice), powered by the Center for Access to Justice and Technology (CAJT), in partnership with the Center for Computer-Assisted Legal Instruction (CALI), walks individuals through a set of interactive questions with an avatar to guide them to determine whether specific forms are appropriate for the individual's legal needs.[7] Some traditional law firms have also begun offering blank forms or interactive forms on their Web sites as a method of drawing in prospective clients.[8]

Web sites that connect members of the public with experts are also gaining popularity as different models are introduced online.[9] For example, members of the public registering on LawGuru.com are able to ask legal questions and receive counsel from lawyers registered on the site and licensed in their jurisdiction. A lawyer wishing to provide legal guidance through these sites must first answer a series of questions and provide proof that he or she is a licensed lawyer in the state in which he or she will be providing online guidance. Other "expert" sites may or may not verify that the individual providing legal guidance to the public is a licensed lawyer. Regardless of the method of delivery, the fact that these resources are growing in number and in demand by the public implies a significant gap in the market for affordable and convenient legal services. It also indicates an opportunity for the legal profession.

Virtual law practice provides a solution to the consumer need for access to justice and also meets the needs of our changing profession. It permits the public to retain the services of a lawyer without having to turn to less secure methods of solving their legal matters. More affordable pricing, convenience, and less intimidation are all factors that make the virtual law office appealing to a large segment of the lower- to middle-income

---

[5]For an analysis of the need for more accessible and affordable legal services in our country, see the Brennan Center for Justice at the New York University School of Law's Civil Justice Initiative, *The Economy and Civil Legal Services Analysis*, May 17, 2010 **http://www.brennancenter.org/ content/resource/the_economy_and_civil_legal_services/** (accessed May 27, 2010).

[6]See also the ABA Pro Se/Unbundling Resource Center's list of online self-help resources, at **www.abanet.org/legalservices/delivery/delunbundself.html**.

[7]Access to Justice (A2J): **www.a2jauthor.org/drupal**

[8]See, for example, the term-sheet generator on the Wison Sonsini Goodrich & Rosati firm Web site: **www.wsgr.com/wsgr/Display.aspx?SectionName=practice/termsheet.htm**

[9]See, for example, JustAnswer.com, at **www.justanswer.com**.

individuals in our country. Likewise, the benefits to the lawyer through streamlined legal work and a competitive advantage with secure online access make it a cost-effective solution for both solos and small firms to implement.

What Is a Virtual Law Practice?

A virtual law practice is a professional law practice that exists online through a secure portal and is accessible to both the client and the lawyer anywhere the parties may access the Internet. Legal services are delivered online using this method. The lawyers and their clients have the ability to securely discuss matters online, download and upload documents for review, create legal documents, and handle other business transactions related to the delivery of legal services in a secure digital environment. A virtual law practice has been referred to in the following ways: virtual law office (VLO), virtual law firm, Web-based law practice, or online law practice.

Virtual law practice and the delivery of online legal services are forms of eLawyering. ELawyering is defined by Marc Lauritsen, the cochair of the ABA's eLawyering Task Force, as

> All the ways in which lawyers can do their work using the Web and associated technologies. These include new ways to communicate and collaborate with clients, prospective clients and other lawyers, produce documents, settle disputes and manage legal knowledge. Think of a lawyering verb—interview, investigate, counsel, draft, advocate, analyze, negotiate, manage and so forth—and there are corresponding electronic tools and techniques.[10]

With future innovations in technology, additional eLawyering capabilities will evolve to expand the concept of virtual law practice and the delivery of online legal services.

What Is a Client Portal?

A client portal is the primary feature of the virtual law office that facilitates the delivery of legal services online. It contains a unique username

---

[10]*Law Practice* (January–February 2004): 36. See also Lauritsen's *The Lawyer's Guide to Working Smarter with Knowledge Tools* (Chicago: ABA, 2010), pp. 97–100.

FIGURE 1   This graphic illustrates the use of a client portal in a virtual law practice.

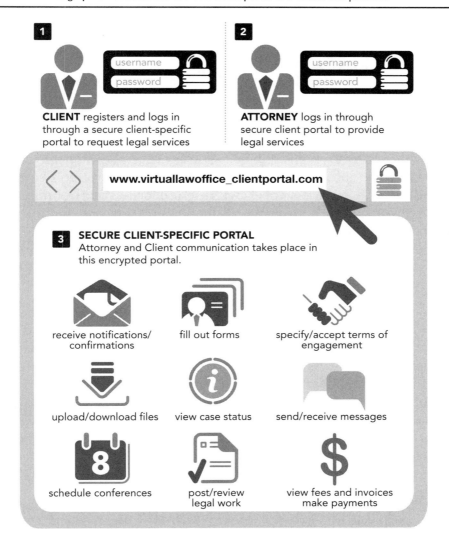

and password that the client uses to enter into his or her own secure account Web site within the lawyer's virtual law office. This client-specific portal where the client and lawyer interact is unique to virtual law practice and is the key to differentiating it from other Web-based services and companies offering legal documents to the public online. End-to-end encryption keeps the clients secure as they log in and work with the lawyer to receive legal services.

In some instances, this same portal may also be used by other lawyers related to the case who are not members of a virtual law office. Opposing counsel or an out-of-jurisdiction lawyer collaborating with the owner of the virtual law office may communicate securely and transfer documents through a case file on the back end of the virtual law office. While the definition, terminology, and features of virtual law practice will evolve with the technology, the client portal is the core feature that will remain out of necessity with each reincarnation.

What Is Not a Virtual Law Practice?

Any law practice, whether a solo or a large law firm, may implement eLawyering methods in their practice, and many do. However, a virtual law office is only one aspect of eLawyering and focuses on the online delivery of legal services to clients. It should not be dismissed as another use of cloud computing for law practice management, because there are unique issues in virtual law practice that extend beyond a discussion of cloud computing or software as a service (the primary method of cloud computing used) in law practice management. Accordingly, the technology, security, and ethics issues raised in virtual law practice are discussed in greater detail in this book.

It is also important to distinguish a professional virtual law practice from the many companies selling online legal forms without lawyer review and from the many new variations of law practice management or client development tools that involve Web-based technology. A virtual law practice is not an online Web site that sells legal documents without lawyer review. A virtual law practice provides direct and personal communication between a lawyer and a client rather than strictly form-generated, unbundled legal documents for sale to the public or single online task management.

Virtual law practice is also not a law firm Web site with an e-mail "contact us for a free quote" form for prospective clients. Communication by e-mail does not constitute a virtual law practice even if sent through a law firm's Web site. E-mail is limited as a method of transacting business and is typically unencrypted and therefore not a secure method of transmitting sensitive data.

A Virtual law practice is also not a rented physical office that may be shared with other professionals along with a receptionist service. Physical office space rented out to a lawyer for a monthly fee for the purpose of meeting with clients is often referred to as a "virtual" law office. While this arrangement allows the lawyer to work from a home office and meet with clients in a shared, remote office space, the arrangement does not use technology to operate the functions of a law office or provide an online interface to obtain and work with online clients.

Likewise, while virtual private networks (VPNs), extranets, and other services, such as GoToPC and LogMeIn, allow a lawyer to access the law office desktop remotely, this is also not a virtual law practice, as that technology is not being used to retain online clients and to deliver legal services online. For years, larger law firms have had client extranets. However, the extranets were not marketed to a prospective online client base and the legal services were not delivered using the technology to establish the attorney/client relationship and complete the delivery of legal services through to the payment and rendering of the final product by the lawyer. A virtual law practice has the ability to encompass the entire process of working with a client online from beginning to end.

The term *virtual law firm* has been popular in the news with the formation of Virtual Law Partners, Rimon Law Group, and FSB Legal Counsel—law firms that are made up of a conglomeration of lawyers that use technology to collaborate online while working remotely and reducing costs.[11] The difference between these larger law firms made up of lawyers working remotely and a virtual law office is the act of delivering legal services to clients online through a secure client portal. These larger law firms use a virtual infrastructure to centralize the management and administrative aspects of their practice and may use software applications piecemeal to communicate with each other and their clients remotely, but they do not specifically market themselves as delivering legal services online.

Virtual law practice is also not a law practice based in a virtual-reality world. Some lawyers and law firms have opened up law offices within virtual-reality worlds, such as Second Life. There is even a Second Life Bar Association with members of the legal profession meeting regularly to discuss issues related to virtual-reality world laws. CLEs and other presentations have also been held by legal professionals in Second Life for educational and professional credit. However, a virtual law office is not based in an online reality world. Some virtual law offices may advertise their services through the opening of a virtual-reality world law office, but at this time there are very few lawyers who are able to make this marketing effort result in paying online clients for their real-world practice. Virtual law

---

[11]Virtual Law Partners, **www.virtuallawpartners.com**; Rimon Law Group, **www.rimonlaw.com**; FSB Legal Counsel, **www.fsblegal.com**

practice is a law practice that is bound in the real world by the jurisdiction of the state bar in which the operating lawyer is licensed to practice law.

These distinctions are important because they affect the security and ethics concerns related to the use of the technology. They are also important because some state bar rules regarding unauthorized practice of law require an examination of whether the services being offered by the lawyer constitute the "practice" of law. Delivering legal services online to clients is the "practice" of law. Furthermore, the online delivery of legal services from start to finish requires a higher standard of care on the part of the lawyer operating a virtual law practice and demands close attention to compliance with the rules of professional responsibility that may not always apply to the structure and processes of a traditional law practice. When interpreting the state bar rules regarding virtual law practice, electronic communication, and unbundling legal services, it is important to have a solid understanding of the structure of the virtual law practice and what services will be provided to clients online.

Changing Technology

Given the rate at which technology evolves, the features of a virtual law practice will continue to expand to provide additional communication and security features for the legal professional beyond what currently may be imagined. However, the core function of a virtual law practice should remain the same—the ability to securely deliver legal services and work with clients and other legal professionals online through a secure online portal. Because of the rate of change in technology and in this area of law practice management, a Web site companion to the book has been set up at **www.virtuallawpracticebook.com** to provide updates to the Appendix.

What Are the Benefits of a Virtual Law Practice?

The benefits of operating a virtual law practice are going to differ based on what the practitioner hopes to accomplish with their practice. Some of the main benefits include the following, which will be discussed further:

- Lower overhead
- Eco-friendly, paperless, less office waste
- Greater work/life balance and flexibility

♦ Ability to expand client base across jurisdictions; competitive advantage

♦ Flexibility to transition between different phases in life and career to meet professional and personal needs

♦ Tap into a broader market of consumers seeking legal services

♦ Serve as an amenity for existing clients of a traditional law practice

♦ Added security of hosted backups and other cost-effective benefits of using software as a service (SaaS)

♦ Lessen malpractice risks through the use of technology to automate checks

♦ Streamline administrative features of a law practice to permit the lawyer to focus on the actual "practice" of law.

What Are the Risks of a Virtual Law Practice?

Many of the risks in operating a virtual law practice are related to either the security or the ethics and malpractice concerns. This book devotes entire chapters to address these topics in greater detail along with providing resources in the topical appendix for further research. Some of the risks that require consideration and mitigation before opening a virtual law office include the following:

♦ Security of the technology, including third-party control and storage of law office data

♦ Retention and return of law office data

♦ Confidentiality

♦ Competency of providing unbundled legal services

♦ Unauthorized practice of law in other jurisdictions

The risks and benefits of a virtual law office will depend on a number of factors, including the chosen management structure, the lawyer's practice areas, the regulations of the lawyer's state bar(s), the years of prior experience that the lawyer has in running a law practice, whether he or she has an existing client base to start with, and what the strategy and goals are for the virtual law practice.

CHAPTER TWO

Choose a Structure for Your Practice

THE FIRST STEP TO setting up a virtual law office is to find the resources from your state bar regarding virtual law practice and other forms of elawyering. Please review the appendix for state bar and other resources to get started. These resources might be in the form of ethics or advisory opinions or in the comments section of the professional rules and regulations for lawyer conduct published by your state bar. These resources may not use the term *virtual law practice* but may relate to the unbundling of legal services, the delivery of legal services using technology, lawyer Web sites, or online advertising. Other terms to search for when researching virtual law practice might include the keywords *Web site, online, electronic, Internet* with *law practice management.*

If you will be practicing in multiple jurisdictions, check with the resources of each state bar in which you will be practicing. If there are no related opinions, you may choose to contact the state bar directly to seek approval for the form of virtual practice you are planning. In addition, the eLawyering Task Force of the ABA's Law Practice Management Section has issued a draft document entitled "Suggested Minimum Requirements for Law Firms Delivering Legal Services Online," which lists the minimum standards for virtual law practice.[1] Once approved, this document will serve as a reference for state bars that have not previously addressed this form of law practice management.

Another preliminary step in choosing the structure of your virtual law practice is to find a malpractice insurance carrier and understand how the

---

[1]October 15, 2009. **http://meetings.abanet.org/webupload/commupload/EP024500/related resources/Minimum_Requirements_for_Lawyers_2009_10_24.pdf** (accessed March 4, 2010).

structure you have chosen will fit in with the carrier's policies. Some carriers may provide discounted rates due to the use of the virtual law practice technology to reduce malpractice risks. Provide them with a list of the malpractice checks built into the systems you use, and emphasize how the use of the technology may, in some instances, be more reliable at preventing malpractice than those methods relied upon in a traditional law practice. For example, the technology requires that certain tasks are completed, such as the conflict of interest check and completion of the formal engagement process, before permitting the attorney to proceed in the case rather than relying on office staff or members of the firm to ensure that all malpractice checks have been handled before the attorney begins work on a case. Be ready to provide the carrier with a walkthrough or explanation of your chosen virtual law practice structure as well as samples of your terms and conditions, disclaimers, and any form of engagement or retainer agreement that you will be using to establish the attorney-client relationship online. Key points to emphasize in your discussion with the carrier include jurisdiction checks to avoid unauthorized practice of law (UPL), conflict of interest checks for online as well as offline clients, and end-to-end encryption to protect client confidences. Refer to the section on obtaining malpractice insurance for more discussion on this topic (see pages 134–136).

Because there are different forms of virtual law practice to choose from, determine the structure for your practice before gathering approvals from your state bar or obtaining a malpractice insurance policy. To do this, you should have a solid understanding of what you are trying to accomplish with your practice in terms of revenue generation, client development, practice management, and creating a better work/life balance for yourself. Consider the following questions to assist in your planning:

1. Will you be providing unbundled legal services to online clients without full-service representation?

2. Will you be working with an existing client base and offering full-service representation as well as online representation?

3. Will your practice have a combination of online clients and in-person clients, both needing access to the VLO?

4. Do you want to provide strictly transactional legal services, such as wills, advance directives, and small-business setup documents?

5. Do you want to communicate with clients online through more interactive discussions, such as real time or IM chat, and provide forms of legal advice in addition to legal document drafting?

6. Will your firm be a multijurisdictional solo practice, or will you be working with other lawyers online to combine resources across jurisdictions?

7. What law practice management tools are most critical for your practice to take online?

8. What administrative tasks would you need to handle through your VLO?

9. Will you need to integrate your existing law office software into the VLO or have a way to synchronize or export from one system to another?

10. Would you like to collaborate with other lawyers or virtual assistants online through your VLO, or will access be limited to lawyers and online clients?

Case Study: From a Traditional Solo Practice to a Web-Based Practice
Dawn Elaine Bowie, Esq.,

*Dawn Elaine Bowie, Esq. is the principal of the Law Offices of Dawn Elaine Bowie, P.C., t/a Maryland Family Law Firm. (**www.marylandfamily lawfirm.com**) She originally began her practice with a traditional brick and mortar law office and met with clients in person and communicated with them through phone and e-mail. After deciding to open a virtual law office, Dawn explained to her clients that she would now only communicate with them through her secure virtual law office, because sending e-mail that was not encrypted was not in the clients' best interests and was not secure. Her clients registered on her virtual law office, and her practice has grown to pull in additional online clients. After almost nine months of practicing law online, she retained a virtual paralegal to assist her in administrative functions of working on her virtual law office.*

Technology: I have a Mac office. My primary computer is an iMac, and I also have a MacBook Pro. Both systems run on OSX 10.6.2. My iMac is partitioned to let me use a single software application necessary to my work in family law (a program that comprises a child-support guidelines calculator). I use Virtual Law Office Technology, LLC, to practice law online with my full-service clients.

Structure of your virtual law office: I have a home office and a geographic (brick and mortar) virtual office. When needed, I can meet with clients and host depositions or meetings at my geographic virtual office for an hourly fee. My mail is delivered to my geographic virtual office and my name is listed in the lobby of that address. Clients do not meet with me in my home office, nor do I routinely have business mail delivered to my home office. However, most of the "nuts and bolts" work of my practice takes place in my home office.

Launch date: February 2009

Why did you decide to open a virtual law practice?

I am working on another line of business that was the initial motivation for my use of a virtual law practice. That line of business is still under development, but it was taking far longer than I originally anticipated to get my new line of business up and running, and when I realized the benefit having a virtual practice could offer my existing clients, I decided to use it for them first. It is a perfect complement to having a home office. My clients love the security and accessibility it provides them and are very happy with this added benefit.

What are the benefits you have seen from this form of law practice?

For me: I have been able to save substantial time and money with potential client inquiries. Before I opened my virtual law office, I spent far too long listening to potential clients in telephone conversation trying to decide if they had a case that was worth an initial office conference. I charge for initial office conferences as a litmus test to determine whether a potential client is willing to pay for my services. Family cases in my jurisdiction can be very costly, and too often potential clients think that they can use an initial office consultation either to get the information they think they can use to represent themselves or simply to try to persuade me that because they have a "just cause" I should reduce or even eliminate the need for them to pay me. So before I started using a virtual law office, not only was I spending far too much time listening to and screening potential clients, but all too often a client would arrive at the initial office conference and "forget" to pay me.

Since opening my virtual law office, I have developed a process that has virtually eliminated the wasted time and effort of responding to clients who are either not serious about retaining me or don't have the money to do so.

The other benefit using Virtual Law Office Technology has had for my practice is that I am freed from the constant din of e-mails from clients. Clients are advised that I check the virtual law office not more than twice a day, absent an emergency. Clients whose cases involve urgent issues or potential emergencies have (prior to my use of the new telephone lines) been given my direct line and sometimes my mobile phone number, although even that will not be necessary using the new telephone lines. If there is an urgent issue, clients can contact me by telephone. Otherwise, I am not compelled to answer electronic mail messages as they come in. Using the technology also ensures that all client communications are easily accessible. It has made it possible for me to ensure that communications with difficult or demanding clients are documented and my responses stored in real time, as they occur, rather than requiring me to write file memoranda or letters.

For the clients: Using Virtual Law Office Technology permits me to ensure that, at a minimum, all client communications, as well as all incoming and outgoing correspondences, court filings, discovery and other documents that have a direct bearing on the client's case, are always accessible to the client whenever the client needs to access it. It also ensures that lawyer work-product information is only available to the client at my discretion.

Using a virtual law office permits me to provide clients with a secure environment with which to communicate with me. There is never any risk that a client's e-mail address will be accessed by a social networking site or, worse, that the client's computer will be infected with a virus carried by an e-mail I may send. The virtual law office allows clients to send me sensitive documents without fear that the documents might be accessed by anyone else. If a client agrees to a telephone appointment, it also allows us to discuss the documents they (or I) have sent while looking at them.

How long did it take for your practice to turn a profit?

I cleared a lot of money my first year in practice as a solo. I cleared more the second year. And more the third year, and the fourth. The fifth was about even with the fourth, as I lost my partner that year. The sixth was better than the fourth and fifth. The seventh (the year I opened my virtual law office) was better than any of them. I'm moving into the eighth, possibly taking on a partner, and I expect it to be better than the first seven by a good margin.

How much did you initially invest in marketing or advertising your virtual law practice?

Not much.

What methods do you use to market your virtual law practice?

I talk about it, and it is featured on my Web site.

Did you have any problem obtaining malpractice insurance for your virtual law practice?

No. Not with respect to either manner in which I use it or plan to use it.

Are there any concerns that you have with your virtual law practice as a form of law practice management?

No. It does require a couple of things that are different. First, I have to be really scrupulous about keeping the database of parties up-to-date. That isn't hard, but it has to be done religiously, and there are still some very early parties, opposing parties, and counsel that need to be [imported] (from my years in practicing with another firm).

Second, I've found it is very important to think carefully about what has to be communicated to potential clients, especially with regard to transactions involving payment of initial office conference fees and the establishment [of the attorney/client relationship](or lack of such) with potential clients. In addition, I make it a point to be sure clients are advised about how the system works, what they need to do to use it efficiently, and so on. I also have had to develop procedures for advising potential clients who don't respond after registering in the virtual law office that I intend to delete their personal home pages.

If you could share any advice with lawyers considering virtual law practice, either regarding the setup or management of this form of practice, what would it be?

Be sure you tailor your virtual law practice to what your clients need. Make sure you explain things to them if they need help. Be open to their suggestions as to how it could be improved and what they would like from it. And check it regularly, whether you get e-mail notifications of activity or not.

Where do you see virtual law practice headed in the future of the legal profession?

There are more small firms and solos out there than big firms. They constitute the bulk of legal professionals in the United States. Given the current economic climate, clients with legal service needs of any kind are looking for three things: efficiency, effectiveness, and responsiveness. The big firms that insist on continuing to do things the way they've always been done, while holding onto the hope that the big money will always come to them, are inevitably going the way of the dinosaur. Lawyers and small firms who use virtual law practice will be able to meet clients' needs with faster, more adaptable and more responsive service than their cousins with the high-rises and the IT professionals, and they will do so at a fraction of the cost. Virtual law practice is the future of law practice.

Below are descriptions of different virtual law practice structures and options, from completely Web-based to integrating a virtual law office with a brick and mortar law office.

Integrating a Virtual Law Practice into a Traditional Law Office

Lawyers who operate a traditional brick and mortar law office find benefits to adding virtual law practice to their existing structures. There are a number of reasons why this might be advantageous. Not only may the practice expand the client base across the jurisdictions where the lawyers are licensed to practice law, but they may also use the virtual law office to compete for local client services by marketing their online services as an amenity to the law office for clients for whom they will provide in-person consultation.

Traditional law practices in many states may now take advantage of electronic filing, service, and access to online dockets. Some courts are even holding virtual hearings, and some lawyers conduct virtual depositions. Adding a virtual law office to a traditional practice can easily fit into a traditional firm's efforts to go paperless and take additional tasks related to litigation online.

Moving Existing Clients from E-mail to the Virtual Law Office

Some clients who continue to make appointments for in-office visits with their lawyer may not be interested in registering for an account with that lawyer online. However, other clients will appreciate this feature of the lawyer's office as an amenity to their in-person visits and a way to keep updated on the status of their legal matter. Existing clients will also appreciate that the lawyer is concerned with protecting their attorney-client confidences by using a secure virtual law office instead of unencrypted e-mail.

When explaining the benefits to your existing clients, emphasize that the online service will help to maximize the amount of legal services the client receives from the lawyer and that it is a cost-effective method of communicating with the lawyer in between office visits. Lawyers may upload and store files in the virtual law office for the existing clients to review at any time. Invoices and payment for legal services may be handled online, providing convenience for clients as well as a way for them to access and view their outstanding balances and invoices for legal services. The lawyer may use a calendaring system to schedule office appointments or to remind the client of deadlines related to the case, such as hearing dates or deadlines for the client to review and return information to the lawyer for response to pleadings. The client may log onto the lawyer's site to view the status of the case or read the last note from the lawyer. Just the ability to check in on their case 24/7 gives the client a feeling of control and security over their legal matters in between office visits. This may result in fewer phone calls to the lawyer's office and fewer office resources expended per client.

Again, emphasizing that these features are optional for clients may help them to transition to using the online component of your practice. More traditional clients may not want to use all of these features, so it may be in the lawyer's best interest to set up a method within their current filing system that tells the lawyer and any paralegals or assistants which features to update for the client online and which matters have been requested by the client to be handled in person.

Adding a virtual law office to a traditional practice may also be used as an effective marketing point for the practice. As the trend in delivering online legal services continues to spread, the general public will continue actively seeking out lawyers who have an online option for providing legal services or at a minimum the ability to communicate with clients online. Because the move toward virtual law practice is primarily consumer driven, lawyers may be able to use a virtual law office in their marketing efforts to distinguish their practice from old-school firms that are not addressing the needs of the public seeking online options.

Transferring Data and Compatibility Issues with Existing Law Office Data

One of the biggest challenges for a traditional law firm seeking to integrate a virtual law office into its practice is finding the smoothest way to migrate critical law office data between the in-house systems that may have been set up for years and the system used to operate the virtual law office. In most cases, it is not practical or cost effective for a traditional law practice to attempt to transfer all of its data to the virtual law office. The firm would not need to nor want to do so. In most cases, the firm would be using the virtual law office as an amenity for in-person clients, a way to collaborate online with other lawyers and assistants, and/or for the collection of a new, separate online client base for unbundled legal services. Transferring all law office data into the virtual law office would not be necessary for it to function as a competitive marketing advantage and to pull in an additional stream of client revenue.

As discussed further, most legal software as a service (SaaS) providers have developed the technology solutions so that data is stored in common file formats, such as comma separated values (.csv) or icalendar. This is done so that law firms can easily import and export data to and from the virtual law office to another in-house system. For example, if the lawyer is using Outlook for contacts and calendaring, this application uses standard file formats that may easily be imported and exported into and from a virtual law office that provides client contact information and online calendaring. The trick here is that many established installed software programs do not provide an easily transferrable file format. They would much rather ensure that the firm is tied to using their product or has to pay in time and money to have the files converted into a compatible format in the event that the firm ever decides to switch to another product. While one criticism of SaaS providers is that the companies have not been around long enough to be considered stable, it could just as easily be pointed out that even longstanding companies producing installed software programs have discontinued support for older versions of their software, requiring firms either to pay for and install the upgraded version or pay the high cost of having the data transferred to another system and into another file format. Simply put, it is one factor to consider, but a traditional firm should not be completely turned off from integrating a virtual law office based on the integration and compatibility of their current in-house systems.

Completely Web-Based Virtual Law Office

A lawyer may choose to set up a completely Web-based virtual law practice and operate that practice from a home office or any remote location where he or she may securely access the Internet. There are many reasons for wanting to operate a completely Web-based law practice. One of the primary reasons is to avoid the overhead of a physical law office. Working from a home office allows the lawyer to save money not only by avoiding an office lease but also by minimizing the cost of office supplies, utilities, and other expenses associated with running a physical law office. A completely Web-based practice is essentially paperless except for the items sent to the lawyer by state bar associations, insurance carriers, and marketing or other organizations that do not e-mail or use digital forms of communication. In these instances when paper is received by the lawyer, he or she may scan the item into PDF format and store the document within the virtual law office system. Again, the amount of paper, ink, envelopes, and postage required to respond to these requests by snail mail are minimized when the lawyer conducts the majority of the business online.

One of the pleasant surprises for many lawyers who practice law completely online is that their clients are appreciative of the opportunity to contact a lawyer at their convenience. The online client does not have to take time off of work or arrange for child care to request legal services from the lawyer. Likewise, the lawyer has the flexibility with the work schedule for his or her law practice, which helps to contribute to a greater overall quality of life.

Not only do online clients find the convenience appealing, but many of them need the ability to pay for legal services online using a credit card. If the lawyer is offering fixed-fee prices or has been clear up front with the online client regarding the amount that will be paid for legal services, then the client is able to more easily budget for those services. Lawyers practicing law online tend to have fewer collection problems because the clients are not surprised by the end cost for services when the final invoice is sent to the client. Being able to pay for those services online with a credit card makes the process both faster for the client and for the lawyer, because electronic payments are nearly instant, rather than the traditional process of waiting for the mailed invoice to go out, the client to deal with the sticker shock and mail back a check, and for that check to clear the bank.

The completely Web-based virtual law office is easy to set up initially but may be more difficult to market to obtain a steady online client base than a traditional law office. Many members of the public may still not be aware that online law offices are an alternative to traditional brick and mortar practices. They may turn to traditional methods of researching to find a lawyer locally, such as print advertising or the yellow pages, where a physical law office may have a greater presence and more visibility locally. There are also limitations with a completely Web-based virtual law practice in terms of being better suited to certain clients and practice areas. Transactions-based practices are going to be more practically suited to a completely Web-based practice. The age and sophistication level of the firm's clientele may also be a factor. The lawyer may need to refer out prospective clients that come through the virtual law office to a full-service firm in their geographic location because the legal matter requires in-person representation. Making such determinations is discussed in more detail in Chapter Six: Ethics and Malpractice Issues.

Contract Lawyers

A virtual law office may also appeal to contract lawyers who could deliver legal services online to clients in addition to their contract work.[2] This method might also be a way for them to ease into creating their own solo practices, or if they are independent contract lawyers to use the technology to deliver their services securely online to current clients as well as bill for and receive payment for services online. Some contract lawyers who conduct legal research and writing may be in an even better position to leverage the technology to provide services that span the country while at the same time obtaining online clients for legal services within the jurisdiction(s) where they are licensed. Contract lawyers may also consider joining forces to deliver legal services online through a common client portal.

Unbundling and Working with Pro Se Individuals

What Is Unbundling?

Providing unbundled or limited legal services occurs when a lawyer breaks out the different tasks associated with a legal matter and provides the client with only specific portions of the legal work. The most common scenario is when a lawyer drafts a legal document for the client. The client is given detailed instructions from the lawyer regarding how to properly execute or file the document, but the client has the responsibility for taking the actions to complete the legal matter. In exchange for providing limited rather than full-service representation regarding the legal matter, the

---

[2]For more information about contract lawyers and for an example of an independent contract lawyer, see Lisa Solomon's Web site, Legal Research and Writing Pro, **http://legalresearchand writingpro.com** (accessed March 28, 2010).

client often receives a discounted legal fee. The practice of unbundling provides greater access to justice for individuals who for a myriad of reasons, such as cost, time, intimidation, or just having a do-it-yourself mentality, might not seek out full-service legal representation.

At the same time, the practice of unbundling also lessens the burden on the court systems' administration. In recent years, courts throughout the country have become swamped with an increasing number of pro se litigants entering the justice system without any legal guidance.[3] Rather than rely on the courts to do the hand-holding of these individuals, unbundling legal services online provides an affordable and efficient way for pro se individuals to receive the level of guidance they need to be able to navigate the judicial system to complete their legal needs. Nonprofit organizations and some state courts have already stepped up to meet this need by providing online forms coupled with online legal guidance to pro se individuals.[4]

While the ABA and many state bars are supportive of unbundling legal services, there are precautions that a lawyer must take to responsibly unbundle their legal services.[5] Before offering unbundled legal services, the lawyer has the responsibility to explain exactly what services will be provided at what cost to the client. Perhaps more important, the lawyer must specify what services will *not* be provided to the client online. A well-designed virtual law practice notifies the client of the nature of the limited services to be provided online as the foundation for all transactions. Multiple steps are required in which the client must read and acknowledge the terms of the representation and/or provide additional information to the lawyer. This permits the lawyer to track the client's progress in understanding and accepting the limited services being offered. Check with your state bar to make sure you are in compliance with any additional requirements

---

[3]See the ABA Standing Committee on the Delivery of Legal Services Pro Se/Unbundling Resource page for documents from the ABA and various state bars regarding the need for unbundled legal services to assist pro se individuals: **http://www.abanet.org/legalservices/delivery/delunbund book.html** (accessed March 23, 2010).

[4]See for example, Law Help Interactive, powered by ProBono.net (**www.lawhelpinteractive.com**) and A2J (Access to Justice), powered by the Center for Access to Justice & Technology (CAJT), in partnership with the Center for Computer-Assisted Legal Instruction (CALI) (**www.a2jauthor .org/drupal**).

[5]The ABA Standing Committee on the Delivery of Legal Services has a Web site encouraging the provision of "unbundled" legal services and assisted pro se representation and a complete index of links to state bar rules and procedures for providing unbundled legal services. The Standing Committee believes unbundling is an important part of making legal services available to people who could not otherwise afford a lawyer. The Web site also features a white paper entitled "An Analysis of Rules That Enable Lawyers to Serve Pro Se Litigants" (November 2009), **http://www.abanet.org/ legalservices/delivery/downloads/prose_white_paper.pdf** (accessed February 28, 2010).

for unbundling that may exist. For example, you may be required to include your contact information, bar license number, and other details regarding your limited representation on any legal documents you provide to the client for filing at the courthouse.

With a virtual law practice, a lawyer has the ability to tailor his or her virtual practice to encompass a variety of limited legal services, including use of a virtual law office in conjunction with a full-service law office. Because each practice will differ in the areas of law practiced by the lawyer(s) and by the chosen design and use of the technology, the responsibility to ensure compliance with state bar rules and regulations will remain with the individual practitioner or law firm.

The rules of professional conduct for many state bars will permit a lawyer to limit the scope of representation if the limitation is reasonable under the circumstances of the individual case. Accordingly, the lawyer must continue to provide competent and thorough representation to the client regardless of the limited nature of the legal services being conducted. Of particular concern with a virtual law practice may be the thoroughness and preparation of unbundled legal services online. Again, the ability of the virtual lawyer to provide unbundled legal services online will depend on the area of law in which he or she practices, the services that he or she decides to deliver online, and the structure of the virtual law office itself.

For example, a lawyer whose practice centers on litigation may use a virtual law practice to generate additional client revenue by answering basic traffic ticket questions while maintaining a full-service litigation practice. The same lawyer might use the virtual law practice technology to provide home pages to existing clients that he or she meets with in person and allow those clients to pay bills online, communicate in a more secure method than through e-mail, and to use the online client portal as an amenity to the full-service firm. However, the lawyer may chose not to use the technology to handle his or her litigation clients.

Another lawyer, however, may decide to enter retirement from a full-service law firm by creating a virtual law practice that handles only transactional legal services, such as drafting estate planning and contracts or setting up business entities for clients who do not want or need to meet with the lawyer in person. The virtual law practice allows this lawyer to work remotely or from home, allowing him or her to ease into retirement or create a completely new online law practice that allows for a better work/life balance. There are a variety of situations where a virtual law practice may be used to provide unbundled legal services, and with each it is possible to combine technology and law practice management to provide quality online legal services in compliance with the rules of professional conduct or other regulations of the lawyer's state bar.

Similar to a traditional law office, the lawyer must use his or her judgment on a case-by-case basis when deciding whether he or she may competently and ethically handle a particular matter online. Some practice areas naturally lend themselves better to unbundling than others. For example, a more transaction-based practice, such as estate planning, corporate law, business law, IP, family law, or bankruptcy, might be more easily unbundled online than a criminal defense practice where the lawyer would be expected to provide more ongoing, full-service representation.[6] Elder law might be another area where completely unbundled services online would be restrictive, because the core client base might not be as comfortable handling certain matters using technology. In those cases, the virtual law office unbundling legal services would work best integrated into a traditional law office. Regardless, if the client's needs would be better suited to a full-service lawyer, then it is the virtual lawyer's responsibility to refer the client out. This is no different from the responsibility of every lawyer, whether unbundling virtually or within a traditional brick and mortar law office.

Case Study: Unbundling Legal Services
Richard Granat, Esq., Owner of Granat Legal Services, P.C., Maryland Family Lawyer Virtual Law Firm
(www.mdfamilylawyer.com)

Richard Granat is the cochair of the eLawyering Task Force of the Law Practice Management Section of the American Bar Association and a liaison member of the Standing Committee on the Delivery of Legal Services of the ABA. He is the coauthor of the "Best Practice Guidelines for Legal Information Web Site Providers," adopted by the ABA House of Delegates, February 2003.

Technology: I operate a completely virtual practice that is based in Maryland and the District of Columbia. I actually operate it from my home in Palm Beach Gardens, Florida. I deal with clients only by e-mail and telephone and not face-to-face. We used the DirectLaw virtual law office platform as our core technology, which is also the company that I created from my experience in running my own virtual law firm.

---

[6]In some states, the courts may still be considering whether unbundling or limited appearance may be allowed for certain matters such as criminal defense cases for the lawyer to satisfy the rules requiring competent legal representation. See, for example, *In re Egwim*, 291 B.R. 559 (Bkrtcy. N.D. Ga. 2003) and *In re Castorena*, 270 B.R. 504 (Bkrtcy. D. Idaho Nov. 28, 2001).

Launch date: May 2003.

What was your reason for opening a virtual law practice?

In the late 1990's I supervised a clinical program at the University of Maryland School of Law that provided assistance to pro se litigants in family law matters. As part of that experience, I envisioned how the Internet could provide legal information and legal forms to consumers who could represent themselves, so I left the university and started MyLawyer.com, Inc., in 1998, which was then an Internet-based legal forms company and which continues to operate to this day, except that the purpose of the company has changed. Subsequently, I saw the need that pro se litigants have for legal advice bundled with legal forms, and I started my law practice based on the technology that was available through MyLawyer.com. More recently we spun off a new company, DirectLaw, Inc., which provides virtual law firm technologies to law firms as a hosted SaaS.

What are the benefits you have seen from this form of law practice?

Convenience, efficiency, a better customer experience, extending the reach of the law practice over the Internet, enabling the creation of legal service developed online at a fixed price to Web-savvy consumers.

What has been the public response?

Pretty good. We have a nice little practice that is a revenue generator and that has a steady flow of business.

What has been the response from legal professionals?

Lawyers in Maryland are not completely aware of what we are doing. We promote our virtual law firm platform through DirectLaw, Inc., and that is receiving increasing interest. I would say that the lawyers who are most interested in this concept are early adopters.

How long did it take for your practice to turn a profit?

Two years.

How much did you initially invest in marketing or advertising your virtual law practice?

Our advertising is approximately 18 percent of gross revenues.

What methods do you use to market your virtual law practice?

We market exclusively online through Google, Bing, and Yahoo!.

Did you receive formal approval or an ethics or advisory opinion from the bar association before opening your practice?

No, I submitted a complete proposal to our malpractice carrier, and they didn't have any problems with what we were doing. In fact, the premium was quite low (less than $600 a year).

Do you have any concerns with your virtual law practice as a form of law practice management?

No, I think it is a great form of law practice and can be replicated for many other kinds of practices.

Do you work with any virtual paralegals or virtual assistants in your virtual law practice?

Yes, I work with a virtual part-time paralegal who also works with my clients and does almost all the paperwork.

If you could share any advice with lawyers considering virtual law practice, either regarding the setup or management of this form of practice, what would it be?

Making it as a pure virtual practice is difficult. I had some special ways of marketing this firm through contacts I had in Maryland. I think the most effective model is attaching a virtual dimension to an office-based law firm, but the challenge is to be able to integrate the two types of law practice.

Where do you see virtual law practice headed in the future of the legal profession?

I believe that at some point every law firm that matters and wants to thrive will have a virtual component so that clients can relate to their lawyers online in a secure Web space. I believe that online legal applications such as Web-enabled document assembly will become more robust and a real option that will increase law firm productivity and enhance the client experience.

Document Automation and Assembly in Unbundled Legal Services

One of the benefits of a virtual law office is the ability to streamline online many of the administrative and routine functions so that the lawyer may focus more on the actual practice of law. Document automation and document assembly may be incorporated into a virtual law office to accomplish this goal. Automated document assembly most commonly occurs when a client who has registered with a virtual law office fills out a secure online form. This form may be "intuitive," meaning that if the client responds affirmatively to a question, the form will automatically know which question to provide next based on the responses. When the client has completed the online form, the lawyer may have the opportunity to edit the responses before completing the process of having the answers auto-generate either back into an original legal document or to create an entirely new document. That final product may then be sold to the client directly online, or instructions and online legal guidance may also be provided. Additional methods of online communication with the client, such as calendaring events, invoicing, and accepting payments for legal services or Web conferencing, may also be available.

Online companies, such as LegalZoom (**www.legalzoom.com**) and Rocket Lawyer (**www.rocketlawyer.com**), use automated document assembly to provide legal forms to clients online.[7] However, without the added review and input from an actual lawyer from the beginning to the end of the process, this model has come under criticism from state bars and other legal professionals and consumer protection organizations.[8] DirectLaw, powered by Rapidocs (**www.rapidocs.com**), a UK-based company, is an example of one software as a service (SaaS) product that provides sophisticated document automation and assembly technology. HotDocs (**www.hotdocs.com**) is another well-known software that provides this service. With some products it may be necessary to purchase state-specific legal forms to create the legal documents. With others, it is possible to customize your own legal forms based on legal documents that you have created for your law practice. This form of document automation and assembly technology may be used as the basis for a virtual law practice providing unbundled legal services online.

Case Study: Document Automation
Marc Lauritsen, President of Capstone Practice Systems, Inc., and Legal Systematics, Inc.
(www.capstonepractice.com)

Marc Lauritsen is the president of Capstone Practice Systems, Inc., and Legal Systematics, Inc.; cochair of the ABA eLawyering Task Force; and

---

[7]See also, MyLawyer.com, **www.mylawyer.com** (accessed on March 4, 2010).

[8]See North Carolina State Bar's Unauthorized Practice Committee's cease and desist letter, dated May 5, 2008, claiming that LegalZoom's practices constitute the unauthorized practice of law in North Carolina. See also the amended class action petition filed January, 2010, seeking refund of fees paid to LegalZoom by Missouri consumers; article in *ABA Journal* (February 19, 2010), **http://abajournal.com/news/article/suit_claims_legalzooms_document_prep_is_unauthorized_ practice** (accessed March 4, 2010).

a Massachusetts lawyer and educator. He is the author of The Lawyer's Guide to Working Smarter with Knowledge Tools (ABA, 2010).

Name some of the document automation products or services available to lawyers.

For the online practice context, Web-based tools like DealBuilder, Exari, HotDocs, and Rapidocs are the leading "platform" options. Services like Contract Express, DirectLaw, and Legal Systematics have emerged to make such platforms available on a software-as-a-service basis.

How can document automation be used in virtual law practice?

Any task involving documents that need to reflect information or decisions gathered from a client can be streamlined by offering the client an interactive questionnaire through which such information and decisions can be specified on their own time and at their own pace. Routine guidance can be provided right in context, and alerts or warnings can be programmed. By using document-assembly technology as part of this process, such information can be easily reviewed by lawyers and used appropriately in documents without reentry, minimizing unnecessary effort and errors.

Are there any legal services, projects, or tasks that you believe cannot be handled as well for the law practice through the use of document automation?

While document automation (and associated intelligent questionnaire technology) can play at least a supporting role in just about every kind of legal service, it is of limited value in "performative" services like negotiation and litigation, and it is no substitute for direct attorney-client interaction in circumstances involving significant emotional and strategic dimensions.

Does document automation permit a lawyer to handle drafting more complex legal matters? Can the lawyer determine the level of automation that he or she needs to add to existing provisions or redraft where needed?

I've seen document automation used effectively in extremely complex transactions involving hundreds of pages. Most of the software tools support arbitrary complexity; the gating factor is human time building and maintaining the models. So it's always a cost-benefit question. Most tools also provide mechanisms for inserting and customizing provisions during or after the automated assembly process. And typically that output is in freely editable word processing form. *Redrafting* sometimes is used to mean reassembling a document with new data or terms after parts of an earlier assembly has been hand edited, while retaining those edits—that is notoriously tricky and only partially supported by a couple of vendors.

Where do you see virtual law practice headed in the future of the legal profession?

I see the term *virtual* itself fading, as the currently novel/unusual approach of operating a practice primarily through the use of electronic media will become standard and obvious.

Collaborating with Other Lawyers in a Virtual Law Firm

Virtual law practice may facilitate collaboration with other lawyers to deliver legal services to clients online and has the potential to create a number of unique Web-based practices. On a smaller scale, two or more lawyers may see the benefit of pooling their resources to form a firm within one or more jurisdictions. On a larger scale, many lawyers could join forces to deliver legal services online in a number of jurisdictions. The flexibility of the technology encourages innovation and entrepreneurship for lawyers willing to invest in a more complex law firm structure.

Here are some examples of virtual law practices with two or more lawyers:

- ♦ A lawyer lives in one state while another lawyer lives across the country. Both lawyers provide online legal services in the same jurisdiction. This allows a lawyer to live in one state where he or she is not licensed to practice law and also maintain a relationship with a lawyer in the state in which he or she is licensed.

- ♦ Two or more lawyers form a single virtual law firm that spans two or more jurisdictions. The lawyers pool their resources to market the practice.

- ♦ Several lawyers in one jurisdiction form a single virtual law firm, where each individual lawyer handles a different legal practice area. When prospective clients register with the virtual law firm, the lawyers take only those clients whose legal matters pertain to that individual lawyer's practice area and refer the others around the firm.

◆ Several lawyers form a virtual law firm that covers multiple jurisdictions where the member lawyers are licensed. When prospective clients register with the virtual law firm, the lawyers take only those clients who are within their jurisdiction and refer the others around the firm.

◆ The "wholesale legal services" model, where the virtual law firm charges an annual or monthly subscription fee to clients for access to the virtual law office and its lawyers. Clients are assigned to lawyers within their jurisdiction and provided legal services based on the package or subscription they have purchased. The lawyers in the firm collect a portion of their legal fees and a portion goes to the firm for operational expenses and to pool resources for advertising. The lawyers in the firm must carefully craft unique partnership and fee structuring agreements, and also consider malpractice insurance policies for all members as well as trust accounting and Interest on Lawyer's Trust Accounts (IOLTA)[9] compliance rules across multiple jurisdictions.

Several of the above examples would work best with a virtual law office that is integrated into a traditional, full-service law firm. Some of these situations are not that different from the arrangements made by larger, physical office law firms that maintain branches in multiple jurisdictions and whose lawyers are also licensed in more than one state. In the above examples, the lawyers are retaining their clients online and delivering legal services through the client portal. This differs from law practices where they use technology to create a conglomeration of legal professionals who collaborate as a firm using the Internet. Instead, in these examples, the technology is used not only for the benefit of pooling the lawyers' resources, but also for providing a way of working with their clients online, in addition to operating an online back-end law office.

The lawyers who are members of a virtual law firm may or may not have access to the client files of the other lawyers in the virtual firm depending on if the technology is a permissions-based system. The lawyers may be assigned to cases individually, but they might also have the ability to communicate with each other through a client file and collaborate on

---

[9]See the IOLTA.org website for state IOLTA programs and frequently asked questions (FAQs) by attorneys. **http://www.iolta.org/** (accessed May 27, 2010).

that client's case file while never meeting with each other or the client. The benefit of keeping this communication completely within the online client file is that the entire file, both the dialogue between the lawyer and client and the lawyer and his or her colleagues, is kept in one place and not scattered around in different hosted systems or files as might be the case if the technology the lawyers were using to collaborate were separate from that of the back-end office.

Collaborating with other lawyers in a virtual law firm that covers multiple jurisdictions raises unique ethics issues, some of which are discussed in more detail in Chapter Six: Ethics and Malpractice Issues. Many of the concerns will be similar to those of a large, traditional law firm that opens branches in several jurisdictions. However, when researching the setup of this type of law practice, lawyers should carefully consider the following:

- ♦ Unauthorized practice of law (UPL) in other jurisdictions
  - ♦ Pay attention to marketing and advertising rules for the jurisdiction that governs each lawyer's law license. For example, there may be requirements for the Web site design or URL registration by one state bar that may not be required in another state.
  - ♦ Jurisdiction checks must be in place for each lawyer to ensure that the prospective clients registering with the virtual law office are routed to the lawyer who is licensed to handle their matter.
- ♦ Conflicts checking
  - ♦ Conflict of interest checking must be run against both online and offline contacts. Ensure that the system used allows for a thorough check on both types of parties and has a way to export online and import offline clients of all of the lawyers working in the virtual law firm so that the check covers any potential conflicts.
- ♦ Online payments and trust accounting
  - ♦ Ensure that the funds are slated to the correct trust account in each client's jurisdiction and that it is in compliance with that state's IOLTA requirements. This takes additional work when there is more than one lawyer with multiple jurisdiction regulations with which to comply.
- ♦ Dissolution of the virtual law firm
  - ♦ Ensure that the digital files are transferred from the online law office to the lawyer responsible for recordkeeping.

Case Study: Two-Lawyer Virtual Law Office
Olea, LLP—Charlene Quincey, Esq., and Kathryn C. Sheehan, Esq.
(www.olealawyers.com)

Olea, LLP, provides accessible, professional legal services related to Washington state law. Services provided online include estate planning, wills and trusts, small business setup, contract and document review, legal research, and family law services, including parenting plans, separation agreements, divorces, and name changes. Olea, LLP, is also a participant in the ABA Military Pro Bono Project, using their online law office to provide pro bono services.

Technology: We practice exclusively online. We do not maintain a bricks and mortar office. In fact, Katy practices out of Olympia, while Charlene practices out of Toronto. We also use electronic faxing and are currently looking into e-signatures to make it easier for clients to send and receive documents. We are big proponents of open-source software and actively search out cost-saving and innovative ways to conduct business.

Launch date: We officially went online in March 2009. We started working on Olea in November 2008.

Why did you decide to open a virtual law practice?

We wanted to offer affordable, accessible, high-quality legal services to underserved individuals. We also wanted to practice law on our own terms, in a positive space and from anywhere we have a secure Internet connection. We are diverse individuals with many interests, so having a mobile office just made sense! Also, there are many advantages for our clients, including the freedom to conduct their legal affairs on their own terms.

What are the benefits you have seen from this form of law practice?

The two biggest benefits are being able to work from anywhere there is a secure Internet connection and offering our clients very affordable legal services because of our low overheard.

How have other legal professionals responded to your practice?

We have received very positive feedback and a great deal of interest, especially within the lawyering community. We were recently featured in *National*, the Canadian Bar Association publication, and in the CUNY School of Law's law journal on public interest lawyering. Our blog, geared toward educating non-lawyers about legal issues that affect them, has garnered much attention and has also been featured and written about by numerous institutions. Most important, however, is that our clients' response to our services has been extremely positive.

How much did you initially invest in marketing or advertising your virtual law practice?

We have leveraged free marketing and advertising wherever possible. To date we have spent about $3,000. A large portion of that was spent on listing our firm on the Nolo directory.

What methods do you use to market your virtual law practice?

We created our online presence using free Internet sources such as Facebook, Twitter, blogging, etc., and we are currently in the process of looking into more traditional marketing techniques and methods.

Did you receive formal approval or an ethics or advisory opinion from the bar association before opening your practice?

We did not receive formal approval, as it was not required by the Washington State Bar Association.

Did you have any problem obtaining malpractice insurance for your virtual law practice?

We acquired excellent malpractice insurance. The fact that we were practicing exclusively through our virtual law office did not affect the insurance rate positively or negatively.

If you could share any advice with lawyers considering virtual law practice, either regarding the setup or management of this form of practice, what would it be?

Our biggest piece of advice is to approach setting up a virtual practice as you would a bricks and mortar practice. Know your market and do a business plan. With respect to setup, we used very little resources but a great deal of time educating ourselves in Web design, online social networking, and familiarizing ourselves with other virtual practitioners and their methods.

There are many similarities to practicing law out of an office—for example, you need to provide quality legal services, you need to market your services, and you need to be organized in your day-to-day management of your firm. Practicing through a virtual law office, however, offers a set of additional and unique challenges. Operating a virtual law office requires a natural interest in the intersection between law and technology——virtual lawyering is constantly evolving, as the virtual lawyer should be.

Where do you see virtual law practice headed in the future of the legal profession?

Virtual lawyering is not a fad and is not going to disappear from the legal scene.

Although we can't predict the number of lawyers or firms that go completely virtual, we have already seen an increase of firms who have added a virtual component to their practice. Moreover, as the younger generation matures and become clients, they will turn to their go-to source of information—the Internet—and virtual law offices will be there offering high-quality and affordable legal services.

Specific to our practice, we see virtual law offices greatly affecting traditionally underserved populations. It is our hope for the future that the virtual law office platform will provide individuals in remote areas, those shut out from obtaining legal services because of how costly they have become, and those who simply don't have access to a lawyer with much-needed, quality legal services performed by actual lawyers. A few specific examples: we just completed a power of attorney for a Marine stationed on a ship overseas, are currently working on a parenting plan modification for a sailor also stationed abroad, and recently wrote a will for a recently retired man of moderate means that had never made a will.

VLO Startup Checklist #1: Putting It Together

___ Research your state bar's rules and regulations regarding virtual law practice and offering unbundled legal services online.

___ Discuss your virtual law practice with your malpractice insurance carrier. Ask about discounted rates due to the use of technology to reduce malpractice risks.

___ Register a virtual law practice Web site domain. Check to see if your state bar requires registration of the URL name or has restrictions on domain name selection.

___ Retain a Web site developer to create a virtual law office Web site. Make sure your Web site content complies with any Web site rules or regulations set up by your state bar. Consider finding a developer with support available to make changes and regular updates to your site.

___ Make sure that any part of your Web site that handles confidential information is protected by an SSL certificate. (Look for the *https* in the URL address and the browser lock symbol.)

___ Establish an account with a credit card processing company to use for your online payments. Ensure that this arrangement complies with your state bar's trust accounting and IOLTA rules. If your site is designed to retain credit card information (not recommended), you must ensure that it is PCI compliant.

___ Draft the terms and conditions, including a privacy statement, for use for your general Web site and any clickwrap[10] agreement or disclaimers used for your secure site. These need to be easily accessible to the public for reference on your site.

___ Consider incorporating your virtual law office as a PLLC, LLC, or other entity depending on the state where you will be conducting business and the management structure you've chosen.

___ Obtain all city and state privilege licenses for your practice.

___ If starting from scratch, educate yourself about starting your own law practice. Review law practice management blogs. Join listservs and forums managed by your state bar practice areas to learn from a collective source of experienced professionals.

___ Write a business plan and have a strategy in place. If you are integrating a virtual law office into a traditional practice, consider writing a separate plan with goals specifically for the online portion of your practice and describe how those goals will be integrated into your firm's overall business strategy.

Case Study: Adding a Virtual Law Office to a Traditional Firm
Mark Spencer Williams, Esq., Rice Law, PLLC
(www.ricefamilylaw.com)

Mark Spencer Williams is an owner and managing member at Rice Law, a North Carolina law firm providing family and education law services. Williams is a family and real property lawyer, and a nationwide education lawyer.

Technology: VLOTech's Virtual Law Office software in conjunction with a brick and mortar office; videoconferencing technology, such as Skype and Microsoft Live Meeting.

---

[10]See the Terminology section in the Appendix of this book for the definition of "clickwrap" and Chapter Six "Clickwrap Agreements" discussing the establishment of the attorney/client relationship online.

Launch date: The virtual law office component to Rice Law, PLLC, launched on February 10, 2009.

Why did you decide to open a virtual law practice?

We saw it as a way to supplement our services for clients and as a method to offer unbundled services in a downturn economy to individuals outside our normal service areas.

What are the benefits you have seen from this form of law practice?

1. We have been able to help clients who could not have otherwise afforded our services in the past.
2. Our clientele is now more diverse, and we have more clients from out of state who have issues within our jurisdiction; it has expanded our geographical market.
3. We find it easier to interact with clients who live overseas in different time zones.
4. We offer more pro bono publico services without significant strain on the firm by answering initial questions at no charge, whereas in-person consultations are billed.
5. Our participation demonstrates to the community our technical prowess, sometimes resulting in the perception that we offer a level of service above non-virtual law office firms.
6. About half of "unbundled" virtual clients become full-service brick and mortar clients.
7. We have been forced to better document instructions for handling certain matters (in part so that pro se litigants can follow them), which has improved our own processes (an unexpected value-added process-improvement strategy).

What has been the public response?

Prospective clients and clients comment positively on the service. When we talk with vendors who provide marketing services for us, they find it of interest, and we often use it as a talking point to educate the public about these services. Online searches for "virtual lawyer" are increasing, and the inference is that the public likes the service. My belief is that the average consumer remains unaware of the existence of virtual law firms. However, they are very aware of services like LegalZoom.

How long did it take for your virtual law office component to turn a profit?

That is very hard to gauge. If we only had a virtual law practice, I could tell you with specificity. But since we have a brick and mortar practice and many of the virtual law clients convert to full-service clients, it is hard to measure. If we had concentrated solely on full-service in the traditional setting, would we have had higher revenues? Does having the VLO cause us more work for those traditional clients who want their documents uploaded to the VLO? Certainly the revenues after the first month were sufficient to pay for the costs of the service, but we can't say that the VLO has made us "more profitable," although we generally believe it has done so.

How much did you initially invest in marketing or advertising your virtual law practice? $3,800.

What methods do you use to market your virtual law practice?

We added our virtual practice to our listings in Nolo, Findlaw, etc. We also paid for Internet-only radio advertising. And we significantly increased our pay-per-click and other Web-based strategies, including marketing via Twitter, blogs, etc.

Are there any concerns that you have with your virtual law practice as a form of law practice management?

My only concern is that a virtual law office seems to attract clients outside our jurisdiction, which is fine if they have a legal issue within our jurisdiction, and you have to appropriately screen for that. I also think that within the context of family law it would be difficult to operate a stand-alone virtual law office. About half of our clients in the virtual law office context find that when they get into trouble because their spouse will not sign a separation agreement or they go to a court hearing and dislike the result, they hire us for full-service. They need a place they can come when they get into trouble.

If you could share any advice with lawyers considering virtual law practice, either regarding the setup or management of this form of practice, what would it be?

You can't just put out an electronic shingle and expect consumers to find you. I think to effectively market yourself you have to have a Web site that adequately describes your services and you have to participate in online forums, Twitter, blogging, etc. to show that you can add value and have expertise, and then potential clients will come to you.

Where do you see virtual law practice headed in the future of the legal profession?

I hope state bars will shut down practices like LegalZoom for the unauthorized practice of law by recognizing that even the preparation of a legal document such as a will is practicing law. And then virtual law offices will replace these programs by not only offering document preparation but by appropriately interviewing the client, preparing a document custom tailored to their needs, giving legal advice, and, when they run into a problem, transferring them to full-service.

CHAPTER THREE

Choosing the Technology

Cloud Computing and Software as a Service (SaaS)

The technology used to facilitate virtual law practice is software as a service (SaaS). SaaS is only one type of technology platform that exists in the general realm of "cloud computing." Cloud computing means that the software application(s) are hosted by a third-party on servers and accessed over the Internet. SaaS applications used to create and maintain a virtual practice on the Internet are secure, hosted systems. A brief, and more technical, background will help explain how cloud computing has evolved from the application service provider (ASP) models of the late 1990s to the current, more flexible and reliable SaaS model that is used today for virtual law practice and help foresee the innovation that may follow in the near future. This background may help dispel the misconception that today's SaaS applications are somehow unreliable because they are an evolution of the technology from the late 1990s.

The term *cloud computing* originates from the explanation that programmers would use to describe complex networks and how data transferred from network to network. The space in which data transferred from one law office's computer network was drawn in diagrams as a cloud to show that this information was now outside the control of the organization. This cloud is actually a known road and location that data travels to and on and does not mean that data is floating out in space unprotected and unobtainable. This was easier for programmers to encapsulate in a cloud in the diagrams than to draw out the entire complex network system for each client. Rest assured, your law office data, if hosted in the cloud, is not actually floating around in an unknown location.

In researching cloud computing or SaaS, you should be careful not to lump together application service providers (ASPs) of the late 1990s with the structure of most current companies providing SaaS. Hardware like your PC that manages data locally is often referred to as a "fat client," and hardware that talks directly to a remote server/mainframe is known as a "thin client." For the last forty years, the tug-of-war between whether to have a fat client or thin client has largely been based on the cost of hardware versus the cost of networks and the management involved with both.

In the 1960s, mainframes were expensive. Accordingly, most offices purchased a "dumb" terminal. This was a terminal that talked to the mainframe, and that was its sole purpose. When personal computers came onto the scene, the industry switched to fat clients. Then when dial-up came along, the trend began to switch back to network-centric systems. In the late 1990s, the industry had a large amount of software developed for fat clients but a burgeoning use of thin clients in the form of Web browsers. Accordingly, many early ASPs tried to put fat software on thin networks. This led to problems that some IT and legal IT consultants may refer to when providing critical opinions of putting law office data "in the cloud."

Currently, the industry is in the stage of moving back to thin clients, and this process is occurring in a mismatched manner. This is one reason why the term *software as a service* has evolved, and *platform as a service* (PaaS) is another variation on the term that is becoming more recognized. While in some ways the names, such as ASP and SaaS, may refer to the same concept, it is helpful to distinguish between what occurred in the 1990s and the goals of the current industry.[1] The key difference is that SaaS means that software is being specifically written as a service designed to work cooperatively in a network environment—i.e., when SaaS products are created, they are designed more in line with the needs of mainframe servers and less in line with the goals of PC software. It is a subtle difference, but this affects the way the IT professionals and the industry think about their users, resources, and security, among other concerns.

---

[1]Many critics will point to the example of Red Gorilla, an ASP company that left small-business customers in a lurch when it suddenly disappeared from the Internet in 2000. The lesson learned from this experience is to find a service provider that has not only solid data return and retention policies in place but that provides export functionality in a number of standard file formats for easy transfer so that the firm using the software is able to acquire copies of their data on a regular basis if they so choose for in-house backup and storage.

The good news is that the hardware and networks are becoming more affordable together in a way that opens up new opportunities. The industry can now produce fat clients that switch to thin clients and back again. This means that professionals have more flexibility and options in terms of complexity and cost when choosing the technology that they are comfortable with to operate their businesses. There are other benefits that have come out of these changes.

Some of the benefits of SaaS include the following: (1) data stored on the server is encrypted using a 128 bit or greater advanced encryption standard (AES) quality cipher algorithm,[2] (2) regular software updates and new features are added without disturbing the workflow, (3) no in-house software installations are needed, (4) the lawyer may securely access the data anywhere the Internet is available, (5) there are regular data backups, and (6) it is less expensive than paying for software, storage, and server hardware and having to run it internally with or without hiring an IT professional for the office. The concerns and risks of hosting law office data in the cloud are discussed in more detail below.

SaaS is becoming an increasingly popular business model as Web 2.0 companies have turned to it to provide their professional clients with the latest technology. This model is ideal for facilitating the delivery of legal services online because it allows the lawyer to focus more on providing quality online legal services to the public without time-consuming in-house software installation, maintenance, and support. In particular, it provides a unique opportunity for solos and small firms to take advantage of the cost savings that virtualization provides without having to hire an IT consultant to install rack units in the physical premises of a brick and mortar law office and set up all of the hardware to create the ability to deliver legal services online. Instead, lawyers are able to leverage SaaS to exploit its benefits while at the same time finding ways to mitigate the risks by creating in-house backups and storage of their law office data that do not require the services of an IT professional.

For every argument against SaaS, you can come up with a similar argument against traditional installed software. Simply put, do your research, understand your comfort level with the technology, and know what your clients need to receive in their online legal services.

---

[2]Rijndael, Serpent, and Twofish are the most common cipher algorithms used.

**Case Study: Advice from a Senior Programmer and
IT Security Specialist**
Benjamin Norman, Virtual Law Office Technology (VLOTech)
(http://www.vlotech.com)

*Benjamin Norman, senior programmer and co-founder of Virtual Law
Office Technology (VLOTech), has over 13 years experience in programming and technology support experience developing secure Web-based
applications. He has developed programs for secure tax and court filing
for government entities and developed and maintained background-
checking software.*

*What security or best practices tips would you provide to a lawyer who is
using technology to handle functions of law practice management
online?*

At home, use a hardware firewall configured to only accept traffic that is
a response to requests made from behind the firewall (change the
default password, turn off the ability to manage the firewall from the
outside, and switch off any features of the firewall that respond to pings
or will otherwise keep the firewall quiet when it is port-scanned from the
outside. If you set up wireless networking, make sure that all wireless
traffic is encrypted with WPA2. Do not use WEP, ever. It can be cracked in
under two minutes.

Make sure that you try to keep all online business computers protected
by only installing just the software you need, keeping antivirus software
up-to-date as well as all software patches, and turn on the software firewall for the computer as well. For people using Windows, use software
like Secunia PSI to keep all other software up-to-date. For Mac users,
many programs will try to find updated versions of the software, and this
is encouraged. For Unix users, programs like rpm or apt can be used to
keep the software up-to-date.

If you can afford to do so, any games and other entertainment software
should be run from a separate computer. I recommend that they have a
dedicated machine for law practice management that is separate from
their other unsecure online activities.

For browsing I recommend Mozilla with the NoScript add-on installed.
Clicking on the S in a white circle at the bottom left will allow JavaScript
and Flash to be run on a page where it is needed (and the settings can
be made permanent for trusted sites). It takes getting used to, but it pro-

tects the browser from an enormous number of Web site attacks. Google Chrome is also proving itself safe with its sandboxing.[3]

When travelling, I recommend a cellular phone modem adapter for wireless connectivity. This is a more secure solution than free Wi-Fi hotspot connectivity and provides better coverage.

Be careful with e-mail attachments as well, and only open items you were expecting to receive. Do not trust an attachment just because it is from someone you know, because the "sender" may be a victim of malware. If you receive something suspicious in Twitter or IM, then e-mail or call the sender and ask if he or she meant to send something to you. You may be helping the sender detect a problem if he or she doesn't know what you are talking about.

Back up your computer regularly. External portable hard drives are cheap, and there are a number of backup software solutions. Keep the backup hard drive safe and take it home with you every night or put it in a fireproof safe designed to store computer media. Alternatively, back up your computer files to the cloud with services like Mozy and a number of others. Do both so you always have your data safe, but be sure that you don't leave your backups in a place where they can be lost or stolen. I also recommend keeping the backups encrypted as well.

What are some of the risks of using SaaS, and for each risk, how can the lawyer mitigate that risk?

The biggest risks for using SaaS software come from the risks the users put themselves in by being unsecure from their side. If someone can install malware, such as a keyboard sniffer, on the user's machine, there is very little SaaS software can do to protect the users from themselves. But this is a risk that applies to both SaaS and any other software solution, although it is even more important to protect passwords when using SaaS software.

Do not share your password with anyone, and never e-mail it, write it down on paper, or share it with anyone. Use a password manager like KeePass to keep your password safe if you can't remember them all. Use secure passwords that are at minimum eight characters long with num-

---

[3]In computer security, this term refers to isolating programs so that they have only limited access to other software or the underlying computer system. Thus if something fails with one program, it will not affect the entire system or any other software applications on that system.

bers and letters as part of the password. Use full sentence passphrases (including punctuation) when you can (these are very secure and even easier to remember, but not every application supports them).

Your SaaS provider should keep your password secure on the back-end server (with a one-way hash)[4] and should never need this info from you. Never give your password to anyone. Anyone using your SaaS software should have their own separate login. If you are asked for security questions to recover a lost password, use your own questions or put in answers that don't match the questions. It can be very easy to find your mother's maiden name or the city you were born in, and this method of password security is very weak, so try to make it stronger. If you can pick your own question, pick one that someone who knows you well couldn't answer.

Before choosing a third-party hosting service, what questions would you recommend that the lawyers ask?

Do you know and trust the person managing your software? If he promises you "100 percent" or "unlimited" anything, he is not giving you the whole story or an accurate representation of reality. Saying "99.999 percent" and providing concrete limits would make me trust that the provider is giving you a better deal backed by real metrics.

Ask what standards and regulations the software falls under and how those have been addressed. Write down the answers, and make comparisons. Rules and standards change all the time, but software providers should all be doing about the same thing.

Ask what happens with your data when you leave, and get it in writing that you get your data back. Ask about the process you use when a problem occurs, and ask how quickly you can expect to get a response. Ask what the process is if their company goes out of business. Do they have a plan in place for emergencies and/or dissolution of the company?

If you could share any advice with lawyers considering using SaaS for law practice management, what would it be?

Find companies that focus on your core values. Do they focus on law, and do they understand your legal needs? What/who is the software designed for? Are they designing software for the general public, or are

---

[4]A one-way hash is a cryptographic algorithm that turns data of arbitrary length into a fixed-length binary value. In doing so, the transformation of the data is one-way so that it is statistically not feasible to recreate the data with the same value. Examples of hash algorithms are MD5 which produces 128-bit hashes and SHA which produces a 160-bit hash.

they focused on a specific sector? If they are offering free software, where does the revenue come from? If you are not paying for the service, you may not have the security, rights, or guarantees that come with a paid license. Be sure you understand the tradeoffs that come with different SaaS pricing models, and act according to your responsibilities.

Where do you see the use of SaaS in law practice management headed in the future of the legal profession?

I see SaaS becoming a natural extension of the law office workflow the same way that telephones and desktops have become ubiquitous. And just like the telephone, everyone will start to forget that they rely on it every day. But unlike a desktop, which has to be upgraded every few years, SaaS will keep up with the times and adapt to new technology innovation transparently for the user.

From a software perspective, I see a focus on portable smart hardware devices taking hold and the software adapting to the strengths of these devices. The software will also become a more helpful personal secretary, keeping a lawyer on track and well informed with easier-to-use interfaces. In a similar way that we are trying to go to a semantic Web, the same tools will apply to helping legal professionals and their clients understand and make the best use of the myriad pieces of information that define our legal system.

The next revolution I see will come when the court systems are connected at every level—from submitting information to the court (some support is already available for submitting items to the court online) to interactive tools inside the courtroom that can tie into the case information prepared for the case by each side. The information that is publicly owned/funded should be available to everyone, and as it becomes more accessible, systems will be need to interact with and make sense of these data. This is similar to the way a search engine works with a Web site, but with interfaces custom to each type of data (the way Google Earth can explore mapping data with a tailored interface relevant to visual data).

Research the Software Provider and Hosting Company

Operating a virtual law practice does not require a lawyer to become an IT specialist. You should find a trustworthy software provider, hosting company, and other IT specialists to assist in updating the virtual law firm

Web site content, keeping the Web-based technology current, and handling any security issues that might affect the online business. New SaaS providers with products developed for the use of the legal profession or other business professionals are emerging daily.[5] This book will not attempt to list every possible technology or product that could be used to deliver legal services online, as it would quickly become outdated. Accordingly, a list of the more well-known software providers is available on the companion Web site for this book (**www.virtuallawpracticebook.com**) and will be updated on a regular basis. The following information applies to any software provider or hosting company related to the setup of a virtual law practice.

Because sensitive attorney-client data will be stored online, you should make sure that the company hosting the virtual law practice is reliable and that the servers are housed in a location that is secure and not threatened by environmental or other factors that would subject the servers to any long-term outage.[6] If the company has geo-redundancy of servers, note the hosting company's backup server locations and the security and reliability of those locations. For more information about Tier 4 data centers that house servers, please see the terminology section of the Appendix.

There are many concerns to address when selecting a legal SaaS provider or company that will be hosting your law office data. Each of these is listed and discussed in more detail below.[7]

---

[5]At the time of this publication, a group of companies providing legal SaaS products has formed an association of legal SaaS providers for the purpose of setting and maintaining high technology standards and security practices for SaaS products created for the use of legal professionals. The founding companies include Clio, Rocket Matter, DirectLaw, and Total Attorneys, whose companies develop and sell legal SaaS products.

[6]Some state bars have addressed the use of third-party service providers having access to and storing confidential client information. The summary of these opinions has been that the lawyer must use reasonable care when selecting a service but that the lawyer may not be required to guarantee that there will be no breach of confidential information through the use of this service. See the State Bar of Nevada's Standing Committee on Professional Responsibility and Conduct, Formal Opinion No. 33 (February 9, 2006), **http://www.nvbar.org/Ethics/Ethics_Opinions_DETAIL .htm#Opinion%2033** (accessed May 27, 2010), and New Jersey Advisory Committee on Professional Ethics, Opinion 701 (April 10, 2006), **http://lawlibrary.rutgers.edu/ethicsdecisions/acpe/ acp701_1.html** (accessed May 27, 2010).

[7]In the summer of 2010, the North Carolina Bar Ethics Committee published North Carolina Bar Proposed Formal Ethics Opinion 7, "Subscribing to Software as a Service while Fulfilling the Duties of Confidentiality and Preservation of Client Property," *North Carolina State Bar Journal*, Summer 2010, Volume 15, Number 2. This proposed Ethics Opinion provides a list of questions that a lawyer should ask prospective SaaS providers before subscribing to the software services for use in law practice management.

Downtime for Maintenance or Upgrades

One of the benefits of SaaS is the regular updates to the software without any cost to the user. Unless you have a support contract with a traditional software company, upgrading to the latest version of installed software can be costly but necessary if the company decides to discontinue support for the older version. While it is a significant cost savings, make sure that when your SaaS provider handles these updates to the software they are not halting your use of the service during that maintenance. A good provider will know how to design the hardware stack so that when it conducts routine maintenance or upgrades the software, you and your customers may continue to operate at full function. At bare minimum, these updates might seem only like a slow Internet connection to you or your clients, but nothing that would hinder normal business operations. They might also involve downtime after business hours, but the provider should be able to provide you with adequate notice.

Case Study: Advice from an Attorney, Author and Legal Technology Enthusiast
Nicole Black, Esq.

Nicole Black is a lawyer, author, and the founder of LawTechTalk.com (www.lawtechtalk.com). She is the coauthor of the book **Social Media for Lawyers: The Next Frontier***, ABA (2010), and is also writing a book about cloud computing for lawyers to be published by the ABA in late 2010.*

What are the benefits for legal professionals that you have seen from this form of law practice?

Virtual law practices offer lawyers flexibility and convenience. Lawyers are no longer tied to their desktops and can access their files and practice management software from virtually anywhere.

What are the benefits to the lawyer's clients from the use of the technology to deliver legal services? What has the public response been to virtual law practice?

Clients benefit from virtual law practices in many ways. First, clients have a sense of more control over their case. They have a greater ability to access and view their case file at any time and no longer need to rely on their lawyer to provide copies of documents. Clients also have peace of mind knowing that they have a secure, encrypted platform wherein they can communicate with their lawyer regarding their case. Finally, virtual law practices offer clients the convenience of accessing their files and seeking information at any time, rather than being limited to trying to obtain this information during typical office hours of operation.

The public's reaction to these types of technologies has been mixed. Some are skeptical of online interactions and transactions, but as people learn more about these platforms and become more acclimated to online interactions and transactions, there will be greater acceptance by the public.

Are there any concerns that you have working with a virtual law office as a form of law practice management?

There are a number of very valid concerns regarding virtual law offices and other types of legal cloud computing applications. Lawyers considering incorporating cloud computing platforms into their practices have an obligation to exercise due diligence in vetting cloud computing providers and must ensure that the cloud computing vendor has practices in place that protect confidential client information. Lawyers also need to stay abreast of ethics decisions regarding cloud computing and must also learn about the security offered by these platforms. Lawyers must understand the security issues and need to ask appropriate questions of the vendors regarding the security methods in place, including whether there is the possibility of transcontinental data flow and whether there is geo-redundancy in place, so that if a server on one coast goes down due to a natural disaster, a server on an alternate coast will have a mirrored backup of the law firm's data.

What methods of marketing would you recommend for a virtual law practice? How would that marketing differ from the methods used by a traditional law practice?

Virtual law offices are perfectly suited for online marketing, including social media, since, presumably, clients who are the most comfortable with this type of platform are already fairly tech savvy. It would follow that many of these potential clients could be more easily targeted using online marketing as opposed to less technologically proficient individuals.

Where do you see virtual law practice headed in the future of the legal profession?

I think that virtual law practices will be increasingly more common as lawyers and clients become more comfortable with the idea of using cloud computing platforms and as cloud computing providers become more responsive to the very valid ethical and security concerns specific to our profession.

Support Future Law Office Growth

Make sure that the hosting provider has the infrastructure or at least the ability to plan for and obtain an infrastructure that will support future growth of online data. If you are starting out as a solo law practice, you may need a minimum amount of online data storage for files and documents in your file libraries. However, if you are transferring in-person clients from an existing firm over into a virtual law office, you may require more storage space as well as room to quickly expand as you take on additional online clients and need to store the increasing volume of documents in your virtual law office. Make sure your hosting company is able to scale their infrastructure to meet the needs of your law practice and future goals for growth.

Cost of the Product

The SaaS model generally operates on a monthly, pay-as-you-go, and for-what-you-need basis. You should check that the provider does not have any hidden fees associated with startup or maintenance or that they don't charge extra for additional technology or training support in addition to the monthly fees. The range of pricing is going to depend on the level of service that you are purchasing and how many features are available in that product. It can run anywhere from $50 a month to $300 a month, and setup fees will depend on the level of customization and training that is provided by the company. If you plan on adding another lawyer user, virtual assistant, or paralegal to work in your virtual law office, find out if there is special pricing for them and if there are any additional costs to adding more users to the system in the future. If it is permissions-based software, make sure you understand the limitations of the licenses you will be purchasing for assistants. You will also want to make sure that you understand the term of any costs, such as if there is a requirement of a one-year contract or if the product is month to month with a cancellation notice requirement.

When researching a product, make a return on investment analysis that takes into consideration the ability of the product to generate client revenue. Some products may be geared more toward practice management tools, such as time and billing, but others may be used to retain and work with online clients. When looking at the price of the monthly fee and any additional costs, consider what the estimated amount of revenue will be each month as a result of using the product.

Data Return and Retention Policies

If you are working with a Web-based application that hosts virtual law office data, including online document storage, you should be familiar with the company's data-retention policy. Should that company have financial troubles or come into a disagreement with a lawyer regarding the Web-based application, you need the reassurance that all of the law office data stored on that Web-based application will be returned to you within a reasonable amount of time. If you prefer the additional security of in-house data retention in addition to the services provided by the hosting company, data contained in the online law office may be available to you to transfer to on-sight digital storage for internal backup or for long-term digital record retention.

If you are storing the majority of the law office documents online through a Web-based application, you should know the hosting company and feel confident about its policies regarding data retention. You should obtain a guarantee from the hosting company that the law office data will be returned in a readable format within a reasonable amount of time. Also note the terms of their policy as it relates to any export features that may be provided by the software. If you are able to manually remove your law office data from the system for your own in-house backup at any time, then the formal return of your data by the company within a reasonable amount of time may not be as critical.

In addition, you should inquire about the technology provider's procedure for handling government and civil search and seizure actions. If the provider is handed a subpoena requesting them to deliver the contents of your law office, there are no legal requirements for them to notify you before responding. The best policy would be for the provider to contact you immediately regarding the request and before taking any action. Make sure you are comfortable with the procedures the provider has in place in the event that this might occur.

Third-Party Hosting

The software provider may outsource the hosting of your law office data with a third-party company. Accordingly, you will want to obtain a copy of any agreements that cover the servers, support and/or maintenance of your law office data that will be in the hands of a third party. In most cases, the third party involved is a company that owns and controls the Tier 4 data center where the servers housing your law office data are located. For practical purposes, the software provider most likely does not own their own data center but is instead leasing or has purchased servers within a secure data center. You may want to fully understand these relationships when considering the terms covered in the software provider's service level agreement (SLA).

Offshore Servers

When asking the hosting company about the location of the servers storing your law office data, be aware that servers located outside of the United States may be subject to international laws. If your law office data were stored on a server located offshore, in the event that something happened to the stability of the hosting company or the company from which the provider leases their servers, there might be some difficulty in retrieving the data from those servers. While this is a very remote possibility, it is another factor to consider.

Some providers may have servers located in the States and then have geo-redundancy or data escrow offered through companies with servers located overseas. In this instance, the servers overseas are being used as a backup protection for accessibility in the event of the failure of the primary server storing the law office data. In such cases, the use of offshore servers is less of an issue, as the data may still be retrieved from the primary server in the States.

Geo-Redundancy

Geo-redundancy is an extra level of security that may be provided by your third-party hosting company. This means that the data stored in your virtual law office would be hosted on servers in multiple locations at the same time. If there were a power or hardware failure or a natural disaster that wiped out one server, another one would be ready to take over its functions in storing and securing your law office data.

Many hosting providers will offer different levels of security, so you may choose to go with one server for your data, understanding the existing data center security in place, and then later add geo-redundancy of servers. In most cases, if you are choosing a SaaS provider of legal products, that company will be leasing their servers from a company and already have geo-redundancy in place. Or they may own their own servers and have relationships with other companies to create geo-redundancy. It is important to find out the relationship that your provider has to the company that owns the servers and how that may affect your data.

Data Escrow

Data escrow is another layer of protection for your virtual law office data. Some SaaS providers will have a data escrow policy in place. In addition to creating a regular in-house, external backup of your law office data from your virtual law office through export features, data escrow sends your data from your provider to a completely independent third-party hosting company, in the event that something happens to your relationship with your primary SaaS provider. For example, if the company should go out of business or into bankruptcy, you would be able to retrieve your law office data from that bonded and separate third-party hosting company. As with geo-redundancy, this level of security may cost extra because it adds an additional expense to your provider to offer the service, but it provides an efficient solution to the concern about ready accessibility of online law office data.

Compliance with Federal Regulations

If your provider will be collecting credit card information for your virtual law office rather than redirecting that service to another third-party hosting company, make sure that they are Peripheral Component Interconnect (PCI) compliant. Most legal SaaS providers do not handle this aspect of your law office management, and you will be relying on a third-party credit card hosting company, typically one connected to a bank or other financial institution that is already in compliance with federal regulations regarding the collection and storage of credit card information.

Unlimited Liability for Confidentiality Breaches— Unreasonable?

Should you hold your provider liable for any and all confidentiality breaches, including those from unforeseen and unpreventable hackers? This is a tricky issue for businesses relying on SaaS to host their confidential data. On the one hand, it is not reasonable to hold a company liable for the malicious breach of security by a hacker that was unpredictable. On the other hand, you are entrusting your law office data, your business, your reputation, and your client's confidential information to the provider and should expect that company to be at the top of its field in identifying and protecting your data from security breaches.

Despite the provider's best efforts, if a hacker is able to access your law office data and you feel that you should be able to hold your provider responsible for this unforeseen attack, be prepared to see that carry over into the cost of your service. Your provider will then need to protect itself with adequate business insurance to cover the cost of providing your virtual law office with the ability to hold the company to unlimited liability for data breaches. You may want to ensure that your software provider has an adequate business insurance policy in place to cover risk that may occur on its end or as a result of its relationship with any third-party hosting company.[8]

Also be practical about this risk based on the size of the online clients you will be working with and the nature of the unbundled services you will provide. Mitigate the risks based on the realistic size of the potential loss. This is covered in the malpractice insurance section below as it relates to coverage in your policy. For example, a data breach due to a hacker may be less likely if you are a solo practitioner unbundling family law services than if you are a large traditional law firm asking your large corporate clients to use the client portal to transfer sensitive information related to their case.

The bottom line when reviewing your provider's SLA is that no hosting company will ever be able to guarantee that there will be no confidentiality breaches of your virtual law office data. Translate this from the cloud

---

[8]Another related issue to consider is the jurisdiction that governs in the case of a data breach. Would the laws apply where the customer is located, where the service provider is located, or where the data is actually hosted in the location of the data center? Required notice of any data breach could be either the responsibility of the lawyer using the service or the service provider. These are all issues to consider when reading through the service provider's service level agreement (SLA), when drafting your terms and conditions for use of the virtual law practice for your clients and prospective clients, and also when asking questions to the service provider to find out how aware they are of these concerns.

into the physical world. While they are insured up to a point, even your other business relationships, such as your firm's bank or your physical storage facility where your retired law office paper files are stored, cannot guarantee 100 percent that there will never be a breach of security in some form. Identifying and finding ways to minimize the risks whether online or in a traditional law office is the safest solution.

Case Study: Advice from a Legal SaaS Provider and Chief Software Architect
Larry Port

*Larry Port is the Founding Partner and Chief Software Architect for Rocket Matter, LLC, a legal SaaS product. (**www.rocketmatter.com**)*

What security or best practices tips would you provide to a lawyer who is using technology to handle law practice management functions online?

When handling any confidential information outside the walls of your office, it's essential to understand who can see the data. Paranoia is your friend. Keep in mind that security doesn't just apply to law practice management software: often, people forget that their e-mail is stored and accessed on remote, unsecured IMAP or POP servers.

For starters, make sure any data transmissions are encrypted. A browser will display a lock icon if the Web site uses SSL to transmit your data through a secure tunnel.

If you're using an encrypted channel, you enjoy the same protection as a virtual private network (VPN). If you must use a computer other than your own, make sure you log out of any program you are using and clear the browser cache, form fields, and cookies. If you're unsure of how to take these precautions, be aware of what kind of browser you're using, and a quick Google or Bing search will help you.

What are the benefits for the lawyers from the use of SaaS for law practice management?

The advantages of using SaaS for law practice management are many, but probably the two most important benefits are reduced IT complexity and a substantial up-front savings of time and money.

When law firms embrace SaaS, they eliminate the need for servers and the networking, security, backup devices, and consultants that come along for the ride. Consider the typical three- to five-year time frame for [the life of] hardware, which adds up to a substantial cost savings over time. In addition, law firms that embrace SaaS don't have to worry about software installations or upgrades since they access the software through a browser.

Properly backing up and securing information is a complex endeavor that most small firms on a budget won't be able to perform correctly, inexpensively, or without headaches. SaaS allows firms to leverage SAS 70-certified data facilities, top-notch physical and network security, constant monitoring, and backups that they would not otherwise be able to afford.

Aside from these more commonly understood advantages of using SaaS, there are many less-known benefits that can have a huge impact on firm profitability. Because SaaS providers depend on month-to-month payments, they need to keep their customers happy by creating efficient, intuitive interfaces. Since both hardware, software, and additional networking is removed from the office, fewer things can break, resulting in less downtime, phone calls, and IT consulting bills. Remote access is enabled via ubiquitous Web access and is also conducted securely, since data are only accessed and doesn't reside on the remote machines. Smart phones with full browsing capabilities, such as the iPhone, Android, and Palm Pre, allow secure access to legal management software via the mobile Web.

What are some of the risks of using SaaS, and for each risk, how can the lawyer mitigate that risk?

Legal professionals should be aware of two major risks with SaaS: connectivity issues and control over data.

It's critical for firms to assess the reliability of their Internet access. Spotty coverage or slow speeds will make SaaS usage irritating at best or unusable at worst. Thankfully, reliable broadband is readily accessible to most people via a variety of means, and connectivity backup devices such as USB modems or MiFi devices are within most budgets.

Then again, you may have the fastest download speeds on the planet, but if your SaaS provider has outages all the time, you won't be able to access your data. Law firms should examine service level agreements (SLAs) of potential SaaS providers for uptime guarantees.

Law firms must ensure that they own their data stored in the cloud and that they can download copies of them on demand. By securely storing local copies of data, lawyers ensure protection against a number of risks: data corruption or loss on the SaaS servers, locking themselves into a single provider for their entire firm life, and connectivity issues. Firms should make sure that their backups come in easily readable formats and that they store and transmit data securely.

Before choosing a third-party hosting service, what questions would you recommend that the lawyers ask?

1) What is your uptime guarantee? This should come in the form of an SLA. Generally, look for guarantees between 99.99 percent and 99.9999 percent uptime. If someone guarantees 100 percent uptime, run screaming. They don't know what they're doing.

2) How often and when do you typically perform server maintenance?

3) Who owns my data?

4) Who has access to my data?

5) What physical security precautions are taken with my data?

6) What network, programmatic, and system security measures protect my data?

7) Can I download my data securely in usable formats whenever I want?

8) Do you perform independent security audits?

If you could share any advice with lawyers considering using SaaS for law practice management, what would it be?

My advice is this: Do what's best for your own comfort level and your firm's efficiency. But when determining your comfort level, assess the true risk of how you conduct business today versus how things would change if you used a third-party SaaS provider.

Here are some reality-check questions for most lawyers: If you keep your data in-house, how secure is it? Who has access to it aside from your staff? Are you able to reliably apply security patches, remove malware, protect against viruses, maintain a firewall, and enjoy the same data, connectivity, and power redundancies as a modern data center? What happens if your office is inaccessible? Where is your e-mail stored? If it's on a commodity mail server, your most sensitive information is already in the cloud and, most likely, unsecured.

Where do you see the use of SaaS in law practice management headed in the future of the legal profession?

SaaS is inevitable. It might take a few years, or it might take twenty years, but most forms of computing are headed in the direction of the cloud. In reality, we're back where we started with the days of mainframes and dumb terminals. Customers leveraging Web-based SaaS apps merely use their keyboards and monitors. All processing is done on a powerful server somewhere in cyberspace.

Creating a Virtual Law Practice by Combining Separate Software Applications

In addition to those products designed specifically for lawyers, there are many SaaS products for general business that may be used piecemeal by legal professionals to take part of their law office management online. Some software applications may be free, and they may have a professional version of their software that will provide more features for a price.

There are some risks associated with the fact that different applications will handle different aspects of the client's confidential data. For example, some lawyers will use Basecamp (**www.basecamphq.com**) by 37Signals to work with clients and other lawyers online, or they may use WebEx (**www.webex.com**) conferencing to meet with their clients.[9] They may then use a time, billing, and invoicing system, such as Rocket Matter (**www.rocketmatter.com**) or Clio (**www.goclio.com**), to provide their clients with online invoices and the ability to pay online. Calendaring and task scheduling with the client's matter may be handled on the same or a completely different application. The data transmitted during these transactions with the client may or may not be securely saved and recorded, depending on what the software provides and what level of security the lawyer has paid for. The lawyer must then find creative ways to ensure that all of the transactions with the client across platforms are easily accessible for future use, link the client and case matter together, and comply with recordkeeping requirements.

---

[9]BaseCamp, **www.basecamphq.com/**; WebEx, **www.webex.com**

While using different software applications piecemeal may cost less in the short term, there may be more risks involved. A lawyer's practice requires a higher level of security and confidentiality for client data than many other professions and in general businesses for which these applications were developed. Consider a popular Google application, for example. Google Docs not only allows individuals to collaborate on a document together, but it also allows them to upload and download files for sharing that are related to the project.[10] However, a review of Google's terms of service provides the warning that Google does not guarantee the security or privacy of the information stored in their applications. Furthermore, the user agreement makes no guarantee that the data you have stored there will be there tomorrow and that it is securely backed up. There is no guarantee of who has access to your data once it is placed in the application.

Other applications similar to Google Docs were created for the purpose of sharing information with family and friends, not for professionals to conduct sensitive business with other professionals and clients. The user agreements or terms of service for these applications will reflect this. Because of the unique risks that the delivery of legal services online may raise for lawyers—such as unauthorized practice of law, conflict of interest checks between online and offline clients, record retention requirements—it may be safer for a lawyer considering virtual law practice to first understand these concerns before attempting to add piecemeal software applications to their traditional law office model. On the other hand, if the law practice's existing software systems easily communicate or import and export data securely with these stand-alone applications, it may be cost effective to take a portion of the law practice management online using piecemeal applications while transitioning other aspects of the practice over to the full delivery of legal services online.

> **Case Study: Virtual Law Office Formed with Piecemeal SaaS and Other Applications Operated in Conjunction with a Brick and Mortar Law Office**
> *Robert N. Grossbart, Esq., Partner at Grossbart, Portney & Rosenberg, P.A., Baltimore* (www.mdbankruptcylaw.com). Grossbart, Portney & Rosenberg, P.A., a Maryland-based firm, provides bankruptcy legal services with a focus on Chapter 7 and Chapter 13 bankruptcy. The firm delivers legal services online and through a traditional law office setting using a variety of technology solutions.

---

[10]See the Google Docs terms of service, Section 14.2: "YOU EXPRESSLY UNDERSTAND AND AGREE THAT YOUR USE OF THE SERVICES IS AT YOUR SOLE RISK AND THAT THE SERVICES ARE PROVIDED 'AS IS' AND 'AS AVAILABLE.'" **http://www.google.com/accounts/TOS** (accessed May 27, 2010).

Technology: It is in conjunction with brick and mortar. I represent primarily consumer debtors. I have a minimum of a one-time visit. That is for me to verify that the person actually exists and if I want to take the case. I use a variety of technologies: Goldmine for general database and calendaring needs; Word to store all scanned and downloaded documents (we attempt to stay paperless); Outlook for e-mail; Pacer as a federal court resource; Firefox as our Web browser; QuickBooks for accounting; Maryland Judiciary Case Search for judgments and liens; Bestcase as our bankruptcy software; Dragon voice recognition; Chaos for billing; MDbankruptcylaw.com is for where clients can learn about bankruptcy and communicate with me; blog; and LogMeIn.[11]

When did you open your virtual law practice?

It evolved. My Web site was launched maybe in 1999. I was using many of the software above prior to the launch. I am a CPA as well, and it was quickly apparent that this could save me money in fixed cost reduction.

Why did you decide to open a virtual law practice?

Because I believe that you must be able to provide a more fluid availability to your clients. It's no different than a retail store that has a Web presence.

What are the benefits you have seen from this form of law practice?

Efficiency, speed, and clarity of communication. Document movement is easier. Clients can receive a password that allows them to go to my site and retrieve documents and court-related information. This makes the necessity of calling decrease for matters that don't require speaking to a lawyer. My office is mobile. Fixed office costs drop dramatically.

What has the public response been to your practice?

The younger the client, the more apt they are to utilize this form of communication. Clients can reach me easier than by phone. They can also hold my feet to the fire, as I can, based on date of communication.

How have other legal professionals responded to your practice?

My accountant loves it. He does not need to come to my office. Everything is by e-mail and scanning. Other lawyers and I can communicate and review documents more easily.

---

[11]LogMeIn is a software company that provides remote access and desktop control for businesses. **http://www.logmein.com** (accessed May 27, 2010).

How long did it take for your practice to turn a profit?

Pretty early, but I was transitioning from brick and mortar to semivirtual, so I had a built-in advantage.

How much did you initially invest in marketing or advertising your virtual law practice?

Very little. I went the old-fashioned way initially by using the phone book and mass mailing. Now I am strictly Internet.

What methods do you use to market your virtual law practice?

The Internet, Google and a few other Web sites that promote lawyers.

Did you receive formal approval or an ethics or advisory opinion from the bar association before opening your practice?

No, but I have spoken to lawyers who work almost exclusively [with virtual law offices] and relied upon their understandings.

Did you have any problem obtaining malpractice insurance for your virtual law practice?

No problems. I can't remember it being a question on my renewal.

If you could share any advice with lawyers considering virtual law practice, either regarding the setup or management of this form of practice, what would it be?

Your Web site is the start. The type of Web site is based on the type of client you are trying to reach. A more sophisticated client wants information. Other clients only are concerned with service.

Where do you see virtual law practice headed in the future of the legal profession?

It is a major component to any law firm. Clients expect their lawyer to be knowledgeable in the virtual world.

What to Expect in a Provider's Service Legal Agreement (SLA)

Expect the following provisions to be found in a standard legal SaaS contract. If they are not there, ask the provider for clarification.

- Service availability (uptime %)
- Customer support response time
- Data retention and return policies
- Confidentiality and nondisclosure statements
- Who has access to your data? There should be a provision stating that the provider will not access the law office data unless the lawyer requests assistance with a matter related to the software that requires the data to be decrypted and viewed or if the provider needs to perform some maintenance or update to the software that requires decryption and viewing of the data. In most cases, the law office data should remain encrypted and only decrypted with the permission of the lawyer. Regarding data center security, see the section above concerning who has access to the servers in a data center.
- Privacy policy
- Subscription and renewal terms
- Terms for payment of the service
- Limitation of liability: The provider should not be held responsible for the lawyers' own decisions and actions taken in regard to the operation of their virtual law office. Nor should the provider be responsible for the actions that the lawyers' online clients may take when working on the virtual law office.
- Define "use of the service" in terms of the following: server memory, CPU time, hard drive space allowed along with provisions for growth of storage space used, reasonable use of the network, such as the computer hardware, network servers, and/or any third-party computer software programs that the provider uses to host the service.

What is reasonable "use"? Reasonable use might be 10 percent of the provider's standard server memory that is being used for the service by the virtual law office. Using 10 percent of the CPU time for the service by the virtual law office would also be reasonable. The amount of reasonable hard drive space is going to depend on the nature of the virtual law office and how you intend to use it for document and file storage. The typical amount of hard drive space that would provide more than enough space with room to grow would be 4 gigabytes for a completely Web-based solo practice. The provider should be able to offer additional hard drive space for an additional fee to accommodate the growth of your virtual law practice. This is discussed in more detail above in the section on evaluating the provider's infrastructure (see page 49).

VLO Startup Checklist #2: Choose the Technology

___ Research the different software providers.

Get answers to these questions:

___ What are your data retention and return policies? What happens to my law office data if I discontinue the service or something happens to the company?

___ What is the pricing structure and history? Is there a cap on the amount that the fees may be increased? Are there any additional costs associated with the setup or additional use of hard drive/server space as my virtual law office grows?

___ Who will have access to my law office data? Does data stay encrypted at all times?

___ Is there end-to-end encryption? What security precautions exist?

___ Will my virtual law office have a dedicated slice of server space?

___ Do your servers have geo-redundancy, or do you offer data escrow? Do these services cost extra?

___ Is there any downtime when I may not be able to access my law office data?

___ How often are my law office data backed up?

___ What type of technical support and training are offered? Does this cost extra?

___ How often are new features added to the software? Where is the development of the software heading?

___ Review the license or user agreement (See above for a list of items to expect in the agreement.)

___ Know your own comfort level with technology. Subscribe for free trials or access to test sites to make sure you are comfortable using the technology and have a practical understanding that you will use to work with clients online.

___ Optional: Have your own backup system for data that resides on your own in-house machines or on portable hard drives.

___ Optional: Have an alternative method of Internet access if you live in an area with regular outage or use a method that is not reliable.

Case Study: Advice from a Practice Management Advisor
Erik Mazzone, Esq.

*Erik Mazzone is a practice management advisor for the North Carolina Bar Association and Director of the Center for Practice Management. He is the author of Law Practice Matters (**www.lawpracticematters.org**).*

Have you ever worked with a lawyer who has operated a virtual practice?

I've worked with a lot of lawyers who run some aspect(s) of their firm virtually. From hosted exchange servers to virtual offices through office suites to SaaS, I find that a lot of lawyers are excited by the idea of not being tied down to a physical location and pile of hardware.

Please provide an example of a traditional task or legal service and how the technology was used to make it more efficient, secure, cost-effective, etc.

I know one firm that uses an online service (RightSignature) to allow clients to quickly and easily sign client agreements without having to come into their office. A small example is the use of SimpleCertified-Mail.com to replace the formerly cumbersome process of preparing and using paper certified mail.

Are there any legal services, projects, or tasks that you believe cannot be handled as well for the law practice through the use of technology? Why not? Please provide an example.

Yes. I still think the act of meeting with a client for an initial consultation is better performed in person when possible. Conducting initial consultations is a sales function, and, in my opinion, sales is still best performed as a face-to-face activity. It's not that it is impossible to make sales over the phone or over the Web; it's just a bit more challenging.

What are the benefits to the lawyer's clients from the use of the technology to deliver legal services? From your perspective, what has the general public's response been to virtual law practice?

There is no question that clients benefit from work that is produced efficiently and with a minimum of errors. Technology is a big help in pursuing those two goals. A lot of lawyers still take a dim view of emerging technologies, but I haven't met too many of them who would trade Microsoft Word for a typewriter.

Are there any concerns that you have with a virtual law office as a form of law practice management?

My primary concern for lawyers with virtual practices is the same as for lawyers with bricks and mortar practices: that they develop enough business to achieve the goals they set for themselves.

What methods of marketing would you recommend for a virtual law practice? How would that marketing differ from the methods used by a traditional law practice?

One advantage of a virtual practice is the ability to serve clients from a broad geographic area (while not running afoul of UPL rules, of course). Marketing that pairs well with that advantage would be the variety of technology-leveraged techniques: social media, blogging, pay-per-click, etc. I also think that lawyers with virtual practices would be well served to use these techniques to humanize their online presence. People do business with people they know and like.

What security or best practices tips would you provide to a lawyer who is using technology to handle law practice management functions online?

Being a lawyer in the twenty-first century means learning the basics of computers and security. From metadata to identity theft, there are a lot of things lawyers simply need to know about technology now that they didn't need to know thirty years ago. Of course, they didn't have iPods back then, so it all comes out in the wash.

What are some of the risks of using SaaS for law practice management, and for each risk, how can the lawyer mitigate that risk?

I think the primary risk of SaaS is that the lawyer is going to somehow lose access to his or her most important data. Most of the reputable SaaS vendors out there take great pains to make sure that this will not happen, and they do that in a variety of ways, from data escrow agents to riding on the infrastructure of a more established company. The important thing is for the lawyer to ask the question and understand the answer.

Before choosing a third-party hosting service or other product used for a virtual law practice, what questions would you recommend that the lawyers ask?

What is my tolerance for risk versus my need to keep costs constrained?

If you could share any advice with lawyers interested in or currently operating a virtual law practice, what would it be?

Market yourself like crazy. Actually, that's my advice for lawyers interested in opening any kind of practice.

Where do you see virtual law practice headed in the future of the legal profession?

To the middle. In some form or fashion, the creation of client relationships and delivery of legal services over the Web is going to be a big part of how all lawyers do business. Remember when we used to call travel agents to plan a trip? Me neither.

CHAPTER FOUR

Practical Setup and How-to Basics

Choose a Name for Your Virtual Law Office

Selecting the name for your virtual law office is going to depend on two factors: (1) your state bar's rules and regulations and (2) what makes the most sense from a marketing standpoint. Most state bars adhere to the ABA's Model Rule of Professional Conduct 7.5 regarding firm names.[1] The key is to choose a name for the virtual law practice that will not be misleading to the public about the nature and scope of the online delivery of legal services.

There has been some discussion among law practice management consultants and marketing experts about whether it is wise to use the word *virtual*, which has the philosophical meaning of "not existing in reality." While the popular and contemporary meaning of the word derives from the IT and computer field rather than the philosophical meaning, the

---

[1] ABA's Model Rule of Professional Conduct 7.5, Firm Names and Letterhead: "(a) A lawyer shall not use a firm name, letterhead or other professional designation that violates Rule 7.1. A trade name may be used by a lawyer in private practice if it does not imply a connection with a government agency or with a public or charitable legal services organization and is not otherwise in violation of Rule 7.1. (b) A law firm with offices in more than one jurisdiction may use the same name or other professional designation in each jurisdiction, but identification of the lawyers in an office of the firm shall indicate the jurisdictional limitations on those not licensed to practice in the jurisdiction where the office is located. (c) The name of a lawyer holding a public office shall not be used in the name of a law firm, or in communications on its behalf, during any substantial period in which the lawyer is not actively and regularly practicing with the firm. (d) Lawyers may state or imply that they practice in a partnership or other organization only when that is the fact." ABA Center for Professional Responsibility, **http://www.abanet.org/cpr/mrpc/rule_7_5.html** (accessed January 17, 2010).

question is whether the term *virtual* is understood by the general public in the context of an online law practice. For this reason, it has been suggested by some that another way to market a virtual law practice would be to use the phrase "online or Web-based law office" rather than the term *virtual*. Before making this decision, the lawyer should know his or her client base and what methods will work best regionally based on other competitive law office's marketing practices. At this time, most virtual law practices are marketing themselves as "virtual law firms" or "virtual law offices." As the number of these practices increases the public awareness, it might also be best to stay consistent with this trend in marketing so that it capitalizes on the terminology currently being presented to the public through other virtual law practices' marketing campaigns.

URL Address

Another factor in choosing a name for your virtual law practice will be the availability of a related URL address. Most of the marketing for a virtual law office will be the direct marketing of that URL to drive prospective clients to your services. Accordingly, you will want the name of the firm and the URL to be somewhat related and easy to remember. Again, this is subject to your state bar's restrictions. Your state bar may require the prior registration and approval of the URL. The state bars may check to ensure that the URL name is not misleading to the public about the lawyer or the law practice. In most cases, as long as the home page of the Web site clearly identifies the lawyer or law firm to which the site belongs, then the URL does not have to contain language that specifically identifies the Web site's owners.

You may also want to purchase additional URLs with similar sounds or spellings that you do not directly market but that may be used by competitive law practices or mistakenly typed in by prospective clients searching for your virtual law office.

Build a Web Site

Your virtual law office Web site is the front door to your law practice. First impressions are important. The image you project on this site will be what instills trust in your prospective clients and prompts them to take action in registering and requesting legal services from you. Investing in the development of your virtual law office Web site will be worth the time and expense.

When building your Web site there are two different standpoints to consider when coming up with the design and content. First, from the marketing side, prospective clients need to be able to easily navigate through the site content and locate the method of registering on your virtual law office without getting lost or overwhelmed with too many design features or gimmicks that distract from the purpose of your site. Second, any content and design on your site has to comply with your state bar's rules and regulations regarding attorney websites and advertising. Below is a list of "must-have" features from the marketing standpoint. A more in-depth discussion of the required Web site components for complying with the professional responsibility rules in most states follows this list. None of the design suggestions should conflict with the features required for compliance with state bar rules and regulations for lawyer Web sites:

- Create a brand through your site. Use your logo design or come up with a tag line that you may display on your site and use in your advertising. That brand will be the link that the public remembers from their first impression of it through your marketing techniques to when they take action and visit your site.

- Ensure quality content. Create educational resources, links, and a general blog educating the public on the legal areas of your practice. If you are not a great writer or do not have the time to develop the copy yourself, consider hiring a copywriter to collaborate with you on the material for the site. There are many experienced copywriters out there specifically with a legal background or who have worked with legal professionals in the past.

- Provide easy-to-navigate links and tabs from the home page to other content. You don't want a prospective client getting lost going from your home page to any of your site's other resources.

- Have a clean design. Do not make the site too frilly or busy with too much text or too many images. This makes it challenging for visitors to find what they are looking for.

- Show your face. Personalize the site by having a professional photo of yourself and possibly your support staff.

- Consider adding a video to record a welcome message introducing yourself and your practice and explaining how your virtual law office operates. Post that video on YouTube with a link back to the site for wider circulation.

♦ Provide useful and free information or tools for clients. One good example of this is the 2010 winner of the ABA Keane Award for Excellence in eLawyering, Rosen Divorce Law Firm, based in Raleigh, NC (**www.rosen.com**). This divorce law firm Web site contains many samples of legal documents, educational articles, free child support calculators, and other tools to allow the general public to gather information online before retaining the services of the firm.

Design Requirements for Professional Responsibility

Your virtual law office Web site must also comply with the rules of professional conduct and other regulations of the lawyer's state bar regarding lawyer advertising. This requires careful scrutiny of the content of a virtual law practice Web site and needs to be taken into consideration from the beginning of the Web site development and ensured before the site launches publically.

The ABA's eLawyering Task Force, ABA Law Practice Management Section, and ABA Standing Committee on the Delivery of Legal Services published the "Best Practice Guidelines for Legal Information Web Site Providers" on February 10, 2003.[2] This publication provides guidelines regarding Web site content that may be applied to a virtual law office. Many of these guidelines are also written into the rules and regulations of many state bars, either under general advertising rules or as separate Web site advertising rules.

In general, the virtual law office Web site should contain adequate contact information to inform the public of the lawyer or law firm providing the services, where they are licensed to practice law, and some method of contact, either by e-mail address or telephone number. This information allows the lay public to conduct their own research regarding the source of legal services being offered and to make an informed decision before retaining that lawyer or firm.

Providing contact information on the virtual law office Web site is one area that can be tricky depending on the structure of the virtual law prac-

---

[2]See **http://www.abanet.org/elawyering/tool/practices.shtml** (accessed May 13, 2008); See also Athey, J. Clayton. "The Ethics of Attorney Websites: Updating the Model Rules to Better Deal with Emerging Technologies," 13 Geo. J. Legal Ethics 499, 505 (2000).

tice and your state bar's requirements. This comes into play usually when the state bar requires a physical address or at least a PO box address on the virtual law office Web site and the lawyer does not actually reside in the state where he or she is providing the online legal services.

Does the lawyer have to retain a PO box and mail-forwarding services in that state? Does he or she have to form a relationship with a traditional brick and mortar law office and use that firm's physical address? Currently, there are several virtual law offices that provide legal services within one state's jurisdiction while the lawyers physically reside in another.[3] Some lawyers may work from home and not wish to publically publish their home address for the general public online or even for their clients. The concern of the state bars seems to be the desire to provide the online client with another method of reaching the lawyer other than through the secure client portal. Imagine the scenario in which a virtual law office exists on a URL one day, and the next when the client goes back, it is gone. While this may also happen with a physical law office—traditional law firms are forever dissolving partnerships, merging, closing up shop, or opening up other branches—the concern is that the online client would not know where to turn.

One simple solution to this issue for the lawyer who resides in one state but provides services in another, or who does not want to list a home address online, is to add a link to their state bar's membership directory. Let's be realistic: it doesn't take much work to discover a person's contact information online if someone really wants to, along with sundry other personal information. Not only does a link to the bar's membership directory usually provide the lawyer's address and phone, but it also provides proof that the lawyer is licensed and sometimes whether that status is in good standing. If nothing else, this link on the site provides a way for the clients and prospective clients to contact the bar to get the contact information that they need should they ever have difficulty reaching the lawyer through the client portal.

As far as providing online clients with additional contact information, if you choose to do so, reserve this for the secure portion of the virtual law

---

[3]See for example, Richard Granat's Maryland Family Lawyer at **www.mdfamilylawyer.com**. Granat resides in Florida and provides Maryland legal services online. See also Rania Combs's Texas Wills and Trusts Law Online at **www.texaswillsandtrustslaw.com**. Combs resides in North Carolina and practices Texas law online through her virtual law office.

office rather than posting it on the static Web site. For example, provide the clients who you have chosen to represent and who have gone through the engagement process with a phone number or a PO box. They may then schedule a phone conference through the online client portal if needed. I would not recommend providing that information to anyone who registers on your site until you have determined that you will be representing them. This helps to limit the number of unnecessary phone calls to your practice and allows you to refer those clients instead through an online referral database that you have created rather than through a phone conversation.

Any content on the virtual law office Web site should include the date the content was last reviewed so that anyone reading the site will have a frame of reference. If the site is set up as a blog, then the date of publication for the content is not only provided automatically with each post but may also be archived and made searchable as a resource for the public and clients. General content and legal advice included on the Web site should state somewhere that members of the public should not rely on this advice and should seek the advice of a lawyer for assistance with legal needs for their individual circumstances. Providing links to other reliable resources for the public to use in making decisions and finding legal assistance is preferable. The jurisdiction of the Web site should be absolutely clear to the public and should be stated in several places throughout the Web site.

Some may ask whether a virtual law office is a direct solicitation to the public for online legal services. The answer is no. A prospective client would have to actively search online to find legal services provided in a virtual law office. Given the large number of online lawyer listings and directories, it is highly unlikely that any member of the public who is capable of conducting an online search for legal assistance would be misled by visiting a virtual law office online for an initial consultation.

Furthermore, most online clients are familiar with conducting highly sensitive transactions online on a daily basis, including online investing, banking, and purchasing and selling goods and services. The steps that a prospective client must take to register with a virtual law office and seek legal services from the lawyer also ensure that the prospective client is made aware of the nature of the legal services provided online through the clickwrap agreement and multiple notices throughout.

Case Study: Advice from a Lawyer and Founder of a National Coaching/Consulting Firm
Susan Cartier Liebel

*Susan Cartier Liebel is a lawyer and founder of the national coaching/ consulting firm Build A Solo Practice, LLC. She is also the founder of Solo Practice University (**www.solopracticeuniversity.com**), a Web-based educational community for legal professionals.*

What are the benefits for legal professionals that you have seen from this form of law practice?

A virtual law office allows for greater demographic reach within a jurisdiction. Being able to cover the four corners of one's jurisdiction or go national, if allowed by the practice area, opens up a whole new client-rich base. Prior to a virtual law office, lawyers were imprisoned by a brick and mortar building. This limited the pool of potential clients unless one was to set up satellite offices through the jurisdiction. It is also much easier to deal with clients, because the interactions can be asynchronous, freeing the lawyer from the traditional workday hours. And no less important, less vulnerability (when used properly) to the number-one reason for lawyer grievance: lack of communication.

What are the benefits to the lawyer's clients from the use of the technology to deliver legal services?

Generally, it is easier for a client who has a hectic life to work with a lawyer in their own time from the comfort of their home or office. It eliminates their having to take time off from work, getting a babysitter, traveling to a brick and mortar building, sitting in a waiting room, and more. I find, if handled correctly by the lawyer, it is more respectful of the client than traditional attorney-client interaction, which constantly requires their physical presence for many matters that could be handled just as effectively, if not more efficiently, online. It also can be considerably less expensive for a client to work with a VLO practitioner because the lawyer has designed a more cost-effective practice.

What methods of marketing would you recommend for a virtual law practice? How would that marketing differ from the methods used by a traditional law practice?

By virtue of being online and wishing to attract clients who are comfortable online, the best method of attracting those clients would naturally be . . . online! This would include extensive use of social media platforms such as blogging, creating and optimizing Facebook business pages, LinkedIn, Twitter, and other platforms that may be hyperspecialized for a given audience. It also may include online forms of credentialing, including teaching online and contributing to online magazines relevant to their practice area. I would also encourage the use of video. When you are dealing with someone online whom you've never met, the opportunity to meet in two-dimensional space, if not the ideal three-dimensional realm, will separate you from others and may be the tipping point in selection if all else is equal. The major difference would be allocation of time and money. Social media engagement requires more sweat equity. This is a significant change.

If you could share any advice with lawyers interested in or currently operating a virtual law practice, what would it be?

Be prepared to be a good time manager. Operating a virtual practice and technically being accessible 24/7 does not mean you *have* to be accessible 24/7. Good time management is key to your emotional and physical health. It is also imperative that you manage your clients' expectations, as there is a tendency to truly believe a lawyer is available 24/7 simply because he or she operates online.

Where do you see virtual law practice headed in the future of the legal profession?

I think it *is* the future, at least for solos and small firms. I also believe it is imperative, regardless of the nature of your practice today, that you will need to be offering some version of your services via a virtual law practice to accommodate the growing demand of clients who will be seeking out these services.

What Are the Startup Costs? Laying Out a Business Plan and Budget

There are several variables that will come into play when estimating startup costs for a virtual law office. These will include the structure of virtual law practice that you choose, the software or technology you implement, your practice area(s), your experience as a lawyer, and whether you are operating an existing law practice before opening your virtual law office or just hanging your virtual shingle straight out of law school and after bar passage.

When Can You Expect to See Steady Client Revenue?

A key component of budgeting is determined by the estimated amount of incoming client revenue. If you have opened a completely Web-based practice and are starting your business from scratch, expect to spend nine months to one year before you see steady online client revenue from your virtual practice. If you are adding a virtual law office to an existing brick and mortar practice, it may take less time to form an online client base because you may be able to include the marketing of the virtual law office in your traditional practice's marketing strategy. Like hanging your shingle on any form of law practice, it takes time to get the word out to the public about the services that you provide online. Just launching a virtual law office Web site publically does not guarantee that prospective clients will know how to find you. It will take time to build the Search Engine Optimization (SEO) of your site in addition to other marketing factors that take time and consistency to kick in.

When budgeting for your practice, you also need to consider the pricing of the online legal services. If you are providing packages for a fixed fee, you may be charging less per client than you might be in a traditional law practice, where you might be using the billable hour or working with clients for a longer duration. Accordingly, determine how many clients you will need to pull in per week or per month to see a decent return on your investment. If you need a larger quantity of clients due to the reduced legal fees you are offering, then you may need to invest in a service that provides leads and add that component to your budget and marketing strategy.

Costs and Your ROI Analysis

Marketing and how much you intend to invest in the launch of your virtual law practice are going to make a big difference in your startup costs. A section devoted in more detail to marketing your virtual law practice is included below. Here we will focus on the costs associated with the setup, maintenance, and daily operation of a completely virtual law practice. If you are operating a physical law office in addition to a Web-based offering, then most of these costs may already be included in what you invest in your current practice and will not be added expenses. However, if you are a completely Web-based practice, you will notice that there are a good number of expenses that you will save by not operating a physical law office.

The largest expenses are going to be the initial investment in your Web site development and the annual and per-transaction fees for your online payment-processing services, depending on which one you choose. Other expenses, such as malpractice insurance coverage, bar and association fees, and CLE costs to maintain your license, should be the same as they would with a traditional law office.

Startup costs have been broken down into two categories: hardware and software costs, with a note in parentheses next to the item when there is a free resource or alternative. Items marked with an asterisk (*) are optional.

Hardware Costs

♦ Computer
  — UPS surge protectors
♦ Internet access
  — Wireless card
  — DSL
  — Backup Internet method*
♦ Mobile devices
  — Smart phones
  — Netbooks
♦ Scanner
♦ Backup methods (in addition to third-party SaaS provider backups of law office data)
  — Portable hard drives
  — TrueCrypt/SyncToy (free open-source software)
  — USB key
♦ Other*
  — Microphone
  — Headset
  — Webcam
    ♦ In computer or separate

Software Costs

♦ SaaS product
  — One product, or use piecemeal products

- ◆ Web browser
  - — Mozilla Firefox with security add-ons, such as NoScripts (free)
- ◆ Third-party credit card processing company's services
  - — Be aware of per-transaction costs and monthly or annual fees.
  - — Factor in the value of the service handling your IOLTA and trust accounting compliance.
  - — PayPal, Google Shopping Cart (free) (See below for a discussion of potential malpractice risks associated with taking credit cards online and using free processing company services.)
- ◆ Software designed for your practice area if needed in addition to the SaaS service*
  - — State-specific programs
  - — Automated document-assembly programs
  - — HotDocs, Pro Docs, Rapidocs, etc.
- ◆ Desktop sharing software*
- ◆ iContact or other service*
- ◆ Quickbooks or other accounting software

Here are a few examples of useful free software applications:

  - — Open Office suite
  - — PDF converter
    - ◆ PrimoPDF
  - — Adobe Reader
  - — TweetDeck
  - — Twitter
  - — Mozilla's Thunderbird E-mail
  - — Skype
  - — Google apps, such as Google Voice, Reader, Docs
  - — Vimeo or YouTube
  - — Slideshare

Office supplies in a virtual law office are minimal. However, this depends on what services you plan on providing your online clients. If you plan on mailing them copies of their documents printed on fine linen paper or in a formal package in addition to providing a digital copy, then this will add to your office supply expenses. Online mailing services and postage will be included here as well as the paper, ink, and any folders, labels, and methods of packaging the product.

Case Study: Solo Virtual Law Office
Bernardo Granwehr

*Bernardo Granwehr, Esq., is the owner of Granwehr Law Firm, PLC, which provides legal services pertaining to Iowa state law through its virtual law office (**www.iowalawyeronline.com**).*

Technology: My practice is completely Web based. Client intake is done via online questionnaires. Clients can also contact me via e-mail or phone. My toll-free answering service is VOIP based. The physical address for my office is the eighth floor of a five-story building—a virtual address that is a step up from a PO box in terms of professionalism. [*Note: Granwehr uses the SaaS services of DirectLaw, Inc.*]

Launch date: The firm opened in March 2008. In September 2008, we launched the Web site.

Why did you decide to open a virtual law practice?

There were two reasons I decided to open a virtual law practice. First, ironically, I wanted a way to experience a more traditional practice of law, but the odd hours of my day job as chief of staff of the Iowa State Auditor's Office would not allow for this. A virtual law practice gave me the flexibility to accomplish this goal. Second, I saw a huge need for legal services among low- to middle-income people. That need only increased with the economic downturn. I saw a virtual law firm as a way to meet the needs of those people.

What are the benefits you have seen from this form of law practice?

For me, the benefit is flexibility. For my clients, the benefit is accessibility. Before my firm opened its doors, Iowans had two main options—pay top dollar for full representation by a lawyer, or go without legal representation and pray that they were doing the right thing. My service fills the gap by putting competent, lawyer-assisted self-representation within the reach of almost anyone.

What has the public response been to your practice?

The public response has been good so far—particularly the response of my clients. They really appreciate the accurate documents and clear guidance provided by my service.

How have other legal professionals responded to your practice?

I have had little interaction with other legal professionals regarding this practice. Most are intrigued or curious, but one of my colleagues who visited my Web site during unrelated research complimented me on the innovative approach of this firm.

How long did it take for your practice to turn a profit?

My first profitable month was January 2009.

How much did you initially invest in marketing or advertising your virtual law practice?

I initially invested $400 the first month. I am now investing $500 to $700 per month.

What methods do you use to market your virtual law practice?

I use keyword search services such as Google AdWords. I find them to be effective because, properly constructed, the ads only target those who are looking for the virtual law service.

Did you have any problem obtaining malpractice insurance for your virtual law practice? If so, what were the issues and how did you resolve them? Were you able to receive any discounts on malpractice insurance due to the use of technology?

I had a problem with the first carrier I approached. Virtual law practice is something the carrier had never seen before. As a result, they refused to insure the practice. I ended up going to an out-of-state insurer that had some experience with practices of this type. The carrier knew that, due to the nature of the practice, it is actually a relatively low-risk practice.

If you could share any advice with lawyers considering virtual law practice, either regarding the setup or management of this form of practice, what would it be?

Remember who your competition is. It's not a brick and mortar law firm but document mills such as LegalZoom. Like the document mills, a virtual law practice can provide legal documents to people, but law firms provide the additional value of legal guidance. The key to success is to provide the legal documents and legal guidance at a price that competes with the document mills. You must leverage technology to provide those services at a competitive price.

Where do you see virtual law practice headed in the future of the legal profession?

I think virtual law practice will grow over the next several years. Full-service lawyers still have a vital role in the future, and the growth of virtual law practices will not change that, but I believe virtual law firms will eventually displace document mills as more people take advantage of those services. This will be a good development for budget-strained courts because self-represented people will be more educated and less likely to waste the courts' time. It will also be good for the clients who, for a comparable price to a document mill, get the additional value of legal guidance.

Having a Home Office or Working Remotely

A virtual law office provides you with the flexibility to work wherever you may securely access the Internet, whether that means having a home office, sharing office space with other professionals, using the public or university libraries, or hunkering down in local coffee shops. But working from a home office is not for everyone. Depending on your situation and work habits, it may be more practical to work from the local coffee shop than a home office. If you are not meeting with clients in person and have established networks of other professionals online, then where you work is really more of a personal than professional decision. As a side note, though, another major benefit to operating a virtual law office from your home is being able to take advantage of possible home office tax deductions.

Expenses That You Don't Need to Start Up Your Virtual Law Practice

There are some expenses that are not necessary to the startup and operation of a virtual law practice. Some of these items, such as formal paper announcements, have been traditionally heralded as good practice for a law firm opening its doors to the community. Because the virtual law office is located online, use of paper announcements and business cards are not as effective at spreading the word about your online practice nor do they generally result in traffic to your Web site. In addition to that, the paper, printing and mailing can be an expensive and time consuming project that may reach other attorneys but rarely pulls in new prospective clients. Other expenses that you might have to purchase to open a traditional law office, such as furniture for the reception or meeting rooms and other office supplies are not necessary. As long as your hardware, whether it is a PC, Mac, Netbook, Smartphone or other device, can open a Web browser and access the Internet, there is no need to upgrade to a new computer before launching your virtual law practice. While some of the items in this list below might be nice extras to supplement your practice, none of them are necessary for the startup.

- Business cards
- Paper announcements that you mail out to other professionals or clients
- A new computer or mobile device
- A separate phone line or fax number
- Listings in costly lawyer directories—print or online versions
- Traditional print ads
- A full-time, in-person assistant
- Furnished office space

Forming the Business Entity for Your Virtual Law Practice

If you are forming a new business entity for the setup of your virtual law practice, you will need to select a form of business entity available in the state where you will be conducting your business. While it may be the simplest method, a sole proprietorship may not work for your online law office. In most states, a sole proprietor must register in the city in which he or she is conducting business. Technically, you are operating your business in each city within the state, so you might be required to register as a sole proprietor in each city in your state to comply with your state's business laws. The cost to do this is clearly not practical. Instead, the better choice might be to form a limited liability company (LLC) or other business entity registered with the secretary of state's office in the state in which you are licensed to practice law. Although it takes a little more work, you may also want to consider a professional limited liability company (PLLC), if that is an option available for lawyers in your state.

If you are licensed to practice law in more than one state, and will be working with clients online in one state while residing in another, contact the corporations division of the secretary of state's office in each state where you hold a license. You will also want to check with the state bars to ensure that you are complying with both state business laws as well as residency requirements that the state bar may have for lawyers practicing law under their jurisdiction.

Billing Methods for Online Legal Services

A virtual law office permits the lawyer to use a variety of billing methods for legal services. These might include the traditional billable hour, fixed fees, a combination of fixed fees and billable hour; payment plans; and even providing online legal services pro bono.

Offering fixed fees for unbundled legal services is the most popular option. Because the technology automates and streamlines much of the administrative processes of providing legal services, the lawyer may find that a fixed-fee option equates to a higher return than attempting to use the traditional billable-hour method. In addition, clients who are seeking legal services online seem to prefer "packaged," unbundled legal services where they know up front exactly what the cost will be. Knowing the costs also allows the clients to budget for the expense of legal services. In the long term, this may help to reduce collection issues for the lawyer after legal services have been rendered.

As with a traditional law practice, some methods of billing will work better with different practice areas, and the methods you choose to provide your clients will also depend on the scope of the legal matter to be handled online.

Online Payment Options

Paying by credit card is often the most popular with online clients, but providing the option of certified check by mail or e-check may also appeal to a certain segment of the online client base.[4]

Be aware that any virtual law practice that accepts credit card payments from clients must be Payment Card Industry Data Security Standard (PCI DSS) compliant.[5] PCI compliance must occur whenever any business

---

[4]E-check is a form of electronic check processing where the client's bank account is directly debited for a purchase.
[5]See PCI Compliance Guide, **http://www.pcicomplianceguide.org/** (accessed June 17, 2008).

stores, transfers, or collects credit card information from clients. Failure to comply with these rules, set by the credit card industry, may result in a business no longer being allowed to take credit card purchases, in addition to multiple fines and penalties. It is unlikely that a virtual law practice would handle the number of transactions that require an audit by PCI DSS security assessors, but the standards in this area are constantly being changed. The responsibility falls to the lawyer to keep any online purchases of legal services by credit card compliant with the most current rules and regulations.

That said, most virtual law offices will use a third-party credit card processing service that will handle the transfer of the credit card information so that it is never stored on the lawyer's virtual law office. This will depend on the technology you have chosen to set up your virtual practice. Most banks provide merchant account services to work with an attorney's bank account, but not all merchant account services are able to work with the IOLTA and trust accounting rules for each state. These services may become costly, as most of them charge both an annual fee and per-transaction fees. Other services, such as PayPal and Google Shopping Cart, offer free accounts and will only charge per-transaction fees, but the level of service needed for a law practice may not be available, and they may not have the ability to transfer funds into the correct account to ensure that funds needing to go straight into the trust account end up there without any transfer fees for the service being deducted from the client's payment.[6]

Accordingly, any online payment options must be set up to comply with the trust accounting rules of your state bar. Because you may choose to use the fixed-fee method of billing, in which the client is provided with and agrees to pay a fixed fee before the services are delivered in full, you may not want to require a separate retainer from clients. If a retainer is

---

[6]While their payment services may use encryption, PayPal, Google Shopping cart and similar credit card processing services do not provide IOLTA or trust accounting compliance and are not set up to handle different billing methods, such as retainers, contingency fees or billable hours for a virtual law practice. These credit card processing services work best for virtual law practice when they are used as a payment method for transactional legal services that are provided to clients on a fixed-fee basis without the need for trust accounting. Most legal SaaS providers and other attorney merchant account services are aware that law firms may use a combination of different billing methods and have addressed this concern as well as trust accounting and IOLTA compliance. See also the discussion in Chapter Three above "Creating a Virtual Law Practice by Combining Separate Software Applications" and the section of the Appendix "State Bar Ethics and Advisory Opinions and Other Resources by Topic: Accepting Credit Card Payments from a Client."

required as part of the initial price quote and must be completed before the lawyer proceeds, then those funds must be placed in the trust account and kept separate from the operating account.

One gray area here is the use of Paypal, Google Shopping Cart, or other credit card processing services that would hold retainer fees but may also collect per-transfer fees from any funds that go through the service.[7] The issue is whether the retainer may be run through the credit card processing company even if that company routes the funds to the lawyer's trust account rather than operating account. Because the funds would first be transmitted to the lawyer's online account at the credit card processing company and then routed to the trust account at the approved federal or state bank, this may be in violation of the trust accounting rules of the lawyer's state bar, because for a short period of time the funds are held by the credit card processing company. Furthermore, the account would have to be set up so that any per-transaction and per-transfer fees were taken out of the operating account and not out of the funds being transferred to the trust account.

While this sounds hypertechnical and the funds would end up in the lawyer's trust account as required, if the credit card processing company in question was not one the financial institutions approved by the lawyer's state bar for the purpose of maintaining trust accounts, then the transaction might be in violation of the bar's trust accounting rules. Given these nuances in the management of online payments, the safest route at this time is either to work with a merchant service designed specifically for lawyers that will be aware of the trust accounting and IOLTA requirements of each state or to use the credit card processing services associated with your bank.[8]

Value Billing—Offering Fixed Fees on Your Virtual Law Office

Some lawyers operating virtual law offices will post their fees for unbundled legal services on the firm's Web site. There is some debate about

---

[7]See, for example, California State Bar Formal Opinion No. 2007-172, **http://calbar.ca.gov/calbar/ pdfs/ethics/2007-172.pdf** (accessed February 22, 2010), and New Mexico State Bar Advisory Opinion No. 2000-1, *Use of Credit Cards to Fund Trust Account Retainer Deposits*, **http://www .nmbar.org/legalresearch/eao/2000-2002/2000-1.doc** (accessed February 24, 2010).

[8]See, for example, Law Charge, which provides merchant accounts for lawyers (**www.lawcharge .com**).

whether this is a good practice. On one hand, it allows the prospective client seeking legal services to know the costs up front and to compare costs to those of other virtual law offices or other online legal service providers without lawyer review of the documents, including those of the popular company LegalZoom. On the other hand, if that prospective client's legal matter is something that falls outside of the scope of the listed unbundled legal services, the client may either not register with the virtual law office to request a price quote for services or may register assuming that their legal matter may be handled at the listed fixed-fee price. At that point, it may be difficult to explain to the prospective client how the scope of his or her legal matter exceeds the listed prices on the site.

Furthermore, as the lawyer needs to increase the prices, he or she would have to edit those in the text of the Web site accordingly. This may lead to some confusion for prospective clients who may have seen the previous rates and will request those rather than the new rates. One way to solve this issue is by ensuring that you label the listed prices as "sample" pricing or include a disclaimer describing the scope of the legal services to be provided in each package or pricing.

The decision to post pricing on your site is a marketing decision that will also depend on the practice area(s) being provided online and how you intend to structure the unbundling of legal services. Even if you decide not to use value billing or to post fixed fees on your virtual law office Web site, you will need to provide a clear explanation of your online billing practices and how they apply on a case-by-case basis to each client during the engagement process. Depending on the technology you choose, this task may be automated for you as part of the online billing process.

Collaborating with Other Lawyers to Create a Virtual Law Firm

Operating a virtual law office may provide the opportunity for a lawyer to collaborate with other lawyers online to form unique law practices that span multiple jurisdictions. Along with this potential comes the need for careful planning. The formation may be similar to the processes used by larger, traditional law firms to create branches and provide services across the states. But the fact that these services will be provided online, and that the lawyers may rarely meet in person with each other or their clients, adds another level of complexity to the structure. Avoiding the unauthorized practice of law (UPL) in other jurisdictions is one risk that must be consciously mitigated with a virtual law firm.[9]

Depending on the type of technology that you choose to create a virtual law practice, there may be a permissions-based system in place that will allow one lawyer to be the "assigned" lawyer to the case. This is even more important with a virtual firm, where the lawyers may never be meeting with each other in person to discuss the firm's cases and may be using their own virtual assistants to manage their online clients. A solid system for assigning responsibility to online clients is critical to ensure that each case matter is handled properly. Lawyers working together in a virtual law practice may not form a single-entity law practice but instead create a relationship where they refer online cases to each other across jurisdictions or where the lawyers review legal documents for each other to avoid UPL.

For example, a lawyer licensed in New York who provides trademark, copyright, and patent legal services has a client who also needs a state-law contract drafted pertaining to the law of California. The lawyer drafts the contract and then has a lawyer from his network in the state of California review the work and approve it for purchase by the online client. The New York lawyer avoids UPL in California by having the California lawyer approve the work, and the New York lawyer is able to provide a full-range of legal services for his or her online client. In return, the California lawyer may have the same relationship with the New York lawyer for his or her online clients needing state-law legal services pertaining to the laws of the state of New York. In this example, it would be important that each online client be provided with notice that their legal work may be subcontracted out to another lawyer and that the client provides permission for this arrangement to occur.

As another example of a multijurisdictional law firm arrangement, a group of lawyers that are licensed in two different states but who practice in different areas of law have formed a virtual law firm. They executed a partnership agreement and signed a fee-structuring agreement among themselves. When a new client registers on their virtual law office Web site, that client is responded to by the lawyer in that client's jurisdiction who handles the area of law related to the needs of the clients. That lawyer becomes the "assigned" lawyer to the case. The other lawyers may be able to review the client's file and communicate with each other through that client file on the shared back-end law office. In this situa-

---

[9]Refer to the ABA Model Rules of Professional Conduct, Rule 5.5, regarding UPL and multijurisdictional law practice.

tion it is critical to provide the client with adequate notice of which lawyer is responsible for his or her case and if other lawyers from the firm will be contributing.

When collaborating with lawyers online, careful planning is needed to avoid UPL through the advertising and marketing of the virtual law firm. Lawyers should review the state bar rules and regulations regarding advertising in each state in which the virtual law firm intends to market the firm as providing legal services. This is not very different from the planning that occurs when a traditional, larger law office opens branches in multiple jurisdictions across the country, but it may involve more online marketing methods than traditional.

Another issue that may be similar is the coordination of taking online payments from clients where the lawyers are licensed in multiple jurisdictions. To comply with the trust accounting and IOLTA requirements of each state bar, the lawyers in the firm may have to set up a complex accounting and tracking system tied into their technology in which the clients are paying their assigned lawyer online and the online payments are occurring in accordance with the firm's fee-structuring agreement.

Case Study: Advice from a Senior Consultant
Jordan Furlong

*Jordan Furlong is a partner with Edge International (**www.edge.ai**) who specializes in analyzing the extraordinary changes now underway in the legal profession worldwide. He is also a senior consultant with Stem Legal (**www.stemlegal.com**) and head of its Media Strategy Service. He authors the award-winning blog Law21: Dispatches from a Legal Profession on the Brink (**http://law21.ca**) and can be reached at jordan @law21.ca.*

Are there any legal services, projects, or tasks that you believe cannot be handled as well for the law practice through the use of technology?

The list of legal services that can't be handled as well by a virtual law firm is much shorter than many traditional lawyers would like to think. But if my practice area required a great deal of personal contact with clients—detailed estate planning, say, or complicated marriage breakdowns, or criminal defense work—I might be reluctant to operate my firm solely in the cloud. Virtual lawyers could get around this by frequently visiting their clients at their homes or businesses, but that's a serious time and resource drain.

What are the benefits for legal professionals from this form of law practice?

First and foremost are the cost savings. Eliminating all the overhead and trappings of a traditional law office dramatically reduces expenses, with two main benefits: entry barriers to setting up and operating a sole practice are lowered, and those lower operating costs can be passed on to the client, creating competitive and access-to-justice advantages. Virtual lawyers also give themselves the option to be flexible in their hours and work habits, although more traditional firms are starting to come to terms with flexible work schedules as well.

What are the benefits to the lawyer's clients from the use of the technology to deliver legal services? From your perspective, what has the general public's response been to virtual law practice?

The client's benefits depend on what technology the virtual firm is using. As mentioned previously, virtual law firm clients should benefit from lower prices, period. If the firm has created extranets for each client by which the client can see the status of her case, the next milestones to be reached, and the progress of her bill, that's a huge advantage over most firms' approaches. Technology should also allow the client to customize the ways in which she interacts with her firm and the legal issues it's handling for her. But again, traditional firms are starting to catch up in this area as well—the use of technology per se is not a competitive hook upon which the virtual client should hang his hat.

Are there any concerns that you have with a virtual law office as a form of law practice management? (These could be concerns with security, conflicts of interest, UPL, ethics, communication issues with the lawyer's clients, etc.)

None of these concerns are unique to virtual law practice—every lawyer needs to take them seriously. Virtual lawyers' challenge is to overcome the perception, fair or not, that they are particularly vulnerable to such concerns. Clients will be inclined to have doubts about the security and professionalism of a virtual firm, since the firm is missing the traditional signals (bricks and mortar office, marble and glass lobby, visible presence in the physical world) with which clients have been trained to identify these characteristics. So virtual firms need to pay extra attention to and resources on double- and triple-checking and -locking client data, creating multiple backups and redundancies for firm information, and, to the extent physical firm assets exist, dramatically demonstrating their security and reliability. Aside from that, there's very little that should concern a client of a virtual firm more than a traditional firm.

What methods of marketing would you recommend for a virtual law practice? How would that marketing differ from the methods used by a traditional law practice?

I would think about focusing on clients more likely to "get it"—younger, more technology-savvy customers who don't need to have the Internet explained to them and who are already favorably inclined toward innovative ways of doing business. I would build my promotional materials around the huge overhead costs of bloated traditional firms contrasted with the cost savings of a lean, focused, streamlined business model like mine. I would emphasize the degree of client control over her information, the ability to have 24/7/365 access to everything her lawyer is doing for her. Traditional firms market themselves through history, brand name, reliability, etc. I can't compete with a hundred-year-old five-hundred-lawyer firm on those counts. So I would focus on being a client-centered, price-conscious, twenty-first-century provider of legal services that does things differently because that benefits the client.

If you could share any advice with lawyers interested in or currently operating a virtual law practice, what would it be?

Focus relentlessly on the client, because most or all of your market advantages lie in making things easier and better for the client. Your services should cost much less because you're not carrying all that extra overhead weight. Your system should allow clients to constantly monitor their work and to access resources (on their own initiative) to help them understand their legal issues better. Make a virtue of necessity by over-investing in security and backups—give the client ironclad guarantees of reliability, so that their peace of mind is never called into question. A virtual law practice, for a few more years at least, will constantly have to battle behemoth law firms that can outspend it a hundred to one. Adopt insurgency tactics: identify the weak points of your traditional competitors, pounce on them, and exploit them to the fullest.

Where do you see virtual law practice headed in the future of the legal profession?

Virtual law practices are not *the* future of law firms, but they are *a* future. Every day, little by little, traditional firms pick up one or two elements of virtual practice, like client-facing technology investments or employee flexibility and remote access. A virtual law firm in 2010 has some real advantages over traditional firms, but by 2020, a virtual firm that hasn't made any changes since 2010 will have no market advantage: both the traditional firms and other virtual practices will have adapted and evolved. Over time, VLPs' greatest impact might well be to change the nature of traditional firms, so that one comes more closely to resemble the other. By 2050, there's a pretty good chance that virtual solo practices will dominate the legal profession—but only if they constantly evolve upward.

VLO Startup Checklist #3: Business Setup

___ Write a business plan. If you are adding a virtual law office to an existing practice, write a separate strategy for the use of the virtual component that fits into the overall plan for your existing firm.

___ Select a name and register a URL.

___ Find a Web site developer and begin the process of creating content for your site.

___ Complete the business formation with your state's corporations division.

___ Draft any partnership agreement or fee-structuring agreements.

___ Obtain state bar approval of Web site design and URL (if necessary).

___ Complete the integration and customization of the virtual law practice technology or client portal into the Web site.

___ Obtain a payment-processing service and set up the transfer of online payments to operating and trust accounts. Ensure IOLTA compliance.

___ Decide on a fee structure, fixed packages for unbundling, and whether to post sample pricing on your site.

___ Set up an e-mail policy. If prospective clients contact you by e-mail first, how will you route them to the secure client portal?

___ Set up a response and turnaround policy for handling online clients.

___ Draft client intake forms, terms and conditions, disclaimers, online engagement agreements, clickwrap agreements, and other firm-specific documents before your Web site launches to the public.

CHAPTER FIVE

Managing and Marketing a Virtual Law Practice

Providing Customer Service in Your Virtual Law Office

This book includes discussion of professional responsibility and ethical practices for virtual law office management, but at least one section must be dedicated to providing quality customer service to your online clients. This is not about receiving immediate rewards for your practice. Good customer service is a long-term strategy of building a strong online client base through referrals and recurring clients.

The goals you should strive for in providing good customer service for your online clientele are (1) build the reputation of your online practice as a secure, efficient, and affordable site to receive legal services, and (2) build your reputation as a responsive lawyer who pays attention to individual online clients' needs. There are simple steps, most of them taking minimal time, that will help your online clients feel more satisfied from their online transactions with your virtual practice.

First, establish a response policy for when the online client contacts you through the client portal. Let the clients know that you will respond to their requests for legal services and other actions in their case file within a fixed amount of time. For example, a twenty-four-hour response policy might be reasonable. Even if the message back to the online client is nothing more than a note stating that you have reviewed their message or received their document online and will get back in touch with them later, this will reassure the client that you are paying attention to their legal needs and concerns. Consider letting your clients know what your response policy is ahead of time so that they know what to expect. At the same time, avoid being too ambitious and making promises that you can't keep. Promising to respond to an online request within an hour after it is received may not be realistic unless you are including auto-responders as part of your response policy.

Knowing the limitations of your virtual practice is important to ensuring that you are able to adequately convey to clients what services you can and cannot provide unbundled through your virtual law office. Be prepared to cordially refer a client to a full-service law practice from the beginning. Being polite and helpful to prospective clients that you are unable to assist may earn you respect and build your reputation. The next time that individual has a legal need that may be handled online or has a friend who could use the services of your virtual law office, these simple actions may win you future referrals.

Learn how to convey sincerity and concern in automated processes. For your practice, come up with simple, standard phrases that you may reuse with online clients in auto-responders that will convey personalized care for each type of case. For example, here is an automated response to a newly registered client on the client portal who is seeking guidance with a divorce:

> Thank you for contacting me. I understand that this is a difficult time for you. In order to find out if I may assist you in my virtual law office, please provide me with some additional information by filling out the attached form online. The information you provide will allow me to make the determination of whether I may be of assistance to you online. If I may assist you, I will provide additional information regarding my representation of your legal matter. If I am unable to assist you in this matter, I will refer you to a full-service law firm that may be able to assist you in your legal needs. If you have any questions or concerns when filling out the form, please do not hesitate to drop me a note online at any time.

If desired, you could provide a phone number along with the auto-responder at this time, or after determining whether to accept representation. Once a formal attorney-client relationship is formed, make it clear that the client may access his or her legal case files securely at any time and should feel free to give you feedback and comments on any legal matters. It is still at the discretion of the attorney how much of the case file and documents are made accessible to the client online.

Some lawyers may be comfortable with their ability to convey sincerity in writing, so such techniques may be enough to reach out to online clients and further personalize their experience with the virtual law office. For others who are more comfortable with conveying sincerity and concern with their voices, they may want to schedule phone or Web conferences with their online clients. This takes longer and consumes more resources than handling the matter completely through the virtual law office interface, but this is a decision best left to the individual lawyer based on his or her personal comfort with technology, practice areas, and the needs of the client base. The process of scheduling phone calls with each client may be automated so that the technology prompts the client for this additional communication after the lawyer has run a conflicts check and is ready to proceed to the next step in determining the scope of representation required for the legal need presented. You may also want to consider hiring a virtual assistant or virtual paralegal to respond to simple online requests for legal services or concerns within a client's case file.

Be flexible and patient with online clients just as you would in an office environment. Your clients may have varying comfort levels using technology, depending on the age, education, and sophistication range of your client base as well as the socio-economic background. That said, most clients will be retaining the services of your law office because it is virtual and providing them with a convenience. You should take care to deal quickly with any complaints or confusion presented by online clients that relate to the technology you have chosen to provide legal services online. In many cases, frustrations will arise from technology issues that you will have no way of preventing, such as the client's own hardware malfunctions or problems with Internet access. You might want to provide some basic guidance on your Web site regarding security and safety for your clients as far as protecting their own computers, backups, and keeping their usernames and passwords secure. Many clients in this day and age have been using secure sites for banking, shopping, and other transactions for many years and are more than aware of these risks and best practices, but it might be seen as good customer service to provide additional guidance and reminders somewhere on the static virtual law office site. You may also wish to create tutorial videos for clients that walk them through different steps of the process, such as registration, requesting legal services, or paying online invoices. At the end of the process, if the client is extremely frustrated, consider reducing the price of your legal services. It might pay off in the long run to return that client to a positive attitude regarding your business.

After delivering legal services to the client, provide an easy and efficient method of closing the online transaction. For example, when a client is ready to pay, try to be flexible with your payment options. Consider offering payment plans for families, or allow the client to send a personal check with the stipulation that it must clear before you process the payment and provide their completed legal services. Allowing clients to pay online with a credit card often helps them to pay for legal services that they could not afford to pay for in cash. After the transaction is complete, allow them to be able to retrieve information through the client portal regarding their online invoice, charges, payments, or other information regarding the status of their payment for online legal services. This helps the client to feel more in control over the process. This is also the type of action that will help to build a strong reputation for your virtual law office.

Terminating the Online Relationship

Do not cut the client off completely after he or she pays for legal services online. The online process may seem cut and dried, and you may certainly run your virtual law office that way, but if you want referrals and recurring clients, then consider the value of staying connected to the client. Consider answering a quick online question at no charge, or check back in with the client to make sure the legal documents they purchased were filed correctly or executed properly. This may be a task that you choose to assign to a virtual assistant or paralegal when it becomes too time-consuming to do so yourself.

At a minimum, provide continued access to the client's legal file online or a way for the client to contact you online following the payment for online legal services. Set up a policy for when you will remove the client's access to their case files. A good date might be the required deadline that your state bar has for client record retention. When the client requests his or her file, be ready to provide export features to remove the files in electronic format.

There is also the question of whether you should provide clients with a paper version of their digital file upon termination of the representation. If the entire file is in digital format, then the client may be able to take the digital version and print it out to paper for his or her own purposes, or, if you wish, you may offer to provide the client with a paper version of the file and add the cost of that to the total fee for legal services. Another good policy might be to include in the engagement process with the client and in the terms and conditions for the virtual law office that only a digital copy of the file will be accessible online and for a specific amount of time. That way the client will have adequate notice of how he or she will be able to access the file and for how long following the termination of the representation.

You may also want to keep in touch with online clients by sending out occasional electronic newsletters or updates to them to keep in touch. If you have a blog on your virtual law office site, you may handle these updates or newsletters in your blog and allow clients to option of subscribing to that blog to receive notification of new posts containing general legal guidance or law office news.

Daily Best Practices

The security of a virtual law office is going to depend on the technology that you select, but just as important, it will depend on how well you and your assistants abide by daily best practices for the use of that technology. Because a virtual law office is located completely online, the lawyer must be educated about security threats when practicing on remote devices and how to mitigate those risks.

Securing Mobile Devices

Working remotely provides great flexibility and opportunity. The use of mobile devices to conduct business online is growing as legal professionals realize the increased productivity that comes with a virtual law practice. The use of mobile devices naturally comes with a word of caution: using mobile devices, such as laptops, BlackBerries, and other handheld devices, to store digital law office data is not typically a secure method because the data on these devices are often not encrypted, and, depending on the setup you are using, access to the data could be left wide open.

Should the mobile device be stolen or misplaced, sensitive attorney-client data would be vulnerable, placing you at risk for malpractice. Even with regular backup of the data, you would not have control over the misuse of the information if the mobile device were stolen. There are some products out there that may be used to reduce this risk. For example, Computrace LoJack (**www.absolute.com/products/lojackforlaptops**) is a company that provides software and service that may track down a stolen laptop and in some cases delete the stolen data. Any lawyer using a laptop to conduct business remotely should consider investigating a similar additional security check. Full-disk encryption is also recommended because it encrypts everything on your hard drive rather than just encrypting specific file folders. Consider using TrueCrypt or PGP. Windows 7 also has a product, Microsoft's BitLocker, that will provide full-disk encryption.

A mobile lawyer may be tempted to use the advertised Wi-Fi available in many coffee shops and other public places to conduct business. Any activity conducted online while using a shared wireless connection in a public place (called a "hotspot") will be wide open to anyone else using that same wireless access. Even if you have firewalls enabled this only prevents hackers from getting access to your computer and does not prevent them from getting onto your network to view your Wi-Fi traffic. Viewing a secure Web site with SSL may be safe, but a wireless eavesdropper[1] could still view any Web sites you have visited and acquire any login information used on unsecured sites (non-SSL). It would be like having a conversation in the open, any search terms you typed into a search engine could be seen by anyone attempting to hop onto your network to see what you are working on. If you are visiting a Web site using SSL, such as your own virtual law office, then any communications will be encrypted and not as susceptible to intrusion.[2] However, unencrypted e-mail and Web pages not using SSL are completely visible to an eavesdropper monitoring your network. Any unsecured ports open on your computer are also vulnerable to attacks if there is no firewall at the computer level. In other words, you are not exposing your virtual law office to vulnerability because the virtual law office itself uses SSL encryption, but you may be opening the door for a potential attacker to access other items on your computer.

A better option for the mobile lawyer needing Internet access would be to purchase a wireless broadband card from a wireless Internet provider.

---

[1] A wireless eavesdropper would use a wireless tool, such as a network sniffer, to acquire data by observing packets that are passing on the network. The hacker then looks for data such as usernames and passwords. He or she takes that information and uses it to impersonate the individual.

[2] There may also be some interference if the Domain Name System (DNS) is controlled by the attacker. In addition to DNS attacks, there are "packet sniffer attacks." Both methods of interference may be used together or separately. These attacks may be used against HTTPS via DNS spoofing or other means if a false certificate is accepted by the user attempting to connect to the secure site. Almost all browsers have visual indicators to alert the user that this may be happening. However, these "red flags" on the browser only work when the user takes them seriously and terminates the nonsecure session.

Connecting this card to a mobile device allows you to avoid the shared hotspot area that Wi-Fi relies on, and it directly connects you to the Internet in a manner less susceptible to wireless eavesdropping by nearby third parties. With any remote-access device, you should install firewalls and antivirus software on your devices and make sure those safeguards are correctly functioning.

Note that no matter how you connect to the Internet—either by landline, Wi-Fi, or AirCard[3]—all confidential communications should be done over secure protocols, such as SSL, from end to end. Even if a connection is secure from the laptop to the Internet service provider (ISP), it is not guaranteed to be secure from the ISP to the end user without additional protections, such as end-to-end encryption.

Checklist of Daily Best Practices for the Use of Technology

___ Use full disk encryption on all computers.

___ Create strong passwords. Change them occasionally. Make sure username and passwords are not written down or are not easily viewable or accessible.

___ Use a daily backup system.

___ Keep antivirus software up-to-date and a firewall in place.

___ Use antimalware protection.

___ Use a pop-up blocker, depending on the browser you use. (Firefox is recommended with the use of security add-ons.)

___ Have a secondary, backup Internet method, such as a wireless AirCard.

___ Secure your wireless.

___ Remove metadata before transmitting documents.

___ Educate and remind your online clients about protecting themselves using their own hardware.

---

[3]An aircard is a device that may be inserted into a computer, smartphone or other device that allows it to connect to wireless Internet access provider. Usually this is to connect to a cellular telephone network.

Marketing Your Virtual Law Office

Methods of marketing are going to depend on the structure of the virtual law practice. Because these differ from practice to practice, below are two of the more common approaches to creating a marketing strategy for a virtual law practice.

1. For a completely Web-based virtual law office, market it only to prospective online clients.
2. For a full-service law firm adding a virtual law office:
   a. market it as an amenity to in-person clients to compete with other traditional firms locally.
   b. market the virtual law office separately, geared to prospective online clients to add an additional revenue stream of online clients to the traditional practice.

Accordingly, the method of marketing is also going to depend on where your prospective online clients are coming from or if you will be transferring in-person clients to use the online offering rather than communicating with them by e-mail and phone in addition to office visits.

Methods used to advertise a virtual law office with a completely Web-based clientele would be the same as used to advertise a brick and mortar law office and must comply with the advertising rules set forth by the rules of professional conduct or other regulations of the lawyer's state bar.[4] Advertising must not contain information that is false or misleading about the lawyer or the services offered by the virtual law practice. Your Web site and blog are forms of advertising your practice. See pages 68–72 and 133–134 regarding setting up your Web site for suggestions on how to do so within the rules and regulations of your state bar.

---

[4]Several state bars have addressed lawyers' use of listservs, forums, and other online social networking applications to advertise legal services. To summarize some of these advisory opinions, if the lawyer is using methods of online communication to advertise for new clients, the lawyer must be careful to provide only general legal advice and avoid creating the expectation of an attorney/client relationship informally by responding to the specific circumstances of an online request for legal assistance. See DC Ethics Opinion 316 (2002), DC Ethics Opinion 302 (2000); Louisiana Rules of Professional Conduct, **http://www.ladb.org/Publications/ropc.pdf** (accessed September 30, 2010); and New York Rules of Professional Conduct, **http://www.nysba.org/ Content/NavigationMenu/ForAttorneys/ProfessionalStandardsforAttorneys/FinalNYRPCs WithComments(April12009).pdf** (accessed September 30, 2010).

Case Study: Virtual Law Office Web Site Design Tips
Dave Ryan

*Dave Ryan, is the manager of online marketing and analytics at Total Attorneys, a technology-enabled service provider for small and solo law firm practices. (**www.totalattorneys.com**).*

What design features should be on a lawyer Web site to attract customers?

The most effective design features will be different for every site—the key is to test the design elements you use and pick the ones that help your site convert visitors into clients. Some design elements that can commonly provide an impact include the color scheme, the location and shape of navigation links, and attention-grabbing graphics. Perhaps the most important site elements are your call to action, phone number, and contact form; be sure to test the location and design of these elements to maximize your conversion rate.

What are some key features of a lawyer's Web site?

1. Phone number. In addition to a form, your Web site should include a phone number that a consumer can call to get in touch with you directly. Different consumers prefer different contact methods, so providing options will help attract customers.

2. Privacy policy. Any time you take someone's information online, you should let them know what you'll do with that information. Your privacy policy should be linked to on the same page(s) as your form, and it should tell a consumer who they're sending their information to and whether you plan on sharing their information with others.

3. Terms and conditions. A terms and conditions page will typically show disclaimers required by any bodies that regulate legal marketing in your areas. In addition, if you have any conditions you want visitors to agree to when using your Web site, this is the place for them.

4. Disclaimers. Most lawyers will need to include some disclaimers on their Web sites. These should be placed at the bottom of the Web site (an area typically called the "footer"), and they should appear on every page of the site.

5. Blog. A blog is an easy way to put fresh content on your site. Updating your site frequently can help visitors find you, and a blog is also a great way to engage visitors or other Web sites.

6. Sharing links. Include links on your pages and blog posts for visitors to easily share what they're looking at on social networking sites like Twitter, Digg, and Facebook.

7. Helpful content. Try to provide your visitors with useful information on your site. There are limits to how many questions you can answer, but if visitors find your site useful, they are more likely to return and more likely to see you as an expert should they want to speak to a lawyer.

How can a site be made easy to navigate?

The most important element to a site's navigation is a well-organized collection of links that appears on every page (this is, in fact, referred to as the "navigation"). Having your navigation links well-organized into categories will help visitors find what they're looking for and also give them an easy way to jump from one section of the site to another. Your navigation should typically be on the top of your site, either stretching across the top or to one side. Put the links you care the most about at the top ("Contact Us" would be a prime example).

In addition to your navigation, link to other pages as appropriate within the content of your site. Do not overwhelm your visitors with too many links; only point them to content you think is important. You may want to provide links at the bottom of a page to related material. Many sites also make use of "breadcrumbs"—links that let visitors jump back to previously visited pages easily.

What services and support should you expect from a Web site development or hosting company?

Assuming you are not familiar with Web site design, development, or maintenance, you are going to rely on your service provider very heavily for your Web site. Look for a provider that will build your site with input from you, host and maintain your site, and also provide help marketing your site. Your Web site is a very public face of your company, and you should demand a high level of service; 99.9 percent uptime (Web sites are occasionally unavailable to visitors; yours should be available 99.9 percent of the time), prompt responses to your questions, and competitive pricing (request quotes from a few providers). Perhaps the most important aspect of your Web site support will be direct control over the content on the site. Never forget that you are responsible for what's on your firm's Web site; you should have direct access to change any content on the site, or at least the ability to request that changes be made immediately.

With any marketing strategy, you will be working on building an online client base several months before you actually see the results. Enjoy the success of incoming online clients, but on a weekly basis be actively working on pulling in the clients you'll see three months from now in your virtual law office.

The free and online marketing tools suggested below often require an e-mail address to join and follow. I recommend that you either set up a filter within your e-mail system to send e-mails to folders specifically set up for these different sources or that you create e-mail accounts separate from your primary e-mail address. There are also services online that allow you to create temporary e-mail addresses that disappear after use or within a set amount of time but that will permit you to register for information or download an application on a Web site without your business e-mail suffering from the marketing spam that typically follows.[5]

Most of the marketing methods listed below are either free or cost a minimal fee. Rather than investing money, they require that you dedicate time and energy and be consistent in your efforts. There are more traditional and expensive methods of advertising a virtual law office from print, radio and television ads to paying for online advertising and referrals. If you have the funds to invest in this form of marketing, then you may want to consult with a marketing professional who will create a marketing strategy for your virtual law practice to capitalize on this advantage.

Before taking part in any advertising or marketing effort, you should check with your state bar regarding its specific advertising rules and regulations. There are varying opinions from state bars regarding online referral services, so be aware of these before joining up with any services for your virtual law office.[6] When researching this topic, be careful to make

---

[5]See, for example, Guerrillamail, **www.guerrillamail.com**, or Mailinator, **www.mailinator.com**.
[6]See in general, ABA Model Rules 7.2(b)(2) and 7.3; see also, for example, Ohio Supreme Court Ethics Op. 2000-5 OH Adv. Op. 2000-5, 2000 WL 1872571, (Ohio Bd.Com.Griev.Disp.), December 01, 2000, Arizona Ethics Op. 05-08 (2005), Nassau County (N.Y.) Ethics Op. 01-4 (2001), North Carolina Ethics Op. 2004-1 (2004), and Texas Ethics Op. 561(2005).

the distinction between a company offering a referral service and one providing online advertising services. Online advertising of a virtual law practice should be permitted by your state bar as long as it complies with the rules and regulations for advertising legal services. But participation in a referral service may not be in compliance with the rules and regulations of your state bar and may be classified as direct solicitation.

Leverage Free Press

Write a press release. E-mail it to local papers and direct it to the specific editors that might be interested in your practice, such as the technology, legal, or business editors. News publications with general public distribution that tend to cover all new business openings may find a virtual law office opening to be newsworthy for their readers. This may lead to a larger feature article or additional coverage. Check out CopyBlogger (**www.copyblogger.com**) or Men With Pens (**www.menwithpens.com**) for tips on how to write a good press release. You might also consider sending a press release to any local or regional legal publications, such as those published by *Lawyer's Weekly* or your state bar association's general practice or technology magazine.

Don't forget that other smaller and often free publications may be interested in writing about your virtual law office or in having you write a guest column. Check out some of the publications outside your local grocery store in the free racks and see if any of them might have readers who could use your online legal assistance. For example, many free local parenting magazines or retirement guides would be interested in an article about online estate planning services for their readers. Many city chambers of commerce have regular business publications that cover new business openings, regardless of whether those businesses join their organization. Many chambers also have specific technology sections. Try sending a press release to the technology business editor as well as the editor in chief, as this could result in a free published news brief or feature article. Keep in mind that most publications now have online versions, which may link to your virtual law office Web site and help drive traffic and prospective clients there.

Free Online Advertising and Lawyer Listings

Many cities have locally run Web sites that advertise a variety of goods and services. Post a free ad for your services. Readers may not be looking for legal services on that Web site, but they may read your name and remember it when they are in the market for legal services. Even some of the larger lawyer listing sites, such as Lawyers.com and Findlaw.com, will offer free basic listings. But they may not advertise that they offer these, so you may have to speak with a representative before being able to obtain one.

Join Online Forums and Use Linking

Find and join an appropriate online forum where your prospective client base gathers. For example, if you are a parent and provide family law or estate planning services, find local parenting forums and join in on the conversations. The same concept would work for different types of forums, such as small business or startup forums, depending on where you believe your clients will be going online to build their social networks. Many well-run forums will only allow advertising of services after making a minimum number of posts to the forum discussions, but while you are joining in on the conversation, your signature should contain a link to your Web site with additional information about your services. This is not direct solicitation of legal services, but it may stick in the minds of the readers over time. To avoid potential malpractice issues, you will need to keep a copy of any general legal information that you provide on the site, and always recommend that members of the forum contact a lawyer for case-specific information rather than rely on your general guidance. Your state bar may have additional guidelines for lawyers taking part in listservs or forums.

Most local and regional newspapers also have Web sites with forums for their readers to discuss published articles and other local news. This might also be a good place to create an online presence. Again, your post's signature should link to your Web site and explain your services. Even when you are not posting on law-related items, your signature will serve as the online shingle for your virtual law office.

Advertising Methods to Avoid

The traditional lawyer listing in a directory is not set up at this time to the benefit of virtual law offices. Most directories require payment for a listing that is for a specific geographic location rather than across the state. Since a virtual law office provides services across the state(s) where you are licensed, these listing are cost prohibitive to advertise in each city and state where you may obtain online clients. Accordingly, you may wish to purchase a listing in your geographic location, but it may be more cost effective to spend that money on search engine optimization (SEO) for your Web site or other marketing services that will drive traffic to your site from across the state.

Yellow Pages print or online listings also may not be cost effective. Individuals looking for online legal services will not be using the printed Yellow

Pages, so the online listing for this is not worth the expense. Most clients who find you by searching online will be coming from Google, Yahoo!, Bing, or other search engines. Instead, spend that money on purchasing Google AdWords or a similar service on a search engine.

Create One or More Blogs That Cover Your Practice Areas

Blogs are effective marketing tools if written on a regular basis. Updating your blog refreshes the page with the search engines. "Top ten" lists and other lists can improve the search engine ranking. Gear your writing toward the general lay public so that you are educating and providing useful information for prospective clients if that is the goal of your blog. If the subject of your blog is geared towards other legal professionals then provide content that is appropriate for that audience's needs. If your virtual law office Web site does not contain a blog that was created by your website developer, consider using Wordpress (**www.wordpress.com**). Google's Blogger is free, but Typepad, Moveable Type, and Wordpress have nicer features and a more professional look for a minimal monthly fee.[7] Once you have established your blog with quality content, republish the feed for the blog on any number of online communities, such as LinkedIn or Facebook, that will repurpose your content for viewing on those sites. You may also want to list your blog in any number of blog directories, including Blawg.com and the ABA Journal's Blawg Directory.[8]

Case Study: Blogging Tips from a Content Writer Manager
Meaghan Olson, Content Writer Manager, Total Attorneys

Meaghan Olson is a content writer manager for Total Attorneys, a technology-enabled service provider for small and solo law firm practices (www.totalattorneys.com).

A Blog Will Introduce You to More Potential Clients

If your Web site is the home of your business, your blog is your handshake. It's where you meet people, share your expertise, respond to potential clients' comments and questions, and strengthen your online brand. Blogs make the online world more human, and they are a vital asset to every Web site.

---

[7]Problogger.net (**www.problogger.net**) has many good tips for using blogs as marketing tools. See also Kevin O'Keefe's Real Lawyers Have Blogs (**http://kevin.lexblog.com/**), Blawging Lawyers (**http://www.blawginglawyers.com/**), Men with Pens (**http://menwithpens.ca/category/better-blogging**), and Copyblogger (**http://www.copyblogger.com/**).

[8]Blawg.com (**http://www.blawg.com**); ABA Journal Blawg Directory (**http://www.abajournal .com/blawgs/**).

How Often Do I Need to Blog?

The general rule is that you should write at least three blog posts a week, and these posts should be at least 450 words in length. The more often you post new content, the more search engines will pay attention to your Web site and increase your rankings on search engine results pages (SERPs). Posting often also increases your trust factor with your audience. Don't let your blog get stale. Fresh content is key to ranking well. Hosting a stagnant blog may even hurt your rankings in the SERPs.

Who's Going to Write It?

Writing your own blogs (versus paying for ghost-blogging services) has its benefits. You know your audience the best, and you, as the subject matter expert, will write blogs that people want to read. When you publish your own blog posts, you are also in control of your own online identity. You speak for yourself rather than having a ghost-blogger "fake" your voice. Unless you're prepared to shell out substantial money, ghost-bloggers typically offer flat, informative pieces that don't do much for getting people interested or excited about your business. Writing your own blog connects you directly with your target audience, which can help get them in the door as clients.

If You Hire a Ghost Blogger . . .

Sometimes people can't commit to writing three blog posts each week. A ghost-blogger can help fill in the gaps and keep your content current. If you're a lawyer and you hire a ghost-blogger, make sure he or she has legal writing experience. It may cost a little more, but you don't want to put yourself in a position where a ghost-blogger publishes something under your name that is legally inaccurate or unethical in its nature. If you decide to go the "ghost route," you should still write your own post every week or two. Don't let a ghost-blogger hijack the voice of your blog. Interject your own posts so you can keep your voice alive and stay connected with your audience. A ghost-blogger can keep your blog current, but, in the end, you're the one who will make it a blog that people will want to read.

Find Your Niche

What are you passionate about in your industry? When you sit down with your professional peers, what do you talk about? There are millions of bloggers out there. You can't compete with them all. Find your niche and stick to it. A good blog has a focus and direction. Write about what you're interested in and you'll receive a genuine following.

Establish Yourself as an Expert

Blogs give you unlimited free online "billboards" to establish your expertise. Offer thoughtful content that's appealing to your niche audience, and you'll be recognized as a thought leader. Comment on current events and relate them back to your core business. For example, if you're a divorce lawyer, offer insight on the latest U.S. divorce statistics. If you're a bankruptcy lawyer, offer your thoughts on the bank bailouts. You can also write about the core facets of your legal field. Be informative and write about how a certain law may be able to help someone in need. Be sure to include your contact information at the end of each post so potential clients can contact you. Reporters also scan the Web for bloggers who are subject-matter experts, so make sure your e-mail address and phone number are prominently placed.

Open Your Door

Give like-minded bloggers opportunities to blog as a guest on your site. Most bloggers will promote their guest post in social media. You'll get more exposure because their followers are likely to hear about the "guest appearance" and visit to your site to check it out. Opening your blog up to guest bloggers will also connect you with other industry leaders, which could lead to you guest posting on their sites or them linking to your content and helping your SEO.

Be a Human

Blogs give Web sites a human touch. Don't be afraid to show your personality. This is your chance to show that your firm cares about people. People will go to their trusted news sites to read news stories, so don't just regurgitate the news—provide a quick summary of the news topic and jump right into your thoughts. Have an opinion and support it with good research. People want to read and interact with blogs that offer new ideas and insight. Post stimulating content and you'll get a response.

Spread the Word

Don't talk to brick walls. Promote your blog posts through social media channels. Immediately after you publish your post, get on social sites such as Twitter or Facebook and let the world know you just posted a new blog and you'd appreciate people's input. Some people are starting to search for information through these social media sites (versus going to major search engines like Google or Yahoo!), so you'll want to make sure you have a decent presence there. Posting your blog posts on those sites can be a good start.

Follow these social media message tricks, and people will be more likely to click on and to read your content:

♦ Use the word *you* in the social media message or present your blog post as a question you'll answer. People respond well if you relate the content to how it affects them.

♦ Post during peak social activity times. You'll receive the best response if you promote your posts on Tuesdays, Wednesdays, and Fridays, rather than on weekends. Peak hours are usually in the early afternoon, between 11 a.m. and 3 p.m.

♦ Ask your friends and followers to repost your blog post link.

Review and Refocus with Each Post

Remember why you have a blog in the first place: to inform people, to get clients in the door, and to enhance your Web site in natural search results. After you write each post, reread it and ask yourself if you offered the world something new or if you answered questions people have. These posts get you noticed. If people like your blog, the search engines will notice the traffic increase (and the increase of inbound links), and you'll be promoted higher in the search results pages for the keywords associated with that post. Also, make sure you set up the post for SEO success by assigning it unique metadata, using keywords in the header, placing a strategic internal link, and making sure your content can't be confused as duplicate copy.

Comment on Blogs Related to Your Specific Practice Area

Use an RSS feed, such as Google Reader or Feedly, to keep current on other blogs that cover your practice area(s) or other topics of interest for your prospective clients.[9] Write comments on posts for those other blogs. The comments will link back to your Web site or blog. Also consider offering to write guest posts on other blogs, and ask for link sharing with other lawyers when appropriate and after careful review of the other lawyer or firm's blog content.

---

[9]Google Reader (**http://www.google.com/intl/en/googlereader/tour.html**); Feedly (**http://www .feedly.com/**).

Twitter

Consider adding Twitter (**www.twitter.com**) to your blog or virtual law office Web site and using a tool such as TweetDeck, hootsuite, or Seesmic to manage it.[10] This may make your clients and prospective clients feel like they are communicating with you on a more personal level. As long as you keep the posts professional, it could be a good way to connect with clients and other lawyers. Even if you don't add it to your Web site or blog, consider joining as a way to network with other online lawyers and to learn from the many marketing and business experts using the network. See the section below on social networking for a more detailed discussion on the pros and cons of using applications such as Twitter.

Make a Video

Recording a quality video is easy and goes a long way to introducing prospective clients to you and your online practice. Place a sample free consultation or discussion about your practice area(s) on YouTube or Vimeo and link back to your Web site to draw traffic.[11] Videos could also be placed in your blog or on your Web site for specific practice areas to provide general education to prospective clients.

Check Out Google's Marketing Tools

Try Google Analytics to track your online marketing and find out what is working best to send you the most customers.[12] This application may be added to your virtual law office Web site to give you valuable information about where your site traffic is coming from so that you may decide which methods you are using to market the site are worth the effort.

Try Google AdWords only if you are willing to spend the time to find out which keywords will place your ad in the best location.[13] The program allows you to set a monthly ad budget and a price per click, which determines the placement of your ad. The downside is that larger law firms with greater online advertising budgets will most likely be using the same keywords as you will for both your state and your practice area for lawyers. Therefore, you would have to invest a decent amount in this program to achieve much of a result or be able to hone in on the best keywords to draw out the clients that are seeking specific online legal services in your practice area.

---

[10]Tweetdeck (**http://www.tweetdeck.com**); hootsuite (**http://hootsuite.com**); Seesmic (**http://seesmic.com/**).

[11]YouTube (**http://www.youtube.com**); Vimeo (**http://www.vimeo.com**).

[12]Google Analytics (**www.google.com/analytics**).

[13]Google AdWords (**https://adwords.google.com**).

Set up a Google Alert to check up on your business's name, your area of law practice, and your own name.[14] This service will send you an e-mail listing all of the appearances in the news and in blogs of the keywords you entered. For example, set up an alert for "[your state] Virtual Law Office" using the quotations marks. This will notify you anytime all of those words are included together in any news article or blog. At least once a month, also run a Google search of your virtual law office's name and your own name to monitor your Web presence.[15] These two techniques could inform you if your name or virtual law office has been mentioned on any other blogs or Web sites where it would benefit you to respond to those posts or e-mail the author. The ranking in the search engines for your name and virtual law office will also give you an idea of the marketing techniques that are working best.

Case Study: Using Search Engine Optimization (SEO)
Meaghan Olson, Content Writer Manager

Blogging and SEO

Blogs can be very helpful in promoting your SEO, which is critical to bringing in new visitors from the search engine results pages (SERPs).[16] Search engines are constantly scanning the Internet to determine which sites are relevant to which specific keyword queries. These search engines consider hundreds of factors to determine relevance, but *the most important factors are having many inbound links from trusted sites and providing fresh, relevant content.* Search engines view inbound links as online personal endorsements. Those links tell the search engines that people believe your site to be valuable. The "anchor text" (the text the link is attached to) also tells the search engines which keywords your Web site or blog post is about. The second factor, fresh content, shows the search engines that you pay attention to your site and offer relevant information on a regular basis. A blog allows you to frequently update your site so you get that fresh content award, and it's a good venue to post content that people will link to.

---

[14]Google Alerts (**www.google.com/alerts**).

[15]Namechk (**www.namechk.com**) is another free monitoring tool with which you enter names into the search field and the site checks every social networking application online for any mention of that name.

[16]See the Terminology section of the Appendix for definitions of search engine optimization (SEO) and search engine results pages (SERPs).

Additional SEO Benefits: Site Organization and Social Media

Another factor to ranking well is good site organization. One way you can accomplish this is through incorporating a network of well-organized internal links throughout your blog posts. A blog gives you a platform to add new content pages to your site, which allows you to internally link those pages to your core "keyword pages."

For example, if you're a trade lawyer and you want to rank in the SERPs for the keyword phrase "international trade law," you would first write a Web page around that topic. Then, in some of your blog posts, you would link that exact phrase—"international trade law"—to that specific Web page. This shows the search engines that your content is well organized and relevant.

Blogs also give you an easy entrance into the world of social media. You can automatically set up your blog posts to update your statuses on social media sites once they're published. When you promote your blog posts through popular social media sites like Twitter and Facebook, you're expanding your reach and giving more people a chance to find, read, and link to your post.

Why SEO?

SEO is about making your Web site accessible to online searchers. The "If you build it, they will come" axiom doesn't work in the search space. To increase traffic to your Web site, you need to get to your site ranking well for search keywords that are relevant to your practice.[17] The good news is that SEO is one of the most even playing fields in the marketing world. Your law firm may not be able to afford to buy fancy television spots or run professional radio commercials like the big guys, but your site can outrank those big guys in the SERPs if you do SEO right. Many top search engines even give local businesses a spotlight in the search result pages. When you start ranking well for keywords that relate to your business, you'll see a rush of traffic coming in from those search engines, which can result in more clients walking through your door.

---

[17]For example, if a Wisconsin firm handles estate planning, when a prospective client seeking online legal services enters the keywords "wills," "attorney" and "WI" into a search engine, that Wisconsin firm's name would appear at the top of the list for the keywords related to a Wisconsin estate planning law practice. Keywords are the words that prospective clients will type in search engines to seek out attorney Web sites. Firms whose names show up at the top of the search engine results page will receive more traffic to their Web site because more prospective clients will click on the top result entries.

If you're already engaged in paid search marketing (such as buying ads to rank for search terms or buying ads on other Web sites to drive traffic to your site), you still need to focus on SEO. Natural search results are seen by some as results that are more trustworthy rather than results that show up in the paid section. If you're only focusing on paid search marketing, you're likely missing a significant number of searchers who may not trust paid ads.

How Much Will It Cost?

You don't have to spend a lot of money to get into SEO. Not everyone needs to hire a full-time SEO specialist to rank well. If this is the first time you've considered SEO for your site, you'll probably need some SEO foundational work to get you started on the right foot. This is where SEO can get a little tricky. There are many factors to consider when setting up a site for SEO success. One wrong setting or a few missed steps can work against you. For this initial work, it's recommended that you hire a professional SEO consultant.

Your SEO consultant can build solid site architecture, create necessary sitemaps, ensure your site is accessible to the search engines, write core page content and metadata, set up analytical tools, create content and link-building strategies, and train your staff on best SEO practices so they can take the reins once you're set up. This foundational work should take a week or two and will likely cost you anywhere from $500 to $5,000, depending on the size of your site and the extent of your needs. These figures are low to midrange, but you shouldn't need to pay more than $1,000 if you have a Web site with less than ten pages of content. Once your foundational work is squared away, you can often maintain your site internally without the help (and the cost) of a SEO firm.

Do-It-Yourself SEO Maintenance

SEO is a specialty field, but it's also not rocket science. Search engines consider hundreds of factors when determining where a site will rank for which keywords, but if you keep these two main pointers in mind, you could easily outrank 80 percent of competing law firm sites.

1. Links, Links, Links

When other people link to you from their Web site, social media profile, or blog post, they're telling the search engines that they trust you and that you're a relevant site. The more links you have coming in, the higher you'll rank in the SERPs. You get links by offering interesting content (also referred to as "link bait") on your Web site. You can increase the chances of others finding your content and linking to it by promoting it on social media sites. There are services that sell links, but it's recommended that you stay away from them. The search engines will heavily penalize you (and possibly throw you off the SERPs for some time) if they discover you bought links to falsely inflate your Web presence. Get links the honest way—earn them by posting good content. If you're having trouble getting people to link to you, there are companies that specialize in creating and promoting link bait, but be prepared to spend a good chunk of change. Those services can cost thousands of dollars for each link-bait promotion.

2. Post Fresh Content Often

Uploading fresh, original content is essential to ranking well. You can forget about having high rankings if you're a stagnant Web site. Search engines love new content, but don't be lazy and repost content from another Web site—your site can actually be penalized for posting duplicate copy. As mentioned earlier, a blog is one of the most effective ways to provide new content. The blog should be hosted on your domain (such as **www.YourWebSite.com/Blog**) so you get full credit for the content you create and the links you receive from it.

Outsourcing SEO Maintenance

If you don't have the resources to write fresh content, you can hire a ghost-blogger. These services can cost anywhere from $5 to $20 per blog post and $15 to $100 per Web page. If you would rather have someone else worry about SEO, you can hire an SEO firm to maintain your site and report analytics back to you. These services usually cost anywhere $1,000 to $4,000 a month, but you can find a few companies that are less expensive (but sometimes less comprehensive).

Rules and Regulations for Online Advertising by Lawyers

A virtual law practice may have more success using different forms of online advertising and marketing than attempting to use traditional methods of advertising a law practice. Because most of the prospective clients registering with the virtual law office will be actively seeking legal services online, the cost-effective way to reach their attention is through forms of online advertising and social networking. Recent state bar advisory opinions have been released that update the professional conduct rules regarding lawyer advertising to apply to online advertising.[18] In addition, the ABA's Model Rules of Professional Conduct 7.1–7.5 cover advertising of legal services. These rules were updated in 2002 to cover advertising by electronic communication. State bar advisory opinions have been released that discuss Web sites, blogging, forums, listservs, and other forms of online advertising such as referral sites. The recurring concern in each of these opinions has been that the lawyer must avoid misleading the general public in any statements that he or she makes and that it is critical to avoid creating attorney-client privilege in any dialogue that is created online.[19]

One risk with using social networking applications as a form of advertising for a virtual law office is that the lawyer's clients may not fully understand what is appropriate in communicating with the lawyer or the firm through these applications. For example, the client may attempt to "friend" the lawyer and then share confidential information over an unsecure and public method assuming that all online communication provides the same level of security. A client may also try to link to the lawyer's Web site on his or her personal blog, which may not be to the best advantage of the lawyer. The lawyer must then come up with a tactful way of declining to reciprocate the "friending" of the client in online networks, such as Facebook or Twitter, or to ask the client to remove the link to the firm's virtual law office from the client's blog or Web site. Some lawyers may want to include a section in their online engagement letter or clickwrap agreement that lays out the social networking policies of their firm and lets clients know up front about the lawyer's practices with regards to reciprocating social networking. This might also be a good place to educate the client about the dangers of attempting to communicate confidential information to the lawyer through nonsecure, online social networking applications.

---

[18]See, for example, Ohio Supreme Court Ethics Op. 2000-5, OH Adv. Op. 2000-5, 2000 WL 1872571, (Ohio Bd.Com.Griev.Disp.), December 01, 2000, **http://www.sconet.state.oh.us/ Boards/BOC/Advisory_Opinions/display.asp** (accessed March 5, 2010); South Carolina Ethics Advisory Opinion 09-10, **http://www.scbar.org/member_resources/ethics_advisory_opinions/ &id=678** (accessed March 5, 2010); Florida State Bar Standing Committee on Advertising, Opinion A-00-1 (August 15, 2000), **http://www.floridabar.org/tfb/tfbetopin.nsf/SearchView/ETHICS, +OPINION+A-00-1?opendocument** (accessed March 3, 2010); Los Angeles County Ethics Op. 514, 21 Law. Man. Prof. Conduct 452 (2005), **http://www.lacba.org/Files/Main%20Folder/ Documents/%20Ethics%20%20%20Opinions/Files/Eth514.pdf** (accessed March 5, 2010).

[19]See ABA Formal Ethics Opinion 10-457, entitled "Lawyer Websites," issued August 5, 2010. This opinion states that "[l]awyers must not include misleading information on websites, must be mindful of the expectations created by the website, and must carefully manage inquiries invited through the website. Websites that invite inquiries may create a prospective client-lawyer relationship under Rule 1.18." **http://www.abanet.org/cpr/pdfs/10-457.pdf** (accessed September 30, 2010).

Comments posted on forums, blogs, and listservs and in any tweets or micro-blogging that is public must be kept general and if possible carry the disclaimer that the public must seek out the advice of a lawyer regarding their specific legal circumstances. To the extent that the state bar advisory opinions attempt to put limitations on lawyers' use of blogging or social networking, they may need to be updated as more lawyers take their law practices online and require online marketing methods to operate successful businesses. As the public becomes more educated about the technology and the online presence of legal professionals, the rules and opinions will also need to be readdressed to reflect the change in client expectations.

Case Study: Social Networking and Law Practice Management
Carolyn Elefant

Carolyn Elefant is an attorney and owner of the Law Offices of Carolyn Elefant (www.carolynelefant.com), and the author of the blog, MyShingle (www.myshingle.com). She is the coauthor of **Social Media for Lawyers: The Next Frontier**, *ABA (2010), and the author of* **Solo By Choice**, *DecisionBooks (2008). She can be reached at elefant@myshingle.com.*

Are there any legal services, projects, or tasks that you believe cannot be handled as well for the law practice through the use of technology?

. . . [I]f *virtual* is defined to include phone conversations (preferably by Skype or some video, but even oral), then I think that it opens up a range of issues that can be handled virtually, since the lawyer can conduct a good, robust client interview with interaction. At the same time, I admit that . . . I am still a few generations behind the Facebook crowd, and since my legal education and early career focused on face-to-face conversations with clients, I may be too limited to figure out how to converse openly with someone by e-mail only. For younger people who are more attuned to this, it may not be a problem. In fact, I think that to ensure that lawyers have the skills to man a virtual law practice (or even work in the digital age), law schools should incorporate skills training like e-mail-based interviews in addition to the kinds of in-person depositions and interviews that are now provided in skills classes.

What are the benefits for legal professions from this form of law practice?

Virtual practice provides greater flexibility and thus enables parents to achieve better work life/balance. Efficiencies of virtual practice (combined with unbundled services) allow a law firm to capture clients it would have otherwise turned away because it would not have been economical. Finally, virtual law practice enables lawyers to have a statewide or even national practice.

What are the benefits to the lawyer's clients from the use of the technology to deliver legal services?

Use of technology empowers clients by enabling them to play a more proactive role in their case. They can access documents and review them at their leisure, ask questions, and send documents back.

Are there any concerns that you have with a virtual law office as a form of law practice management?

No, none whatsoever. My greater concern for law practice management relates to lawyers who have not kept up with the times and do not know how to use e-mail or create forms to run a practice more efficiently.

What methods of marketing would you recommend for a virtual law practice? How would that marketing differ from the methods used by a traditional law practice?

Virtual law lawyers providing unbundled services need to explain and educate clients on their value add. Because some clients who go to virtual providers may be DIY types, the education about value that a lawyer can bring is important.

In observing the rise of virtual practices, the marketing issues and economics have been a conundrum for me. It seems to me that if a lawyer is running a fully virtual and unbundled practice (i.e., no full-service work or brick and mortar practice), that he or she would have to generate a large volume of cases. Based on some of the prices I've seen, the average cost for incorporations, pro se divorce, or wills/estates is around $200 to $500 per matter—let's say an average of $350. Assuming a Monday through Friday work week and a 50 week/year schedule, a lawyer would need to bring in five cases a week—or one case a day—to gross $87,500. Now, granted, with technology, the lawyer could probably dispatch those cases in eight to fifteen hours/week. But to generate that kind of volume—twenty to twenty-five cases a month—a lawyer would need a "feeder" (e.g., referrals from court pro se programs or other law firms turning these clients away), would have to invest a substantial amount in generating an Internet presence, or would have to collaborate with several other lawyers or firms to share marketing costs and cover a broader area. In that regard, the marketing would differ a little from a traditional practice in that it would be largely Web based and more focused on ways to generate a stream of business and volume.

My answer would differ if the virtual practice served as an adjunct to a full-service firm. There, a firm could employ a traditional suite of marketing—from online blogs, Web, and social media to in-person seminars, articles, and bar events to generate referrals—to generate clients for the traditional practice, and those who could not pay or wanted more streamlined service could go the virtual route.

What security or best practices tips would you provide to a lawyer who is using technology to handle law practice management functions online?

To be honest, I think that many security concerns are overblown—there are always risks, and our information is rarely secure. For example, there's a video on YouTube showing a courtroom proceeding in Maricopa County, Arizona, where the defense lawyer is arguing her client's case to the court and behind her two courtroom deputies are lifting her file and removing documents. All in open court! Likewise, several businesses located in the World Trade Center lost all of their files following the 9/11 attacks. In short, I have yet to see any evidence that putting client files in the cloud compromises confidentiality any more than any other situation.[20]

I think that rather than focus on airtight security, lawyers are better off controlling the type of information that they transfer online to minimize risk. For example, lawyers should not even request Social Security numbers or credit card information from clients unless absolutely necessary (e.g., for cc, use a third-party provider). In matters (e.g., Social Security cases) where the information is necessary, I would choose a provider very carefully or perhaps only store redacted information online.

This approach is similar to the compromise that the federal courts made when they implemented PACER (online document storage). Before PACER was implemented, many courts routinely asked litigants for Social Security numbers and other identifying information. Rather than require parties to seek protective orders, the federal courts changed their policy and now limit the amount of confidential information that is to be filed online to avoid that problem.

---

[20]Author's Note: No law practice is immune from risk regardless of size and whether virtual or traditional brick and mortar. The traditional firm that employs a nightly janitorial service entrusts the security and confidentiality of their paper files to the care of the cleaning crew for those hours. When the office's IT assistant is called in to help update an installed software program or work on hardware on the firm's premises, there is a level of risk involved. Using cloud computing to store law office data is another management decisions that should undergo the risk versus benefit analysis, and if selected, the firm then finds ways to mitigate the risks as it would with other management tools.

What are some of the risks of using SaaS for law practice management, and for each risk, how can the lawyer mitigate that risk?

I see very few risks. In general, SaaS systems are much easier to use than the clunky desktop models or than pen and paper, and a law practice management (LPM) system is only good if people actually use it. I suppose there is the possibility that the system could go down and data could be lost, but I think the best practice is to build in redundancy (e.g., the files stored on SaaS should not be your only copies). There could also be problems with granting access to virtual assistants and lawyers working remotely—that they might either intentionally or inadvertently compromise security. In that situation, the appropriate solution is proper training and perhaps requiring all system users to sign some kind of agreement memorializing their commitment to use the system properly.

Before choosing a third-party hosting service or other product used for a virtual law practice, what questions would you recommend that the lawyers ask?

How long has the vendor been in business, is the product designed for lawyers, and do they have experience with lawyers as customers? What kind of backup and security does the vendor's system have, what kind of insurance/guarantees are provided in event of breach, what kind of tech support is available, is there a mechanism by which the lawyer can download data regularly, what happens if the company goes out of business, and how does the company handle transfer of files if the lawyer changes services?

If you could share any advice with lawyers interested in or currently operating a virtual law practice, what would it be?

If speaking to new lawyers (either just out of school or new to a particular practice area) starting a virtual-only, unbundled practice, I'd say look closely at the economics. How many cases will you need to generate to make the practice financially viable, and what will it cost you to generate that level of business if you are working on your own? Also, if you are providing unbundled or low-cost service, do you have the skills to process these matters efficiently, since economic viability will depend on your ability to handle these matters efficiently? On the other end of the spectrum, I would advise lawyers with full-service firms to ask themselves whether they are "leaving business on the table" in the form of clients who cannot afford full-service—and to consider capturing them with virtual services. I would also advise lawyers who want to practice part-time while raising a family to consider a virtual firm to earn some money while keeping a foot in the door of the practice of law.

Where do you see virtual law practice headed in the future of the legal profession?

This one is tough for me to call. We will definitely see much more in the way of virtual legal services as well as consumers eager for a virtual option. But whether those services will be provided by lawyers or by LegalZoom-type services remains to be seen. As technology improves, services like LegalZoom may be able to generate more quality products, and as consumers grow comfortable with do-it-yourself applications (like self-checkout at supermarkets and video kiosks), they may decide to avail themselves of forms instead of paying a little bit extra to have a lawyer involved in the review.

By way of analogy, my husband and I prepare our own taxes using Quicken, which has become much more sophisticated over the years. But about three years ago, we had a slightly more complex tax problem (my husband had been working in another state for most of the year and had not changed over his withholdings), so we went to an H&R Block–type company. Though we did receive the peace of mind that the company would pay any penalties if there were a mistake, we did not think that the $300 or so that we paid to have an "expert" review the forms really added much value over doing it ourselves. Now, granted, we are both well educated, and my husband has some accounting know-how, so DIY was a legitimate option, whereas it might not be for some clients (particularly those in pro se divorce). In short, I am not sure at what point even the reduced cost of lawyer review of a discrete legal matter like a lease or LLC or will becomes enough of a value add over a pure DIY option.

With regard to whether a virtual lawyer can replace forms, I do not think that the technology for forms employed by LegalZoom or the matters that forms address have yet reached the level of sophistication to make a lawyer irrelevant. In fact, some of the problems I've seen with these forms suggest that a lawyer is more relevant than ever. One problem I'm referencing would probably not become an issue for another decade or more. The same is true of the tax software. Indeed, now, the software has improved once more such that it addresses the issue for which my husband and I sought out an accountant.

Set Up a Social Networking Policy for Your Practice

Whether you are a solo practice or a part of a multi-lawyer virtual law office, establish a social networking policy and stick with it. The key to marketing with online methods is consistency in the online image that you present to the world. Having a policy in place helps you to maximize your efforts in this area and to avoid sending the wrong image to other lawyers and prospective online clients.

A Starting Point for Developing Social Networking Policies

There are different forms of social networking. I would recommend categorizing the most popular online social networking tools in terms of those that are going to be limited to legal professionals (internal social networking) and those that are accessible by the general public (external social networking). Any policy for social networking that you establish should reflect the varying degrees of security and malpractice risks that the different social networking methods provide. Understand the benefits of each form and weigh them against the risks. Build the policy around the methods of social networking that your virtual law office will be committed to using to build its online presence.

Internal social networking includes social networking that is limited to legal professionals or members of your virtual law office, such as associates, virtual assistants (VAs), and virtual paralegals. It is not open to the general public. This is going to be safer and more secure but also more time-consuming because it may require administrators and moderators to set up and maintain. It would not be practical for the solo or small firm to implement, but these lawyers may wish to participate in other private networks of legal professionals. Some examples might include forums, such as those offered by the state bar, or that are specifically created for lawyers in your specific practice areas. The benefit is that the discussion is limited to only the audience you want, and it requires confirmation and registration to post, so there are few security risks. The disadvantage is that lawyers are not often interested in taking the time to contribute to a Web site forum. Listservs such as the ABA's Solosez or legal professional communities such as JDSupra and Legal OnRamp, and other Web sites where lawyers may share and collaborate with other legal professionals, are all forms of internal social networking.[21]

---

[21] ABA Solosez (**www.abanet.org/soloseznet**); JDSupra (**www.jdsupra.com**); Legal OnRamp (**www .legalonramp.com**); See also Martindale Hubbell Connected, **www.martindale.com/connected**.

External social networking is any social networking method that is available to the general public. It is going to have more risks as far as security. For example, with this form of networking you will have to avoid having members of the general public provide confidential information or ask for legal advice that will be viewed publicly. But these methods will also have more results as far as marketing your services, building your brand, and networking with other legal professionals. External social networking includes blogging, which may be used to create and control the online presence for your organization. It provides an opportunity to educate the public regarding your virtual legal services. You may control who posts and who comments, but you must be careful what is written on the blog, realizing that the general public is the audience. You will need to create adequate disclaimers on the blog as you would on any Web site to advise the public to seek out the services of a lawyer to evaluate their unique legal circumstances. (See the section above with tips about blogging for your virtual law practice.)

Twitter is another example of an external social networking site. It is a quick way to create relationships and networks with other lawyers and legal professionals. But it may be more time-consuming than blogging because for it to be effective and to acquire a number of followers the posts must be more regular and contain useful and interesting content. The big risk here is that the general public may request legal advice online when there is no private or secure transmission of the confidential information.

Suggestions for social networking for your virtual law practice include the following:

1. Decide on a consistent image to promote and stick with it. That image could be your firm's logo or you personally as a representative of your practice.

2. If you decide to use one of the social networking tools that is open to the public, set a clear policy up front for yourself and anyone working for your virtual law office about the face that your practice wants to present to the world. Then keep that image consistent throughout the methods of social networking that you use.

3. Instead of trying to monitor your associates' or assistants' actions online, make a daily practice of monitoring your virtual law office's online presence. You may do this by keeping active, daily searches on the name of your virtual law office on Twitter and through Google Alerts. This will notify you daily or several times a day if your name or your virtual law office name is referenced on

any Web article, blog post, or Twitter tweet. Using these monitoring tools is the best way to keep track of any criticisms or negative comments that are made about your virtual law office. While you cannot prevent these from occurring, you will then have ample opportunity to find out the source and to contradict those negative comments and defend your online reputation.

4. Set security protections. The first step after the organization or employee has registered for an account or profile with any social networking site is to go to the "settings," "privacy," or "security" option. The default setting may not be the safest option. Set the security options so that members of the general public cannot comment on your organization's profile page or so that employees cannot post comments or photos that you would not want viewed on your profile or site.

Create an Online Network of Lawyers for Referrals and Support

There are many wonderful opportunities to collaborate with other lawyers online both in your jurisdiction and across the country. Here are a few to consider:

1. ABA's Solosez listserv: Often this listserv is like an online office water cooler for lawyers, and the large volume of e-mails means you have to be comfortable with the delete button. But there is a wealth of knowledge on here if you know how to ask the right questions. Sign up with a separate e-mail account or have your e-mail filter out all the Solosez e-mails into a separate folder for daily maintenance. There are other ABA listservs online that might be useful, but Solosez is one of the most active.

2. Your state bar association's general/small firm practice section listserv or online forum. Depending on what your state bar association offers, this could serve as a great source of information from peers on state-specific laws and also as a source of referrals from lawyers across the state.

3. LinkedIn is a networking site for professionals that permits you to join professional groups and connect with others for potential referrals and business collaboration.[22] Your LinkedIn account allows you to link to your Web site and blog and to join similar groups of lawyers interested in virtual law practice and other forms of eLawyering.

---

[22]LinkedIn (**www.linkedin.com**).

Many lawyers are also now joining Facebook and using it as a more personalized version of LinkedIn to communicate with other lawyers and network.[23] You may want to create a Facebook account in the name of your law practice rather than using your personal Facebook account to keep any networking professional. Some firms are also creating "fan" pages for their firms. The security and features of these public social networking sites change quickly, and new forms of networking are always on the immediate horizon. Keeping current on the most used applications by legal professionals is the least time-consuming strategy for your practice, rather than trying to join and keep up with each new online community.

Keep Your Clients Updated

Rather than mailing out holiday cards in bulk once a year, consider sending out quarterly e-mail blasts either in the form of announcements or short newsletters with basic legal information. The cost to do this would be about the same or less than ordering holiday cards with your business name printed on them.

Avoid sending out mass e-mails to clients who are registered on your virtual law office. This will most likely result in placing your e-mail address on a blacklist, which means that anything you e-mail to those clients from that address will be marked as spam, and chances are they will never see it. iContact, AWeber, and Constant Contact are examples of companies that will help you to send out e-mails that comply with the anti-spam regulations.[24] This method is affordable and also offers other useful tools to store your clients' e-mail addresses and to track who has opened your e-mail, how many times, and when. It also allows your clients to unsubscribe from your updates or newsletters if they choose.

Update Your Business Plan

The delivery of legal services online is an area that is growing and evolving at a fast pace. Expect your business plan to change as your online practice grows. However, as with any traditional law practice, it is useful to have a five-year projection in place from the beginning. If you are adding a virtual law office to an existing practice, consider creating a separate plan for the

---

[23]Facebook (**www.facebook.com**).
[24]iContact (**www.icontact.com**); AWeber (**www.aweber.com**); Constant Contact (**www.constant contact.com**).

goals associated with the virtual component of your practice and integrating that into the overall business plan for your law practice.

Write down a marketing strategy and advertising budget for the year. Even during months when your virtual law office is busy with new clients, you should have a checklist of ongoing online marketing methods that you actively pursue to ensure that the upcoming months are just as busy.

Consult with a Marketing Professional

At some point you may wish to retain the services of a professional marketing team to assist you in any number of services. Some of these services might include branding for your virtual law office, creating an image and logo to improve the site, writing and circulating press releases, redesigning your Web site, writing general content for your blog, or improving the search engine optimization of your Web site. The cost for professional marketing services will vary by the scope of the project. You might want to seek out a professional that is familiar with working with the legal profession and who understands the technology and how virtual legal services differ from traditional law practice so that he or she may help you to market it competitively.

Marketing a Multijurisdictional Virtual Law Firm and Avoiding UPL

An expanded client base is the main benefit of opening a virtual law firm that provides legal services pertaining to several states' laws. One example of a lawyer doing this is Kelly Frame, a lawyer licensed to practice law in South Carolina, Georgia, and Illinois.[25] While Frame maintains a brick and mortar law office in South Carolina, he also has a virtual law office that caters to clients in all three states in which he is licensed. Thus he is able to work with Georgia and Illinois clients online while offering the virtual law office features as an amenity to his in-person South Carolina clients. Another example is Harrill Law.[26] Jonathan P. Harrill maintains a full-service Southern California law practice and combines it with a multijurisdictional virtual law practice that provides legal services online to clients in both California and North Carolina, where he is licensed to practice law.

---

[25]Frame Legal, (**www.framelegal.com**).
[26]Harrill Law, (**www.harrill-law.com**).

A lawyer operating a virtual law firm that caters to clients in more than one jurisdiction needs to carefully review the advertising and marketing regulations for each state in which the legal services are being offered on the Web site. This is important to avoid risk of unauthorized practice of law in other jurisdictions as well as running afoul of one state's requirements for Web site design or URL registration that may differ from another state in which the lawyer is licensed. See the section below regarding Unauthorized Practice of Law with Multijurisdictional Virtual Law Firms for more unique concerns raised by this form of law practice.

Working with Virtual Assistants and Virtual Paralegals

As your virtual law office grows, consider retaining the services of a virtual legal assistant or a virtual paralegal. A virtual assistant, often shortened to VA, is a professional who provides office administrative services remotely through the use of technology.[27] A virtual paralegal also provides support for the lawyer remotely using technology, but he or she is also a licensed paralegal and will be able to provide assistance more closely related to the creation of legal services. VAs and virtual paralegals are typically technology-savvy professionals who are capable of advising a virtual practitioner as to the most efficient methods of handling the tasks that the lawyer would like to outsource.

> ### Case Study: Virtual Assistants
> *Tina Marie Hilton, Owner/Virtual Assistant of*
> *Clerical Advantage Virtual Assistance Services*
> **(http://clericaladvantage.com).**
>
> *Clerical Advantage provides virtual assistant services to solo and small businesses, with a focus on business creatives (writers, coaches, speakers and teachers) and legal professionals.*
>
> *What technology do you use to work with lawyers online?*
>
> I use a combination of technologies depending on what my clients prefer. Online secure file-sharing sites like Dropbox, secure project-management sites like MyClientSpot, and e-mail all play a large part in my work

---

[27] See the e-book *An Introduction to Virtual Assistance for Businesses*, by Tina Hilton, owner of Clerical Advantage Virtual Assistant Services. **http://clericaladvantage.com/services.aspx** (accessed July 1, 2008).

with lawyers. I also frequently use the password feature in Adobe Acrobat to secure files transferred via e-mail. I've found that working online allows for a much more secure atmosphere than a traditional office. No files lying open on desks or conversations overheard by clients in the waiting area are just two items that working online eliminates.

What projects or tasks do you handle for the virtual law practice?

At the beginning of my virtual assistant career, I provided more traditional legal assistance, including processing and preparation of real estate closings. Over the course of time, my knowledge of WordPress, blogging, and Internet applications has transformed my services to focus more on blogging assistance, PowerPoint presentation assistance, and information product development. I do, however, still have several clients whom I assist with scheduling meetings, document formatting, and preparation as well as other tasks that would be considered more traditional types of legal assistance.

How is that work handled differently through the use of technology?

Many of the meetings that I'm scheduling for clients now are teleconferences, and the contact I make with the participants is done through e-mail and the use of the online scheduling application WhenisGood.net. I'm also preparing documents for electronic filing and submission in many cases.

How has the technology made traditional tasks more efficient?

Traditionally, scheduling meetings would require multiple phone calls or e-mails, trying to find a date and time that works for everyone. This can take days or even weeks to finally decide on a suitable schedule. When using the online scheduling application, an e-mail is sent to all recipients directing them to a Web page where they are given a choice of dates and times to choose from. They can then input the dates and times that work best for them. As a virtual assistant, I compile all of the responses to determine the best choice for the meeting and then send out the scheduling information. All of those back-and-forth e-mail exchanges between multiple participants is now pared down to two e-mails. Less time spent equals lower cost for that task to be completed as well.

Are there any projects or tasks you have found that cannot be handled as well for the law practice through the use of technology?

It really depends on how "computerized" the practice is. If they are already pretty much paperless, scanning all documents into electronic format, etc., then the use of technology is going to be a natural extension of the practice. But those practices that haven't started really utilizing electronic documents and files will still require more traditional in-office help for organizing and filing.

For example, many real estate lawyers or title companies might think that title processing would be something that must be done in house due to the many parties involved providing documents, etc. In the past, I have successfully provided processing services easily, utilizing e-fax to receive supporting documents from parties involved. Most lenders now provide closing packages electronically, and with the use of a good processing program installed on a network that can be securely logged onto, everything that is available in office is also available remotely. Phone calls for the processor can easily be redirected to their own phone number without clients ever knowing the processor is remote.

Have you ever worked with a lawyer who has operated a completely virtual practice, or have most practices been operated in conjunction with a brick and mortar law office?

To date, I've had a mix of those that are strictly virtual and those that maintain a brick and mortar office as well. Even those with the traditional office spaces do much of their work outside the office.

How long have you been a virtual paralegal or virtual assistant?

I opened my virtual assistant business in September of 2007.

What are the benefits for virtual paralegals and virtual assistants that you have seen from this form of law practice?

A virtual law practice is a perfect fit for a virtual assistant. The fact that the lawyer is practicing virtually means they already are open to using technology to run their practice, which can be a big stumbling block with other potential clients. They are also going to see the natural wisdom of teaming up with a virtual assistant rather than having to provide equipment, benefits, and the space that hiring a traditional assistant or paralegal would require.

Do you work with the lawyer's clients online or communicate only with the lawyer? If you have worked with the lawyer's clients online, what have the clients' responses been to using the technology?

My business has evolved so that currently most of my communication is with the lawyer only due to the nature of services I'm providing. In the past I have communicated extensively with lawyers' clients online. My experience was that clients embraced the use of technology, as it generally made things easier for them as well.

Are there any concerns that you have working with a virtual law office as a form of law practice management?

I certainly have to keep all of those concerns uppermost in my mind when working with a lawyer. Separate backup of files and making sure my system and network are secure are important concerns. And when required to communicate with lawyers' clients, I never lose sight of my need for the same professionalism and ethics that I operated with during my years as an in-office assistant.

If you could share any advice with virtual paralegals or VAs considering offering their services to a virtual law practice, what would it be?

Be professional. When you keep professionalism at the forefront you are just naturally going to make sure that ethics, security, and other concerns are addressed appropriately. Just because your desk may now be in your living room, never lose sight of the fact that you are a professional businessperson.

If you could share any advice with lawyers considering practicing law online and working with a virtual paralegal or VA, what would it be?

Take the time to really determine exactly what your needs are. That applies to both the work and the personality of the assistant you are looking for. Even if a virtual assistant or virtual paralegal possesses all of the skills you need, if his or her work style and personality doesn't match yours, it's not going to work well. And be willing to really spend some time in the process.

Where do you see virtual law practice headed in the future of the legal profession?

I think virtual law practices will eventually be the norm rather than the exception. Especially for solos and small firms. Meeting with clients won't require a brick and mortar office with the advent of more "virtual office spaces," which offer rental of professional offices for meetings on an as-needed basis. And much like the medical field is doing now, the legal profession is going to eventually move to requiring electronic files rather than traditional paper documents. Courts will require electronic filing rather than simply offering it as an option. It will just make sense for law practices to be virtual as well.

A virtual law office might have permissions allowing the back-end law office to be accessed by a VA or virtual paralegal and also allow the lawyer to lock those functions of the practice that the lawyer may not want the support to have access to. Because of the accessibility of a virtual law office, the VA or virtual paralegal could be located anywhere in the United States or even in another country, depending on the type of work the lawyer needs handled. If the legal work involves state-specific law, then a virtual assistant with paralegal experience in that state would be advisable. On the other hand, if the project is transcription or other administrative tasks, the virtual assistant's home state would more likely be irrelevant and the focus on hiring would be the virtual assistant's level of experience and referrals from other lawyers. A virtual legal assistant working with a virtual law office may be retained on a per-project basis, or a more permanent working relationship may be established, depending on the lawyer's needs.

With any virtual assistant relationship, the lawyer must comply with his or her state bar's rules of professional conduct or other regulations regarding management of non-lawyer assistants. Appropriate instruction and supervision should be given to any virtual assistant hired to work in a virtual law office. One of the safest methods for the lawyer to protect him- or herself is to keep good digital records of communication of instructions to the virtual assistant from the beginning of the relationship. If the virtual assistant will be working through the virtual law office application, the lawyer needs to emphasize the importance of nondisclosure and security for the online clients and that the virtual assistant should closely guard his or her username and password to permissions-based virtual law office access.

Again, most professional virtual assistants, especially those with legal training and experience, are more than aware of these issues. Many of them will even provide the lawyer with a confidentiality agreement from the beginning of their services, which the assistant will have signed, ensuring the lawyer of his or her knowledge of and concern for this critical aspect of providing online legal services. You may also wish to visit the Web site for the International Virtual Assistants Association (**www.ivaa.org**). This organization provides educational resources for businesses interested in retaining the services of a virtual assistant and contains a code of ethics and best practices for its members as well as a member directory.

Case Study: Virtual Paralegals
Denise Annunciata, Owner of Virtual Paralegal Services, Inc.
(http://www.virtualparalegalservices.com/)

Virtual Paralegal Services, Inc. has a team of senior-level paralegals that provide on-demand paralegal services™ to lawyers and their clients.

What technology or methods do you use to work with lawyers online?

Virtual Paralegal Services uses MS Office Suite and MS Sharepoint.

What projects or tasks do you handle for the virtual law practice?

Virtual Paralegal Services has a team of paralegals specializing in general corporate, transactions, real estate, intellectual property/trademarks, securities/blue sky, and litigation. We generally provide full-service to lawyers from more clerical projects to junior associate-level assistance.

How is that work handled differently through the use of technology?

Other than sharing documents via a virtual server, our work is handled and feels very much like it did when we worked for large firms/companies. We correspond mainly via e-mail and phone.

Can you give an example of a traditional task and how technology has been used to make it more efficient, secure, cost effective, etc.?

There are a few examples. One is using Google, LeapLaw, or some other Internet services to obtain information. Information and forms that can be obtained via the Internet make a world of difference in costs and efficiency. And diligence and large projects are easily handled via online deal rooms or via our virtual workspace.

Are there any projects or tasks that you have found cannot be handled as well for the law practice through the use of technology? Why not?

That largely depends on the client. If the client is willing to send original documents or minute books to us, we can handle anything. In cases where clients need on-site assistance, we can provide it only to local companies/clients. For the most part, this hasn't been a big problem.

Have you ever worked with a lawyer who has operated a completely virtual practice, or have most practices been operated in conjunction with a brick and mortar law office?

Our clients are both—completely virtual, and some have a brick and mortar law office.

How long have you been a virtual paralegal or virtual assistant?

Virtual Paralegal Services was incorporated in 2006. I was a virtual paralegal for two years prior to that.

Do you work with the lawyer's clients online or communicate only with the lawyer? If you have worked with the lawyer's clients online, what have the clients' responses been to using the technology?

We have communicated directly with some lawyers' clients. It's completely up to each lawyer how they handle our communications. When we do communicate with them, although we are virtual—the communication is either via e-mail or phone.

Are there any concerns that you have working with a virtual law office as a form of law practice management?

Security is a concern, but when that issue arises we will work through our virtual, secured workspace.

If you could share any advice with virtual paralegals or VAs considering offering their services to a virtual law practice, what would it be?

I guess I would just say that being a virtual paralegal probably isn't best suited for entry-level paralegals. And any virtual paralegal should be technically savvy and keep abreast of technological advancements.

If you could share any advice with lawyers considering practicing law online and working with a virtual paralegal or VA, what would it be?

Just like in the brick and mortar legal world, all paralegals are not created equal. So lawyers should be careful who they chose to work with, particularly when it's a virtual relationship. But, of course, most lawyers would know that. And, like I mentioned already, I think an experienced paralegal is going to work out better than an entry-level person, mainly because experienced paralegals bring more to the table.

Where do you see virtual law practice headed in the future of the legal profession?

Since the early 2000s, virtual law has grown significantly, and I would expect that with vast technological advancements it will just grow exponentially over the next decade.

Case Study: Virtual Secretarial and Paralegal Services
Laurie Mapp, Owner of Halo Secretarial Services, and
Virtual Legal Assistant

*Halo Secretarial Services is a virtual assistance practice, specializing in providing virtual legal assistant and paralegal services (**http://halo secretarialservices.com**)*

What technology do you use to work with lawyers online?

My main technology is a project-management system with SSL encryption (Teamwork PM), through which my clients and I upload and download files for sharing. I also have clients who send work simply by e-mail.

What projects or tasks do you handle for the virtual law practice? How is that work handled differently through the use of technology?

I do very similar tasks to those I performed working in a traditional law office. I draft court and client documents and then upload the final versions to my project-management site. I do dictation, using Express Scribe software. I think one of the main efficiencies my clients see is that they are only paying to have work done on an as-needed basis. I'm not sitting in their office filling my day until they actually need me—they send work when they are busy, and I complete and return it within a specified time frame. Costs are reduced for the client, as I maintain all of my own systems, software, and hardware. An example of this would be when a client uploads a digital audio file to my secure project site. I download it, transcribe the material, and then upload it for them to access the completed work.

Are there any projects or tasks that you have found cannot be handled as well for the law practice through the use of technology?

Certainly there are some tasks that cannot be managed by a virtual legal assistant. For example, I have a client who puts together bound material for sending to a client. I can draft, edit, and even send the digital file to her printer for her, but I cannot physically put the package together. It *could* be done, but time and cost of sending would have to be factored into the equation.

Have you ever worked with a lawyer who has operated a virtual law practice?

The lawyers I work with are brick and mortar law offices with virtual components.

How long have you been a virtual paralegal or virtual assistant?

Close to a year and a half. I worked as an in-house legal assistant for over ten years prior to starting my virtual legal assistant business.

What are the benefits for virtual paralegals and virtual assistants that you have seen from this form of law practice?

There are so many benefits! Most paralegals and legal assistants are employees, but virtual paralegals and assistants are able to be self-employed, giving them the opportunity to work in the areas of law that they prefer and giving them a great deal more flexibility in their work arrangements. I am able to work when my children are sick without missing a beat, and I no longer have to waste any of my day commuting.

If you could share any advice with virtual paralegals or virtual assistants considering offering their services to a virtual law practice, what would it be?

My biggest piece of advice is always to be ready to run a business! It's not enough to be good at being a paralegal; you absolutely must be ready to do all of the related business tasks like marketing, bookkeeping, etc., or you must at least must be prepared to hire help in areas you are not able to take on yourself.

If you could share any advice with lawyers considering practicing law online and working with a virtual paralegal or virtual assistant, what would it be?

A virtual legal assistant or paralegal is a wonderful option in so many ways. We can assist when there is a temporary need, we can assist with overflow work that in-house staff can't keep up with, or we can be your main support person. A virtual assistant will be more invested in your practice than most in-house staff, as we need your practice to grow and be busy in order for you to want to continue partnering with us.

Where do you see virtual law practice headed in the future of the legal profession?

I think there is going to be incredible growth in the area of virtual law practice, as it provides a wonderful opportunity for both the lawyers and their clients. It reduces travel, by allowing the lawyer to avoid his or her commute, and allows the client to schedule meetings online without having to travel to the lawyer's office. It reduces the restrictions of geography and allows people to truly work with someone who is the best match for their needs.

CHAPTER SIX

Ethics and Malpractice Issues

AS WITH ANY TRADITIONAL law practice, it is the responsibility of the lawyer delivering legal services online—not the hosting company, the software provider, the state bar, the ABA, or any other entity—to ensure that the daily online practice avoids malpractice and complies with the high ethical standards required by the lawyer's law license. This responsibility often means that the lawyer must take ethics or advisory opinions from his or her state bar and interpret them to apply to the use of new technology and forms of eLawyering. If the lawyer's state bar has not directly addressed virtual law practice, there may be other directives related to unbundling, limited legal services or forms of eLawyering that may answer the lawyer's ethics questions as they relate to online law practice. Please see the state-by-state opinions and resources listed in the appendix.

Where Do State Bars Stand on Virtual Law Practice?

If you have questions about your state bar's opinion on virtual law practice, you should contact them directly for a formal or informal advisory opinion. In many cases, they may want you to educate them on the structure of the virtual law practice and how the technology will be used to deliver legal services online. Be prepared at this stage in the development of virtual law practice to provide detailed information in this regard.

The state bar may also want to review the virtual law practice's static Web site before it is launched and may also require the approval and registration of the firm's URL with the state bar. These steps may be necessary for a traditional law firm's creation of a Web site or use of online advertising, but there will be additional scrutiny of the terms and conditions or disclaimers and other notices to the public on the virtual law practice Web site. Items that the state bar may look for in the static Web site include the following:

♦ Adequate notice of the jurisdiction that the practice covers

♦ Terms and conditions and disclaimer that are always accessible to the public on the site

♦ Current contact information for the lawyer or the firm

Regarding current contact information on the Web site, with some state bars, this may include a physical office location. This is an issue that some lawyers who reside in one state and practice law in another are dealing with. Residency requirements are discussed in more detail below. It may be necessary to negotiate with the state bar to add a line to the Web site explaining that the lawyer is not physically located in that state where the legal services are provided. If this is the case, then the lawyer must emphasize in this disclaimer that the site only provides limited legal services and not the representation of a full-service law firm. In other instances, the state bar may be satisfied with providing a PO box address as contact information, and the lawyer must then be responsible for retaining a service that mails the contents of the PO box on a regular basis to his or her home office or other physical address.

The problem is that the rules of requiring contact information for the clients in many states have not been updated to recognize the delivery of legal services online. With so many other methods of communication available aside from snail mail, these rules seem outdated and in need of updating. Furthermore, individuals seeking online legal services are not typically members of the public that will then be turning around and communicating by writing letters and mailing them to the lawyer. In the event that a document needed to be mailed to the lawyer rather than electronically uploaded to the virtual law office and handled completely online, then some lawyers will have a PO box near their physical location and may give that address out to the occasional client and other entities that still mail out invoices, licenses, notices, and other transactions related to the business that are not handled online.

Malpractice Insurance Coverage

Malpractice insurance for your virtual law practice is just as much of a no-brainer as it is in a traditional law office. You should have it. The good news: The use of technology may actually help to limit the risk of malpractice in delivering legal services online. When discussing malpractice insurance coverage, the lawyer may want to mention the automated checks and processes set up within the technology that are designed to prevent malpractice.

For example, a jurisdiction check may occur upon registration of a prospective client to the virtual law office Web site, which may throw up a red flag warning to both the lawyer and the prospective client to ensure that each individual is aware that the physical location of the prospective client may not be within the jurisdiction in which the lawyer is licensed to practice law. This system does not prevent the lawyer from taking the case. There are many instances when a client residing in one state may need the assistance of a lawyer licensed in another state—for example, if the client owns property in a state outside of his or her primary residence and needs legal assistance related to that real property.

Furthermore, the high-level security of a virtual law practice when compared to the use of unsecure methods of electronic communication, including unencrypted e-mail, also helps to prevent malpractice risks when communicating with clients online. The added protection of this level of security helps to protect client confidences. Please refer to the section of the book related to security and privacy of the technology for additional information.

When approaching the malpractice carrier, if the entity has not directly addressed a virtual law practice, be prepared to educate the representative on the topic by including walkthroughs of the software, samples of how the lawyer works with clients online, copies of the terms and conditions for your site, examples of how the engagement process works, how your conflict of interest checking works, and any other processes that might assist the company in understanding fully how you deliver legal services online. Some lawyers taking this educational approach to obtaining malpractice insurance have found that they qualified for a discount due to the use of the technology to automate many of the malpractice concerns in their practice. While this may not be available with every carrier, as more virtual law practices emerge, we may see different policies being offered to address them directly.

When evaluating the policy for your virtual law practice, make sure to read through the exclusions to ensure that the insurance company is not attempting to reduce its risk by adding in provisions that may exclude aspects of your technology used for practicing law online. Consider, too, that depending on the type of practice that you structure, you may be dealing with more "quantity" of online clients than with a handful of "quality" clients, meaning that you may be dealing with many smaller online drafting projects rather than one or two online clients who are paying larger total legal services. This may mean that in any instance the total loss might not be as large as if you were working with larger paying clients. Again, it completely depends on the structure of the practice and how automated you will be in delivering legal services. If you will be working with higher paying online clients, then you will want to check that the coverage is sufficient to address that risk.

If the virtual law practice is structured as a firm or partnership of other lawyers, whether multijurisdictional or not, your malpractice insurance policy should cover all of the members of that virtual law practice. This will ensure that the firm itself or all the members will not be held responsible for the acts or omissions of one of the other lawyers in the virtual law firm. This is an important safeguard even if the lawyers are located in different states to form the virtual law practice. The challenge will come in finding a malpractice carrier that will be willing to write a policy for lawyers that crosses over several states. Given the additional risks that this structure of virtual law practice brings, any carrier may likewise be hesitant to draft a policy that provides adequate coverage, or, if they do, the cost may be significantly greater than what would be provided to a traditional multimember firm. Another option would be for the lawyers within this larger firm to draft into their fee structure, partnership agreement, or other governing document a provision that every lawyer will be individually responsible for their own acts or omissions as well as individually responsible for obtaining insurance coverage for their section of the virtual law practice.

Insurance for Your Hardware

Your law practice is located online, and you can't access it without your hardware. You may also have other law office data stored on your computer or hard drive as backup. Protection for the loss of the use of this hardware may be something to consider in an insurance policy. At this time, coverage by most insurance companies is limited when it comes to loss related to electronic data, use of computers, software, or access to backups and other law office data. Another area for loss with a virtual law practice might be the risk of a security breach associated with the activities of a malicious hacker or online identity theft. Again, these are risks that most insurance carriers are not willing to take on at this time.

There are ways to protect your law practice in this regard. Make sure that you have more than one method of accessing your law office data. Reducing your risk means being meticulous about backups and choosing a service provider that offers geo-redundancy, regular daily backups and data escrow. The service agreement you have with the software provider will more than likely not protect you from the risk of the loss of data if it is related to your own acts or omissions or the failure of your own hardware in the operation of your virtual law practice. Make sure that your virtual law practice abides by daily best practices for the use of the technology. The best measure is to come up with your own methods to minimize the risk of loss in these areas that will most likely not be covered by an insurance policy. Please see the section entitled "Daily Best Practices" in Chapter Five above.

Case Study: Malpractice Insurance Carrier
Camille Stell, Director of Client Services, with the contributions of the underwriters and claims lawyers, at Lawyers Mutual Liability Insurance Company of North Carolina (www.lawyersmutualnc.com).

Lawyers Mutual provides financial protection from professional liability for more than 8000 lawyers throughout the State of North Carolina.

The basic idea among myself and our underwriters that we would not consider a virtual practice more problematic than any other sort of practice. In some ways, it could be considered like a niche area of practice.

A couple of thoughts: (1) general/basic risk-management principles apply, such as client screening—you need to beware of "red flag" clients, but so do all lawyers. You need a clear understanding of the fee up front, but so do all lawyers. There is a thought that maintaining privilege and confidentiality can be more challenging in a virtual world; an example might be since all communications are via e-mail, the risk of sending, replying, or forwarding to the wrong person might be higher; (2) anytime you unbundle legal services, clearly defining the scope of the representation is critical, as is revisiting scope of services as that can change (lawyers also need to be careful about not unreasonably limiting the scope); and (3) in theory, documentation should be easier, given the virtual nature of the relationship, which could be good or bad, but it definitely means that e-mail content should not be an afterthought.

Do insurance policies for a virtual law office differ from those offered to traditional law practices?

No.

Is there anything unique that you require from a lawyer prior to providing policy estimates?

No.

What should a lawyer look for from their malpractice insurance carrier when shopping for a policy for his or her virtual law practice in terms of policies, premiums, support, services, etc.?

You want to make sure that you are purchasing the right amount of coverage for your area of practice. If you handle commercial real estate deals in excess of a million dollars, you want to make sure that you get more than $300,000 in limits. Likewise, if you are in a criminal defense practice, you probably don't need as large limits, and you might feel more comfortable with a large deductible, as you are in a safer area of practice. You also want to think about continuity of coverage. Legal malpractice insurance policies are claims-made policies as opposed to occurrence policies like your car insurance. The coverage is not when the act or omission occurred but when it is reported. You want to make sure that if you change companies, and even if you are remaining with the same company, that when you complete a new application every year to respond properly to questions about potential problems of which you are aware. "Prior acts coverage" can prevent gaps in coverage when a lawyer is changing companies or changing employment. Is this provided, or something you need to purchase separately? Is your malpractice company approved or recommended by your state bar association?

Many companies do have special relationships with their bar association, and they are "bar approved" or "bar related." NABRICO is the National Association of Bar Related Insurance Companies, and many of the companies that are members are "mutual" companies, meaning that their policyholders are the owners of the company.

Does your malpractice provider offer risk-management resources or CLE? Can you call with a question when you run into trouble? Do they have claims-repair efforts—before suit is filed—when they will offer assistance to avoid a malpractice claim? Do they have local claims counsel? The ABA Standing Committee on Lawyers' Professional Liability has a section on the ABA Web site with helpful articles and resources.

Are you aware of any complaints or grievances that have been brought up against a lawyer delivering legal services online? If so, what was the nature of those actions, and how could they be prevented?

No malpractice claims. I am aware of issues that the NC State Bar Authorized Practice of Law Committee is looking into that involve Web companies such as Ask.com and whether lawyers who participate in those are aiding in the unauthorized practice of law. The same issues arise with debt-relief companies that offer a "marketing" opportunity for lawyers to belong to a network where you are referred cases in a geographic area. Some of these are document-preparation companies who do all the work with no lawyers involved, then they need a local lawyer to "sign off" on the work product. The economy is driving some lawyers to make poor choices to get involved with some of these companies, but I would not view these as virtual law practices.

Can you recommend any tips to avoid malpractice when delivering legal services online?

Develop proper forms for checking conflicts, client screening, and engagement, non-engagement, and disengagement. Understanding the scope of the representation is important for both client and lawyer, and if the scope changes, update the engagement letter. Fee agreements are key. Keeping client expectations reasonable early in a case usually leads to a more satisfied client. Do they know what to expect in fees? Do they know how they are going to be billed? Do they understand what the final work product will look like? Do they understand how the virtual relationship will work? Documentation will be key in defending against bar grievances or malpractice cases when the client complains about things that are the very essence of a virtual practice—"I never met my lawyer. My lawyer didn't return my phone calls," etc.

What would you identify as the key ethics issues that may arise in the operation of a virtual law practice?

Staying up-to-date in your practice area so that you are offering competent services. Conflicts of interest issues are always problematic for lawyers.

Do you see the potential to prevent malpractice through the use of technology to deliver legal services online? In what ways may the technology be used to prevent malpractice?

The common areas of malpractice are not those cases where lawyers don't know the substantive areas of law but those where lawyers miss deadlines or have a conflict of interest. Technology is great for dealing with these kinds of problems. Having a calendar system is important, but also important is building in advance warnings—it's not helpful to determine that a major deadline is today; you need to factor in prep time. Having a conflict-check system is important, and technology is a great tool to manage your client and adverse relationships. If we know that certain clients are problematic, you can develop questions on your intake form to help with client screening.

Where do you see virtual law practice headed in the future of the legal profession?

I think there is a generation of lawyers who are not interested in high compensation but more in a lifestyle that suits their personality. I believe those individuals will chose careers of interest, then make them fit into their lifestyle. You may have lawyers who have a virtual practice for a season of life—while they have children at home or aging parents—then they may return to a more traditional practice. I think our current economic situation has also shown lawyers that they don't need to pay for fancy reception areas and conference rooms and that virtual practices make economic sense even when the economy rebounds. I also think when you look at many consumers today, they expect to make most purchases online—not just books or DVDs, but they choose colleges online, they make major purchasing decisions (such as cars) online, and they will expect this to translate into professional services as well.

Preventing Malpractice through the Use of Technology

Unauthorized Practice of Law

One of the foremost ethics issues is the unauthorized practice of law (UPL). To be at risk of UPL, the lawyer's actions must constitute "practicing law" as defined by the rules and regulations of his or her state bar.[1] Some state bars have a different definition of "practicing law," and there has been some question about whether providing forms to clients to fill out online with no other lawyer interaction constitutes the "practice" of

---

[1] See the ABA's Task Force on the Model Definition of the Practice of Law Web site for resources and a list of the different state definitions of the practice of law: **http://www.abanet.org/cpr/model-def/home.html** (accessed May 30, 2010) and the Task Force's Report issued April 2003: **http://www.abanet.org/cpr/model-def/taskforce_rpt_803.pdf** (accessed May 30, 2010).

law under those states' rules. But with a virtual law practice, the lawyer is not providing online forms or other law-specific interaction with the client until the attorney-client relationship has been established. The lawyer is conducting work with the client just as he or she would in a traditional law practice, only in the online environment using the processes set up in the technology. There should be no question that these actions constitute the "practice" of law.

Aside from this, there are two main issues related to UPL. The first is UPL in other jurisdictions. This arises when the virtual law practice Web site is located on the Internet and therefore is accessible by anyone who has Internet access. This is discussed in greater detail below.

The second issue is UPL by non-licensed individuals. Companies such as LegalZoom and Nolo, Inc., providing legal forms for sale online take up a large portion of the market for online legal services because of their ease of use by the public and their affordability. But neither service provides the customer with the benefit of legal advice or review of the legal documents being purchased. The question is whether the general public understands the value and importance of having personalized consultation by a lawyer. In many cases, it may be acceptable for consumers to use those services, but in others there is the danger that the consumer is not filling out the forms correctly and believes that the provisions in the legal documents he or she has purchased are providing protections that do not exist.

At the same time, there is an increasing need for affordable access to justice, which the legal profession alone is not able to meet. This problem continues to grow as more court administrations become overburdened with the handholding involved in working with the large number of pro se litigants flooding their court systems. The legal profession cannot step up to meet this public need without the use of technology to assist in automating many of the transactional legal advice and form generation that that is needed in most basic legal matters.

A virtual law practice provides a balanced and safer alternative for consumers seeking online legal services because it includes the ability to consult directly with a lawyer regarding the individual circumstances of the customer's legal issue. Any legal documents provided to the client as unbundled legal services are not released to the client until after the lawyer has released them and in some cases not until the payment for legal services has been rendered. In addition, because there is lower overhead to operating a virtual law practice and because much of the process may be automated, the lawyer providing these services should be able to provide lower fees for the services that they provide, whether that is through fixed fee, billable hour, or a combination fee structure.

Another concern with UPL by non-licensed individuals may be the ability of individuals to open a virtual law office who are not qualified or licensed to do. As more virtual law practices emerge, it may fall to the responsibility of the individual state bars to ensure that any virtual law practices within their jurisdictions are being operated by legal professionals who are licensed and in good standing. Because of the ease and low cost of setting up a virtual law practice, it may be tempting for a lawyer who is not qualified or not in good standing with his or her state bar to open up a virtual law practice. But just as with a traditional law practice, that responsibility for enforcement should fall to the state bars.

UPL in Other Jurisdictions

The main concern regarding UPL relates to the risk that the lawyer may be practicing law outside his or her jurisdiction when contacted by an online client who is a resident of another state where the lawyer is not licensed. The responsibility of avoiding UPL falls to the lawyer delivering legal services online, even with a jurisdiction check in the software, so that he or she is able to handle the requested legal services without committing malpractice.

In many respects, the analysis does not differ greatly from the process that a lawyer in a traditional law office would go through to avoid committing UPL. But there are two primary differences of which a lawyer practicing law online should be aware.

One difference is that the notification to the prospective client of the lawyer's jurisdiction to practice law is handled online rather than in person or through a mailed engagement letter. The other difference is that the scope of potential online clients registering for legal assistance will be greater in number, requiring added careful examination for the unauthorized practice of law in each online request for legal services presented by a prospective client.

ABA Model Code Rule 5.5(b) states that "[a] lawyer who is not admitted to practice in this jurisdiction shall not: (1) except as authorized by these Rules or other law, establish an office or other systematic and continuous presence in this jurisdiction for the practice of law; or (2) hold out to the public or otherwise represent that the lawyer is admitted to practice law in this jurisdiction."[2] This rule applies to any law firm Internet presence, not just a virtual law practice. But because clients will be able to work with and purchase legal services from the Web-based law office, the virtual law practice Web site needs to be even clearer to the public about the services that are provided and the nature of unbundled legal services in general.

To comply with the ABA Model Rule 5.5(b) and the rules of most state bars, the lawyer setting up a virtual law practice should pay close attention to the Web site content and advertising rules established by the state bar(s) in which he or she is licensed. Regarding UPL in other jurisdictions, it is the responsibility of the virtual law practitioner to provide clear notice throughout the virtual law practice Web site that he or she is only licensed to practice law in the state(s) in which the lawyer holds an active bar license. Furthermore, to also guard against UPL in other jurisdictions, the virtual law practice should contain the name of the lawyer(s) practicing law online and current contact information. By providing adequate notice, the lawyer should not be found to be soliciting clients from a state where he or she is not able to practice law.

To prevent UPL, a virtual law practice should contain some form of automated jurisdiction check for the benefit of the client and the lawyer. This is best handled from the very beginning of the process of engaging the prospective client during the initial registration on the virtual law practice Web site. For example, when the client registers on the Web site, a simple check for the zip code would notify the lawyer that the client is a resident outside his or her jurisdiction. A notice would then appear to the client stating that the lawyer may only be retained to answer legal questions and handle legal work related to the laws of the state for which the lawyer has an active law license.

Any jurisdiction check should not prevent the client from continuing with the registration process, but it serves the purpose of providing more than adequate notice of the lawyer's jurisdiction. Through this process, the lawyer is provided with a red flag on the back end of the law office to let him or her know that the client resides in a different state and may have a legal matter that the lawyer is not permitted to handle.

---

[2] ABA Center for Professional Responsibility Web site, **http://www.abanet.org/cpr/mrpc/rule_5_5 .html** (accessed January 3, 2010). See also the ABA Commission on Multijurisdictional Practice Report to the House of Delegates. The recommendations in this final report were all adopted on August 12, 2002. **http://www.abanet.org/cpr/mjp/201b.pdf** (accessed January 3, 2010).

The unauthorized practice of law in another jurisdiction would occur if a lawyer used his or her virtual law office to draft a legal document that pertained to the laws of another state where the online client was a resident but where the lawyer did not have a license to practice law. But if the lawyer operating the virtual law office were partnering with lawyers and legal assistants on his or her virtual law office who were licensed in other jurisdictions, then this should prevent UPL. For example, a virtual paralegal could work on the virtual law office to draft a will or other estate planning document for a client in a jurisdiction where the virtual paralegal was familiar with that state's estate planning laws. The virtual paralegal would then flag the document for review by the lawyer on the virtual law office who was licensed in that online client's state. The review and approval of that legal document by the lawyer licensed to handle that state's laws would permit the virtual paralegal to complete the transaction for the online client without it constituting UPL in another jurisdiction.

UPL with Multijurisdictional Virtual Law Firms

UPL must be carefully considered when virtual law practice is structured as a multijurisdictional practice. In some respects it operates no differently than a traditional firm with offices in different states. But the key here is in ensuring that the prospective client registering for legal services online is connected to the lawyer who is licensed to handle the legal matter at hand. This may mean a more robust system for checking the jurisdiction or the use of a virtual paralegal or assistant to handle the initial filtering of requests for legal services from new registrants.

Residency Requirements and UPL

Residency requirements exist for a handful of state bars and are another example of a restriction on the legal profession that may need to be updated to reflect changes in law practice management.[3] These residency requirements focus on the lawyer "actively practicing law within the state" or maintaining a "bona fide office."[4] How should this be interpreted if the lawyer physically resides in one state and actively practices

---

[3]See, for example, Missouri State Bar Informal Advisory Opinion Number 970098 regarding Rule 5.5; *Tolchin v. New Jersey Supreme Court*, 111 F.3d 1099 (3d Cir. 1997); *Lichtenstein v. Emerson*, 674 N.Y.S.2d 298 (App. Div. 1998); *Parnell v. West Virginia Supreme Court of Appeals*, 110 F.3d 1077 (4th Cir. 1997).

[4]See, for example, Mich. Comp. Laws Ann. § 600.946 (the lawyer must show intent "either to maintain an office in this state for the practice of law, and to practice actively in this state, or to engage in the teaching of law").

law from a virtual law office providing the legal services pertaining to the laws of another state? He or she is actively practicing law, just not physically within the state.

In some instances, the residency requirements have been reduced to only lawyers who are handling litigation in that state. If the lawyer is required to appear before a court in that state, then he or she is required to have a physical residency in that state. This makes practical sense, but New Jersey's Advisory Committee on Professional Ethics and the Committee on Attorney Advertising have gone one step even more backward. They released a joint opinion stating that even when a lawyer hires a virtual assistant or receptionist or shares a rented office space for conferences to attempt to create an office presence in the state, this does not create a "bona fide office" that complies with the state's residency requirements practicing law.[5] The opinion significantly limits lawyers licensed in New Jersey to having a physical law office where clients may call during regular business hours. This restriction on business discriminates against many solos and in particular women lawyers who may need to practice law from home, but for personal and security reasons, they do not want to provide their home address or phone number to clients. How this restriction will affect solos and small firms wanting to form completely virtual law offices is yet to be seen, but the joint opinion does allow for lawyers with a traditional law practice to also operate a virtual law office with adequate notice to prospective clients of the firm's physical office location.

For other virtual law practices where their state has a residency requirement, this may be met by forming associations between the virtual law firm and a physical, traditional firm in that state. In that case, the virtual law practice Web site should include in the disclaimer that there is not a physical law office location for the virtual law practice itself, but that in the event of the client requiring a full-service firm for the purposes of litigation or in-person representation, the virtual law practice will refer the client to the firm associated with it that is within the geographic location of the client. But as in New Jersey, other state bars may require out-of-state lawyers to maintain an office as a condition of practicing in the jurisdiction. While these rules have survived constitutional challenges to

---

[5]Joint Opinion, ACPE 718/CAA 41 (March, 2010), **http://www.judiciary.state.nj.us/notices/2010/n100326a.pdf** (accessed March 30, 2010). The opinion refers to "virtual law offices" but does not specifically define a virtual law office as a Web-based practice and instead refers to rented office space.

date, many need to be reconsidered in light of new advancements in law practice management and to reflect the needs of both the public and members of the profession.[6]

Providing Competent Online Representation

Depending on the structure established for your virtual law practice, there may be some practice areas and legal matters that do not translate as well into the services offered through a virtual law practice. You may also have a client base in your practice that is less comfortable using technology. In those cases, the key is to know what level of legal assistance you may provide online and then to adequately inform the prospective client of the limitations of those services. As with a traditional law practice, you must comply with your state bar's rules of professional responsibility to provide competent and diligent representation, one time phrased as "zealous representation."

If you are operating a virtual law firm in addition to a traditional law practice, this is easily accomplished by meeting with your client in person and then handling smaller matters associated with the administration of the case online, such as payment of invoices, calendaring, and document review, if the client so chooses to use the virtual law firm as more of an amenity to working with you rather than as the sole method of communicating. If you are providing strictly unbundled or limited legal services online, then it is important to know when the online client's legal matter requires in-person representation for competent and diligent representation to occur. For example, a client would need to be referred offline if he or she had a criminal defense case that would require continued and consistent full-service representation.

Can you adequately convey the nuances of a legal matter online, or does it require at a minimum that the lawyer pick up the phone and speak with the client? The answer to this question raises the biggest difference in the generation gap between lawyers. Lawyers who attended law school with their laptops and smart phones on at all times during each lecture, and maybe even took their bar exam on a computer, feel more confident that they can adequately communicate using technology, even if it is

---

[6]For further research, see *Supreme Court of New Hampshire v. Piper*, 470 U.S. 274 (1985); *Supreme Court of Virginia v. Friedman*, 487 U.S. 59 (1988); *In re CARLTON*, United States District Court, D. Maryland, No. 10-mc-160, 2010 WL 1707722 (D.Md.) (April 26, 2010); *Schoenefeld v. State of New York*, 1:09-CV-0504 (LEK/RFT), United States District Court, N.D. New York, (February 8, 2010).

only limited to text or a combination of instant messaging, text, video, and real-time chats. Online forms on a virtual law practice Web site both provide legal guidance to clients and prompt them to answer additional questions to guide the lawyer through their individual circumstances. Armed with these collected data, the lawyer then may follow up with additional online communication to verify the situation and clarify anything that is needed with the online clients.

Lawyers who did not begin their legal careers with this comfort level with technology may be more accustomed to speaking with clients in person or by the phone. They may claim to hear certain inflexions in the tone of voice of the client that hint to them that the client is unsure or hiding something from them. At the same time, the lawyers who are used to communicating online know how to use online methods to comfortably determine the underlying emotion or motivation of the person they are communicating with. The same doubt and resistance between generation gaps occurred when phones were new to the law office and another older generation of lawyers swore that it was impossible to gauge the client's motivations and veracity without looking the client directly in the eyes.

The best response to this argument against completely Web-based delivery of legal services is that lawyers should know their own comfort level with technology and consider the methods of working with each client on a case-by-case basis. If the legal service requested online requires the lawyer to call the client or if the lawyer feels more comfortable calling each client by phone, then the lawyer should do so. If it is necessary for the legal service requested, then it is the responsibility of the lawyer to speak with the client by phone to competently handle the matter or refer the client to a full-service law practice.

As far as the ability to streamline the delivery of legal services online, this extra step of picking up the phone may slow up the delivery process and add a level of inconvenience to the client and the lawyer that was not there when both parties could handle the matters 24/7 and without having to schedule an appointment within the business hours of a work week. This added step would also need to be taken into consideration with any fixed-fee or value-based billing system, as it may take additional time to conduct a phone conversation and the client then would have access to a phone number to contact the lawyer at any time following that initial call. This would thus defeat another benefit of virtual law practice, which is the ability of the entire transaction and conversation to be documented, with date and time, online within each client's case file.

Many states have given formal approval to unbundled legal services.[7] At the same time, many of them have added requirements that the lawyer provide notice of lawyer authorship on the unbundled legal documents to be filed with the court system and provide adequate contact and bar license information for the lawyer that provided the unbundled legal services. Several of the existing ethics and advisory opinions by state bars were written before virtual law practice had expanded beyond the communication between lawyers and clients by e-mail. The main concern in these opinions is that it might be difficult to provide competent representation online with limited client contact.

Virtual law practice and other forms of eLawyering, however, provide for a great deal more personal interaction with clients than the use of e-mail exchanges. A secure virtual law practice does not rely on e-mail, which is unencrypted, to handle any attorney-client communications or transactions. A virtual law practice permits extended communication between lawyer and client through the interface and provides an additional method of online communicating that extend beyond simply sending text notes between the parties.

For example, within the client portal, every client has their own home page where they may store communications between the parties; documents that are uploaded by clients or by the lawyer; an interactive calendar; sticky notes with reminders for invoices, deadlines, and other billing items; and client information. The lawyer might conduct Web conferences or Skype calls in which the lawyer and client may speak and see each other while online. In addition, through the use of other online social networking tools, such as LinkedIn, Facebook, and Twitter, a lawyer has the ability to let clients know what he or she is doing on a minute-by-minute basis. While this may not be desirable in most cases, the ability to form close business relationships through Web-based applications is fully available. Accordingly, written concerns by state bars regarding the ability of a virtual law practice to provide competent limited legal representation may not recognize these advancements in technology. They may be tailored more toward e-mail communication between client and lawyer and may not relate to the ability of the virtual law practice to assist the lawyer in identifying conflict of interest issues or providing personalized, competent online representation.

Another safeguard provided by the technology is the use of an online referral database that may be built into the online back-end law office.

---

[7]See the appendix topic "Unbundled Legal Services" for a list of state bar ethics and advisory opinions approving of unbundling.

This allows the lawyer to build a network of other legal professionals and easily and quickly refer prospective online clients to other virtual law offices or full-service law firms if the lawyer is unable to provide competent legal representation online. The use of a virtual paralegal or assistant to filter through prospective online clients and refer unqualified candidates to other resources may be a more efficient method of handling a large influx of online clients.

Other options toward helping to avoid malpractice is to partner with another virtual law office that will handle practice areas that you are not familiar with or to partner with a full-service firm in a different geographic location that will send referrals to you when clients want to work online in exchange for your referrals of clients needing in-person representation. The key to avoiding this malpractice risk is the same as with any traditional law practice: the lawyer has the duty to determine, on a case-by-case basis, whether he or she has the requisite legal experience to provide quality legal representation to the client requesting services.

Conflict of Laws

Conflict of laws raises one of the more complex issues as it relates to virtual law practice. The issue comes up when a lawyer opens a virtual law practice with the intent of providing federal law–related legal services, such as in the practice areas of immigration law or intellectual property law. The lawyer is able to handle the online client's matter as far as it relates to the federal law matter.

For example, he or she may file the patent application for the online client who may be a company or small business instead of an individual. But if that same online client then asks the lawyer to draft a contract through the virtual law office, the lawyer is faced with the question of whether he or she may handle that aspect of the legal services that extends outside of federal law. The contract for the online client should be drafted in accordance with the state law in which that online client is a resident or where the client who is a business or company does its primary business. Therefore, the lawyer must run a jurisdiction check to make sure that he or she is able to assist the client based on the state(s) in which he or she is licensed to practice law.

If the virtual law practice is being marketed nationally or regionally as providing federal law legal services, then it may become frustrating to the online client to be restricted in the amount of work the contracted lawyer may legally handle for the client online. The client would be required to go to another lawyer, full-service or virtual, within the proper jurisdiction for the state law–related matters, which may end up costing more than if the client were able to go online to obtain all of the business-related legal services that were needed.

What if the service that the online client was requesting included a privacy policy and disclaimers for the online client's Web site? The client's Web site is accessible to customers across the world, and the client conducts business though that site nationally. There is not a lot of precedence for providing a solution to this issue within law practice management or ethics texts. While technology has already erased state boundaries for conducting business and other transactions, the regulations and state laws have not kept up. The safe answer would be that the virtual law practice is not able to work with that online client to draft that document unless the client is located within the lawyer's jurisdiction. The state in which the privacy policy or any other online contract would be expected to be enforced would be whose law would have to be applied.

One safer solution to conflict of laws issues as they arise in virtual law practice is for the federal law–focused virtual law offices to form networks with other virtual law practices in other states. Online clients requiring state law contracts could be referred to other virtual law offices or partnerships could be formed between virtual law offices wherein the lawyer not licensed in the state could draft the document and forward it to the lawyer contact in the correct jurisdiction for review and approval. Then that contract could be provided to the online client through the same virtual law office without that online client having to transfer the file to another lawyer. This is provided that the online client has notice that the lawyer will need to have another lawyer review the draft first and has approved this practice.

Another issue related to this form of multijurisdictional virtual law practice is the application of the attorney-client privilege. If the lawyer licensed in one state is providing the client who resides in another state with legal services related to federal law, which state's attorney-client privilege applies? Since the primary purpose of the privilege is to protect the client, the simple answer might be that it would be the client's state's laws regarding attorney-client privilege that apply.[8] But this is another

---

[8]In the event of a case that comes up in the federal court system, the Federal Rules of Evidence, Article V, Rule 501, would be applied, and this would determine whether the attorney/client privilege law of the state or federal common law would apply. **http://www.law.cornell.edu/rules/ fre/rules.htm** (access on May 30, 2010).

area related to multijurisdictional virtual law firms and conflicts of law issues that are being worked out as more of these virtual firms emerge.

Conflict of interest checks on the drafting lawyer in this transaction would need to be handled as well. The additional step in this process before the online delivery of legal services to the client may mean that the cost for the legal services would be higher than it normally might be. These are all ideas to take into consideration as the first group of innovative lawyers begins to forge the path for virtual law practices that cover both federal and state law matters for online clients.

Authentication of the Client's Identity: Is It Our Duty to Prevent Fraud?

The Internet facilitates the potential for individuals to commit fraud regarding their true identities. Accordingly, a lawyer with a virtual law practice should conduct some form of online verification to ensure that clients are who they claim to be. But it is not the lawyer's duty to identify and prevent fraud. Lawyers should be allowed to rely on the contact and other information provided to them online by clients. If a client is signing a clickwrap agreement confirming his or her identity and accepts the terms of the representation, then the lawyer must be able to rely on this contract just as he or she would a written engagement letter in the mail. The reality is that lawyers will encounter dishonest individuals in a traditional law practice just as they do online. While a lawyer cannot ensure that the final use of the legal documents he or she has created never falls into the wrong hands, the lawyer may draft legal documents to the best of his or her ability with the information provided by the online client.

There has been some question of whether anti–money laundering regulations (AML compliance), such as those implemented in the 2001 U.S. Patriot Act, would apply to a virtual law practice, but the list of businesses affected by these provisions at this time does not include law firms, only banking and financial institutions.[9] Furthermore, the application of

---

[9]See IRS, *Uniting and Strengthening America by Providing Appropriate Tools Required to Intercept and Obstruct Terrorism (USA Patriot) Act of 2001* (Public Law 107-56), **http://www.irs.gov/businesses/ small/article/0,,id=154565,00.html** (accessed March 28, 2010). Because this may change in the near future, see also Financial Action Task Force Risk Based Approach (FATF RBA) 2008 Guidance for Legal Professionals, **http://www.fatf-gafi.org/dataoecd/5/58/41584211.pdf** (accessed September 30, 2010); and *Voluntary Good Practices Guidance for Lawyers to Detect and Combat Money Laundering and Terrorist Financing*, Recommendation of the ABA Task Force on Gatekeeper Regulation and the Profession, approved on April 23, 2010, **http://alturl.com/4xy2q** (accessed September 30, 2010).

these provisions would not appear to be practical because the money paid by the clients for legal services rendered online would most likely be processed with a credit card online and be reviewed through PCI compliance and other federal regulations during that process. Any funds collected and held through the virtual law practice would go through the same process of being deposited in the lawyer's trust account as would occur in a traditional law firm. Again, fraud occurs in person as well as online, and in both instances, the lawyer must be able to rely on the information collected from the client during the intake process without being expected to run extensive, costly, and impractical background checks on each prospective client.

Because the legal services purchased through an online client portal may be largely transactional or unbundled legal services, it is often left to the online client to complete the final steps to execute the prepared legal documents. Including detailed instruction regarding proper execution of the documents, as well as the assurance that the client may return to the lawyer with any questions or concerns until the matter is completed, is good virtual practice procedure. In addition to any identity check conducted by the lawyer through the registration process, a notary public assisting the client in executing the legal document will be required to check the driver's license of the individuals signing the documents. In many cases, witnesses may also be required in addition to the notary public to sign the legal document verifying that the client is who he or she claims to be.

In addition, there are other methods that a lawyer may use to verify the online client's identity. A lawyer may choose to request that the online client upload a copy of his or her driver's license to the virtual law practice so that the lawyer may check the client's identification and contact information. There are online services that a lawyer may purchase that provide additional verification measures, but in most cases this is not practical for the daily operation of a virtual law office, and in most cases, the prospective clients will not appreciate the inconvenience of taking this additional step before consulting with the lawyer when it is a step that would not be required if the client visited a traditional law office.

Frankly, if individuals seeking legal services online are going to commit fraud, they would be more likely to purchase the less individualized services of one of the companies selling legal forms online without lawyer review. They would have the option of purchasing legal do-it-yourself kits or software from an office supply store or simply going online and running Internet searches to cut and paste together their legal documents. They are probably not going to register with a virtual law office to pay for legal services provided by a licensed professional when there are cheaper and less risky methods for them to accomplish their nefarious goals.

Defining the Scope of Representation Online

A traditional law practice uses an engagement or retainer letter to define the scope of the representation and to notify the client of the billing procedures, deadlines, and other information about working with that law firm. Providing unbundled services online requires that the lawyer pay extra attention to ensure that prospective online clients understand the scope and nature of the legal representation being offered and provide informed consent. The notice will depend on the structure of the virtual law practice—if it is completely Web based or being run in conjunction with a full-service firm. Please see the Appendix for two sample terms and conditions for a virtual law practice—one for a completely Web-based practice and the other for a virtual law office integrated into a traditional law firm.

Notices should be provided to the prospective online client, and the lawyer should receive assurance that these notices have been read and accepted by the client. The scope of representation may be communicated and further refined multiple times through secure online messages from lawyer to client. There are multiple ways that this may be accomplished with a virtual law practice, and the method will depend on the type of technology used as well as the methods that your online client base is most comfortable handling. In many cases, given the different levels of comfort with technology that your clients may have, the best approach would be to offer more than one method of providing notice to clients and having them accept and return that agreement.

For example, a traditional limited scope of representation agreement may be uploaded for the client to sign and return to the lawyer online, either by scanning and uploading to the virtual law office, or it may be returned by traditional mail or fax. An online form may be used to allow the online client to click through and accept each individual provision of the agreement, ensuring that each term was read and accepted before proceeding. This would work like a clickwrap agreement but require more active acceptance by the online client of the entire document. Another method would be the use of digital signatures to send a traditional agreement for the client to sign digitally. Copies of that signed document could then be stored in the client's file in the client portal. A combination of two or more of these methods might be used by lawyers who require added assurance that the client has read, understood, and provides informed consent to the nature of the unbundled legal services being provided online.

If you are operating a virtual law practice in addition to a traditional law firm, it is critical that the clients using the client portal for any form of communication with the lawyer sign some form of understanding that describes the use of the technology, privacy, and confidentiality of the virtual law office in addition to the traditional engagement letter provided by the full-service firm. This may be an addition to the traditional engagement letter discussing the firm's offerings and terms and conditions for its online use, or the lawyer may choose to have the client read and accept two different letters—one for the traditional law office services and another for the use of the online client portal.

Establishing the Attorney-Client Relationship Online

Clearly establishing the attorney-client relationship when delivering legal services online is key to avoiding malpractice risks.[10] One ethics concern may be that the virtual lawyer may create an unintended client/lawyer relationship.[11] This issue is addressed by the use of multiple clickwrap agreements and communications with the prospective client, which require that he or she acknowledge and agree to the terms of use of the virtual law office and client portal. Further, it is the responsibility of the lawyer to limit and define the scope of the representation following the initial online consultation. This process is no different than if a lawyer were to accept or decline representation of a client in person. The scope of representation or decision to decline representation is presented to the online client. If the client accepts the services of the lawyer, then the client is required again for an additional time to acknowledge that he or

---

[10]See, generally, ABA Model Rule 1.18, Client-Lawyer Relationship, Duties to Prospective Client.
[11]See *Barton v. U.S. Dist. Court for the Central Dist. of Cal.*, 410 F.3d 1104 (9th Cir. 2005) (holding that the attorney/client relationship was formed and a duty of confidentiality arose when prospective clients filled out an online form that the law firm had posted on its Web site. See also Kelcey Nichols, *Client Confidentiality, Professional Privilege and Online Communication: Potential Implications of the Barton Decision*, 3 Shidler J. L. Com. & Tech. 10 (Feb. 14, 2007), at **http://www.lctjournal.washington.edu/Vol3/a010Nichols.html** (accessed May 30, 2010).

she has notice of this arrangement and is agreeing to it through a tailored clickwrap agreement.

In addition to using a clickwrap agreement to establish the attorney-client relationship, the lawyer may also use a combination of online and traditional methods to ensure that he or she has covered all of the bases. A written engagement letter could be uploaded to the client for his or her signature to store in the client's online case file. The lawyer could have the online client execute this agreement by electronic signature rather than a physical signature that would need to be scanned in and uploaded back to the client file on the virtual law office Web site. While only one process would mostly likely provide adequate notice to the prospective client of the terms of the representation, the flexibility of the technology allows lawyers to design their own additional methods of protecting themselves from professional malpractice based on their own comfort levels and what their state bars require.

In addition to the notice and acceptance process provided to each client, the process itself may be audited. The full history of each transaction may be viewed in both the lawyer's online case files and in an audit log managed by the technology company used to host the software. In the audit log, the lawyer may review if there were any overrides conducted by him- or herself or another lawyer, such as if the terms of the engagement and other billing process were ever bypassed, if management features were reset, or if terms for the representation were provided to the client for another notice and acceptance process. In other words, the technology may provide an additional trail documenting the establishment of the attorney-client relationship. This documentation would extend beyond the online dialogue between the lawyer and the client in the client's case file to maintain a record of the transactions to establish the attorney-client relationship.

This process of establishing the attorney-client online relationship is required before either the client or the lawyer may proceed to engage in any transactions related to the online delivery of legal services. By this method, a virtual law practice may provide more protection for the prospective client than a telephone call, unencrypted e-mail communication, or even a short in-person office visit.

Clickwrap Agreements

As with most online businesses offering services over the Internet, the lawyer relies on a clickwrap agreement, which online clients are required to review and accept in the client portal before proceeding with the online delivery of legal services. A clickwrap agreement or "click through" agreement is the common method of clicking on a button on a Web site to accept the terms or user agreement associated with the use of that site or the online software application provided on that Web site. Clients are familiar with clickwrap agreements from registering for online banking, signing up for profiles on social media sites, such as Facebook or LinkedIn, or have encountered it before purchasing items online with a credit card.

A typical clickwrap agreement in a virtual law practice provides the client with notice of the terms and conditions for use of the client portal and the online legal services being offered. The online client is required to assent to the agreement by clicking on a button in a dialog box or pop-up window that reads "OK" or "agree." Many clickwrap agreements require that the client scroll down the entire text of the agreement or check an additional box, such as one stating "I am over the age of 18," before clicking on the "OK" or "agree" button to finalize the agreement. If the online client declines to accept the agreement, he or she has the option of clicking on "cancel" or closing the window containing the agreement. When first introduced, the clickwrap, or "shrinkwrap," agreement was viewed as a contract of adhesion, but this form of agreement is now accepted as a valid and enforceable contract form, as long as the terms and conditions related to the agreement are accessible at all times by the online client.[12]

A clickwrap agreement contains the terms and conditions of the lawyer's online representation to the client, explains the nature of unbundled legal services, defines the scope of representation, and may contain other provisions tailored to the lawyer's virtual law practice. For example, the online client is required to accept a clickwrap agreement before registering on the client portal and again when agreeing to the purchase of specific legal services. The lawyer should take care to define the scope of legal representation (or clearly decline representation) with each individual client who contacts the lawyer through the virtual law office. This process may be handled securely on each client's home page, and the complexity depends on the legal work the client is seeking.

As more lawyers go online with their law practices, the use of the clickwrap agreement will most likely be a standard on virtual law offices. While retainer fees, payment arrangements, and further definition of the scope of legal representation are communicated to the client through the client's secure home page, the standard clickwrap agreement for the vir-

---

[12]See *ProCD, Inc. v. Zeidenberg*, 86 F.3d 1447 (7th Cir., 1996).

tual law office serves as the legal contract between the lawyer and his or her online clients and should be a stagnant feature on the lawyer's virtual law office. Think of it as the replacement for a traditional engagement or retainer letter.

The ABA Committee on Cyberspace Law, during a panel discussion at the ABA's Annual Meeting in 2007, provided these recommendations for forming legally binding online agreements:

1. The user must have adequate notice that the proposed terms exist.
2. The user must have a meaningful opportunity to review the terms.
3. The user must have adequate notice that taking a specified, optional action manifests assent to the terms.
4. The user must, in fact, take that action.

Lawyers must draft the terms and conditions for use with the virtual law office Web sites and clickwrap agreements that conform to their individual practices and the services that they intend to offer online. The ABA Cyberspace Law Web site has a searchable archive for members that contains many good resources to assist lawyers in researching this topic and drafting their online engagement agreements.[13]

Unique to a virtual law office, the terms and conditions for use of the site and client portal should explain or provide, at a minimum, the following information for the prospective client:

1. Notice of the jurisdiction in which the lawyer is licensed to practice law
2. Nature of unbundled or limited legal services
3. How and when the attorney-client relationship and scope of the relationship will be defined
4. Confidentiality policy
5. How client funds and payment of invoices for legal work are handled online
6. E-mail policy
7. Security of the site, PCI compliance if accepting credit cards
8. Web tracking, including cookies, information collection, and privacy policy

---

[13] ABA Committee on Cyberspace Law Web site: **http://www.abanet.org/dch/committee.cfm? com=CL320000** (accessed on May 13, 2008).

9. Registration process and the nature of a clickwrap agreement
10. Contact information for the lawyer operating the VLO and a helpdesk e-mail or contact for technical matters related to the client's use of the Web site

Furthermore, each individual solo or small-firm practitioner may want to use an additional retainer or engagement agreement or other contracting method with clients after registration that conforms to a more traditional contract. The flexibility of the Web-based technology allows for the operation of both a clickwrap agreement and additional methods.

For example, the lawyer may want to upload a traditional engagement or retainer agreement to the online client through the online client's home page. The client may then sign the contract, scan it to PDF, and upload it back to their online case file. If the lawyer prefers to have the original signature of the agreement, there is no reason why the lawyer may not request that the client send the contract via snail mail to the lawyer before the legal work is commenced. A retainer fee may be paid by the online client at any point in the process. The lawyer permits the client to pay this fee when appropriate, and steps must be taken to ensure that the retainer payment is routed to the lawyer's trust account. See the section in Chapter Four discussing online payments and billing options for a virtual law practice.

Protecting Client Confidences

The virtual lawyer should take reasonable precautions to protect confidential information that is transmitted between the lawyer and the client and to preserve the attorney/client privilege. All state bars have rules of professional conduct requiring that communications transmitted from the client to the lawyer be kept confidential.[14] In this regard, e-mail is not the safest method for lawyers to rely upon to transmit confidential client data. Most e-mail is not encrypted and is therefore not secure. A virtual

---

[14]Rule 1.6 (a) of the ABA's Model Rules of Professional Conduct states, "A lawyer shall not reveal information relating to the representation of a client unless the client gives informed consent, the disclosure is impliedly authorized in order to carry out the representation. . . ." See, in particular, comments 16 and 17 to Rule 1.6. Comment 17 provides that lawyers must take "reasonable precautions" to safeguard confidential information and prevent it from going to unintended recipients during the transmission. **http://www.abanet.org/cpr/mrpc/rule_1_6.html** (accessed January 17, 2009); For a detailed analysis and review of ABA Model Rule 1.6 (a) and other state bar opinions related to the duty of confidentiality, see Washington State Bar Informal Opinion 2080 (issued 2006) **http://mcle.mywsba.org/IO/print.aspx?ID=1553** (accessed May 30, 2010), This opinion specifically addresses confidentiality issues arising from inquiries through a law firm's website.

law office should have an SSL certificate and provide the client with secure transmission of data. See the above Chapter Three: Choosing the Technology, which discusses security used to protect sensitive lawyer and client data.

As an example of what may be coming down the pipeline in terms of protecting confidential client information, a 2010 Massachusetts law was passed that provides regulations for how entities owning or processing personal information of Massachusetts residents need to protect those data.[15] The Massachusetts Office of Consumer Affairs and Business Regulation (OCABR), which passed the regulation, determined that personal information must be encrypted in order to provide adequate security for the confidential data. Nevada also updated its encryption law in January 2010 to require any businesses storing personal information where the storage is outside of the control of the physical business to ensure that the data is encrypted.[16]

If the encryption requirement is seen as standard for business professionals entrusted with their client's personal information, then it may be only a matter of time before the state bars recognize that lawyers should be held to the same if not higher standards for protecting the confidentiality of their clients' data. If lawyers know that unencrypted methods of communication with clients, such as unencrypted e-mail, are not the most secure methods of protecting confidentiality, then wouldn't those lawyers be in violation of most state bar rules and regulations requiring lawyers to take reasonable precautions to protect their clients' confidential information?

Accordingly, the same technology used by online banking and government tax authorities to provide services is the same level of security that should be used in operating a virtual law office. With a virtual law office, the only individuals who should have access to confidential attorney-client information are the lawyer and the client. The company hosting the law office data should keep the data encrypted even during updates to the software application that protects any attorney-client confidences from being viewed by a third party. By following these guidelines and conducting careful research of the third-party provider as discussed above in Chapter Three: Choosing the Technology, the lawyer may be confident that he or she is complying with the reasonable care standards required by the ABA and most state bars regarding protecting client confidential information.

---

[15]See the General Law of Massachusetts, Chapter 93A, Regulation of Business Practices for Consumers Protection, **http://www.mass.gov/legis/laws/mgl/gl-93a-toc.htm** (accessed May 30, 2010).
[16]See Nevada Revised Statute Chapter 603A—Security of Personal Information, (2009) **http://search.leg.state.nv.us/isysquery/irl5021/1/doc** (accessed May 30, 2010).

There is some debate about whether a law firm should disclose to its clients details about the technology and any third-party service providers that it has chosen to create and maintain the firm's virtual law office. The author is of the opinion that it is not the duty of a law practice to disclose its professional practice management decisions to prospective clients and no state bar ethics or advisory opinions could be found to indicate otherwise. In the event that prospective clients request specific information about the technology, security or the user agreement with any third-party provider, the law firm will need to make the decision about which management aspects of the firm the clients need to make an educated decision about using the virtual law office for legal services. Rather than incorporating this information into a clickwrap or engagement letter, another option might be for the firm to provide reassurance and adequate notice to prospective clients through an educational page or section on the virtual law office Web site that discloses the nature of the technology, addresses security concerns and details how client data is handled and stored by the firm.

Storage and Retention of Client Data

The case file organization and document retention in a virtual law office may actually protect a lawyer from the malpractice risks that could be associated with a traditional law practice using basic e-mail as the only form of digital communication with clients. The lawyer has a duty to safeguard client property throughout the legal representation and for a number of years following the completion of the client's legal matter. The client's files and documents related to the case are the property of that client.[17] Recent state bar advisory opinions address the fact that not only are lawyers communicating with clients using technology, but they are also retaining their clients' case files and other data related to their clients' legal matters digitally.[18] For example, the Association of the Bar of

---

[17]See ABA Model Rule 1.16(d): "Upon termination of representation, a lawyer shall take steps to the extent reasonably practicable to protect a client's interests, such as giving reasonable notice to the client, allowing time for employment of other counsel, surrendering papers and property to which the client is entitled and refunding any advance payment of fee that has not been earned. The lawyer may retain papers relating to the client to the extent permitted by other law." **http://www.abanet.org/cpr/ethicsearch/file_retention.html** (accessed May 30, 2010).

[18]The Association of the Bar of the City of New York Committee on Professional and Judicial Ethics, Formal Opinion 2008-1, "A Lawyer's Ethical Obligations to Retain and to Provide a Client with Electronic Documents Relating to a Representation," NYC Eth. Op. 2008-1, 2008 WL

the City of New York Committee on Professional and Judicial Ethics Formal Opinion 2008-1 addressed the lawyer's ethics obligation to retain and provide the client with electronic documents related to the legal representation. The opinion stated that the lawyer must take affirmative action to preserve any digital communication regarding the representation that may otherwise be deleted or lost from their digital filing system. The opinion also recommended that the lawyer discuss storage and retrieval of electronic documents and data at the beginning of the representation. The Arizona State Bar Committee on the Rules of Professional Conduct also published an advisory opinion concluding that lawyers may store law office data online and use a system that allows their clients to access the information online as long as the lawyer takes "reasonable precautions" to safeguard the security of that confidential information.[19]

Lawyers operating virtual law practices are easily able to comply and go beyond what the ethics opinions recommend through the digital storage and recording of the case files within a virtual law office. Inside the client portal, each communication between the lawyer and the client is stored in a separate discussion section of the main case file. Each communication is labeled with the date and time of the transmission as well as the name of the individual who entered the message into the file. Likewise, any files that the lawyer has placed in the case file are labeled with the date and time of the online storage as well as information such as whether that document is a draft or a final legal document. Forms provided for the client to fill out online may also contain information regarding the last time the documents were edited and who edited them. Clients should be unable themselves to delete anything from their online case files in the client portal, which allows the lawyer to properly store data covering the entire representation.

Because most state bars require that lawyers retain their case files for a period of years, all of the data stored in the virtual law office remain on the hosted system and are subject to regular backups on the server host-

---

3911383, (N.Y.C.Assn.B.Comm.Prof.Jud.Eth.), July 2008, **http://www.nycbar.org/Publications/ reports/show_html.php?rid=794** (accessed January 17, 2009). See also the State Bar of Wisconsin, Professional Ethics Opinion E-00-3, **http://www.wisbar.org/AM/Template.cfm?Section= Wisconsin_ethics_opinions&TEMPLATE=/CM/ContentDisplay.cfm&CONTENTID=48462** (accessed January 17, 2009), and the appendix "State Bar Ethics and Advisory Opinions and Other Resources by Topic: Electronic Storage of Law Office Data."

[19] Arizona State Bar Opinion 09-04 (December 9, 2009), **http://www.myazbar.org/ethics/opinion view.cfm?id=704** (accessed May 30, 2010). See also Rule 1.6(a) of the ABA's Model Rules of Professional Conduct and specifically Comment 17 related to "reasonable precautions."

ing the virtual law office. In the event that the lawyer wants to discontinue his or her use of a virtual law office, wants to switch technologies providing virtual law practice management tools, or wants to leave the practice of law completely, he or she may contact the software company to return all of the law office data in encrypted format to the lawyer for storage and retention. It is recommended that a lawyer first check with the company providing the technology to ensure that the data collected and stored on the virtual law office during the course of the online practice may be easily returned to the lawyer in encrypted, digital format. See the above Chapter Three: Choosing the Technology.

Complying with the "reasonable precautions" requirement to safeguard client property and protect confidential client communications means that lawyers delivering legal services online have the responsibility to keep updated on what is "reasonable," given the speed at which technology is developing and the increasing number of security risks. Furthermore, it may be in the best interests of the virtual law practice to draft an additional provision in the clickwrap or other engagement agreement related to client data storage, return and retention. The virtual law firm could require that the prospective client agree to the nature of the online storage and digital format of their case file and acknowledge that the return of client data will be in digital format and most likely through electronic delivery. Considering that most clients seeking online legal services expect this feature from a virtual law firm and see it as a benefit to selecting a firm that delivers legal services online, it should not be a problem to add these details to the clickwrap or other engagement letter. For a law firm operating a virtual law office in conjunction with a brick and mortar law office, clients could be offered their files in paper and/or digital format depending on what the firm decides would be best for its clients.

Electronic Discovery

Consider that all data transmitted through and stored in a virtual law office has the potential to become electronic evidence in a legal case. Electronic discovery (ED) has crept into every law practice, including solos and small firms. Electronic activities may hang around longer than contracts written on paper and stuck in a file and may be easier to obtain if needed. Electronic discovery, as with any discovery, must be produced in a timely and proper manner when required. In the case of ED, much of this issue comes down to proper electronic data management and the ability to retrieve the necessary data. Accordingly, ED business standards and best practices are critical for a virtual law practice. Lawyers operating a virtual law office should be familiar with ED and its potential impact on their businesses as well as their clients'.[20]

> ## Case Study: Impact of Virtual Law Practice on Electronic Discovery
> ### Sharon D. Nelson, President of Sensei Enterprises, Inc., a computer forensics and legal technology firm in Fairfax, Virginia (www.senseient.com)
>
> *Sharon D. Nelson is the coauthor of* The Electronic Evidence and Discovery Handbook: Forms, Checklists and Guidelines *(ABA, 2006) and* Information Security for Lawyers and Law Firms *(ABA, 2006), as well as* The Solo and Small Firm Legal Technology Guide *for 2008, 2009, and 2010 (ABA, 2008, 2009, 2010). She is also a co-author of* How Good Lawyers Survive Bad Times *(ABA, 2009). Ms. Nelson is also the author of the noted electronic evidence blog Ride the Lightning (**http://ridethelightning.senseient.com**) and is a co-host of the American Bar Association podcast series called "The Digital Edge: Lawyers and Technology."*
>
> The virtual practice of law is a fascinating development. Keeping costs low has allowed virtual firms to offer very competitive rates. This new and exciting model for practicing law is changing the face of lawyering in ways that lawyers of the last century could not possibly have imagined. Virtual lawyering has many potential implications. I've been thinking about the possible effects of a completely Web-based practice on electronic discovery.
>
> Certainly virtual lawyers will use hosted electronic discovery repositories and SaaS versions of electronic discovery tools. In that, they will be no different than many other lawyers. They will, of course, want to carefully vet the pricing, capability, and security of these repositories and tools. Curiously, I think the biggest impact of virtual lawyering will come when the virtual law firm itself is a party to litigation. Simply because everything is outsourced, the virtual law firm will have data everywhere.
>
> Ruby Receptionist may have phone data, Legal Typist may have documents, Clio or Rocket Matter may have a wealth of information about

---

[20]Comprehensive information on this topic may be found in *The Electronic Evidence and Discovery Handbook*, by Sharon D. Nelson, Bruce A. Olson, and John W. Simek (Chicago: ABA Law Practice Management Section, 2006), and also at DiscoveryResources.org (**www.discoveryresources.org**).

cases and clients, VoIP providers will also have phone data, cell phone providers will have data, Google Wave or any other application function of Google will have data. Live data may be stored perhaps at one data center and backup data may be stored at another center. The law firm may not even know the location of these data centers, just the names of the companies they contracted with. The tentacles of data just go on and on.

Large law firms always have a lot of data in many places, but that was typically not true of smaller firms. Generally, the firm held its own data. It might outsource payroll, have a CPA and, today, cell phone and Internet providers. Not a lot of third parties tended to be involved. In the electronic discovery world, one of the major headaches is simply locating the data, always a nightmare with a large entity. Virtual law firms will have to be looked at carefully to ascertain all of the third parties who have relevant data, depending on the nature of the case. The law firms themselves will have to do this in response to discovery requests, and the requestors would be well advised to look at their standard discovery requests and perhaps retool them for virtual law firms.

I would retool in such a way that I identified in the request the kinds of third parties who might be involved. One of the biggest potholes in ED is overlooking a source of relevant data, often innocently. So if I make a request for data, it is prudent to carefully identify all possible sources of relevant evidence to prevent anything from being overlooked.

The other aspect I would mention is security. At this point, I'm assuming that the law firm is representing a client in an e-discovery matter. If trial strategy and privileged documents are located "in the cloud," cloud security is always being penetrated by hackers and by those who perform electronic business espionage, which is an increasingly lucrative profession. It is very hard for a virtual law firm to truly know how secure its data are. I am not suggesting that brick and mortar law firms always secure their data well, just that they at least know what security measures have been taken. Every day brings us a new "data breach" story in the news, so security must be a prime concern. I also find that lawyers don't generally scrutinize their contracts with providers very carefully from a security standpoint. Sometimes providers provide soothing and incomplete assurances that a security specialist would quickly unravel. In any event, virtual lawyers should tread carefully when placing their data in the hands of others.

CHAPTER SEVEN

Conclusion

The development of the online delivery of legal services is consumer driven. There is a continual need for expanded access to justice in our country. Virtual law offices, both those completely Web based and those integrated with a traditional law practice, provide a secure and cost-effective solution.

As with any form of business, there are risks associated with the delivery of legal services online. There are also benefits that surpass those found in a traditional brick and mortar practice and ways to mitigate the risks. It is up to individual lawyers to decide for themselves whether this form of law practice is appropriate for their legal careers and for the clients that they serve.

The technology will continue to change methods used to deliver legal services online to our clients. We cannot predict the new features in communication or risks in security that will inspire additional innovation, but the fundamental component of virtual law practice will remain the same—a secure method of delivering online legal services from lawyer to client, from start to finish. In the future, the word *virtual* or even *online* may not be used to describe the process of delivering legal services using technology, but the delivery of legal services online is more than a passing trend, as has been noticed by more than one luminary in the fields of legal technology and law practice management. Richard Susskind in *The End of Lawyers? Rethinking the Nature of Legal Services* discusses disruptive technologies as a factor that will force legal professionals to find more innovative ways to provide legal services or face the consequences of losing their practices to the competition who will find ways to embrace the changes occurring in society and the legal marketplace.[1] To maintain a competitive advantage in the growing legal market, solos and small firms will need to provide some online means of serving their clients, whether or not it is offered in conjunction with a brick and mortar law office.

As more virtual law practices launch, we will begin to see more state bar ethics and advisory opinions helping to guide lawyers through the setup and operation of their virtual practices. In an ideal world, these opinions and any regulations and rules that arise will be broad and well educated from a technology standpoint. If innovation in the delivery of online legal services is to be encouraged, then this is a necessity to avoid the suppression of entrepreneurship and innovation in our profession. At the end of the day, virtual law practice is about providing the public with another option for access to justice and giving lawyers the ability to build unique practices that enrich their professional and personal lives.

---

[1]Richard Susskind, *The End of Lawyers? Rethinking the Nature of Legal Services* (London: Oxford University Press, 2008).

Appendix

Terminolgy

auto-responders—A service that is set up to automatically send a response to a set action as defined by the person setting up the responder. The most common example is the "out of office" e-mail message that may be sent from one e-mail address in response to an e-mail received at that address. In virtual law practice, auto-responders may be used to send a prospective or existing client a customized notice that the lawyer has noted their action and will respond within a fixed amount of time.

clickwrap agreement—A clickwrap agreement or "click through" agreement is the common method of clicking on a button on a Web site to accept the terms or user agreement associated with the use of that site or the online software application provided on that Web site. Clients are familiar with clickwrap agreements from registering for online banking, signing up for profiles on social media sites, such as Facebook or LinkedIn, or have encountered it before purchasing items online with a credit card. Clickwrap agreements have been held to be binding and enforceable contracts, provided that the online clients have continued access to the terms that they are clicking to accept. See *ProCD, Inc. v. Zeidenberg*, 86 F.3d 1447 (7th Cir., 1996).

client portal—An online space provided to a client that is accessed with an unique username and password. The client may securely log into this space, an encrypted and restricted Web site, for the purpose of requesting legal services and communicating with an lawyer online.

cloud computing—A term used to described software applications that are hosted by a third party on servers and accessed over the Internet rather than with installed software. Software as a service (SaaS) applications are the most common example of software that permits cloud computing. The term originates from the IT field when network administrators would attempt to diagram complex network systems. The diagram would picture a cloud shape to represent where the data went when they were transferred from one network to another. This cloud shape did not represent the unknown, just a simpler way of diagramming network systems and a way to indicate when that data was outside of the control of the organization. Unfortunately, as a result, the term "in the cloud" tends to carry with it a sense of the unknown, which is not an accurate description of the secure storage and transfer of electronic data.

cyberlawyer—A lawyer whose practice focuses on a combination of different areas of the law involving computers and the Internet, including intellectual property, privacy, and security.

data center—Servers holding electronic data are housed in data centers. These facilities are typically million-dollar investments with highly regulated environments with fire suppression, backup power, redundancy, security, and 24/7 monitoring. There are different levels of data centers labeled as Tier 1 through Tier 4 with different requirements at each tier. The highest requirements and the best security are found on the Tier 4–level data centers. Only high-level administrators have access to the server rooms of a data center. Junior-level administrators are not allowed in the data center without a senior-level administrator escort. The facilities are typically nonpublic and unadvertised. The building itself may have redundant climate control, a redundant physical power plant, generator backup, and encrypted electronic door locks. Rules of access will be set by the company owning the data center.

eLawyering—This word encompasses all of the methods that lawyers may use to practice law online, from the delivery of online legal services to online law practice management. ELawyering includes collaborating and communicating with lawyers and clients through the Internet, drafting legal documents and providing legal advice online, case and client management, and any new methods that a lawyer may invent to use the Internet within the legal profession. The ABA has an eLawyering Task Force that convenes regularly to discuss the development of eLawyering in the legal profession.

encryption—Data that have been converted into a state using a cipher (an algorithm) that is not readable without the key to decrypt the cipher. Encryption is used to protect data as is they are transferred from one secure place to another. There are different levels of encryption depending on the level of security needed and whether the data are in storage.

end-to-end encryption—A method to describe the transfer of data that remain encrypted from the time they leave one point until they are received at the other point and are decrypted so that they may be read.

geo-redundancy—Data are hosted on servers in multiple locations at the same time as an extra level of security. In the event of a power or hardware failure or a natural disaster that caused the failure of one server, the remaining server would take over the function of storing and securing those data.

mobile lawyering/mobile lawyer—A lawyer who makes use of mobile devices and other technology to practice law either on a virtual law office or in conjunction with a traditional law office.

online social networking—Networking using methods that are hosted on the Internet to form connections with other individuals, both personal and professional. Examples of online social networking include listservs, forums, blogs, online communities, collaborative platforms, micro-blogs, and instant messaging, among others.

paperless law office (also termed a "green" law office or eco-friendly law office)—A law practice that attempts through the use of technology to reduce or eliminate the amount of paper and law office waste that it generates.

search engine optimization (SEO)—An Internet marking strategy that involves driving and increasing traffic to a Web site from different search engines using techniques that are not paid for directly but are imbedded in the source code of the Web site or blog.

search engine results page (SERP)—The results that a search engine will provide in response to entering a keyword and performing a search. The results usually include a title, link to the Web site, and brief description. As an Internet marketing strategy, the goal is to obtain a high ranking on a SERP, which means that the Web site appears at the top of a SERP in response to keywords associated with the services provided by that Web site.

secure socket layer (SSL)—An encryption protocol used to provide security for communications over the Internet. SSL certificates may be purchased from companies that verify the identity of the Web site and certificate owner through unique authentication identification.

server—This is a broad term that may be used to describe any combination of hardware and software set up for the purpose of running a service for clients. Servers that house data requiring the highest levels of security are stored in data centers.

software as a service (SaaS)—A business model in which the company provides the customer with a license to use its software, which is hosted on the company's servers. When the customer discontinues the use of the service, the company removes its data from the company's servers.

unbundled or limited legal services—This form of delivering legal services is when a lawyer breaks out the different tasks associated with a legal matter and provides the client with only limited portions of the legal work.

virtual law office, VLO, or virtual law firm—A Web-based law practice that allows for the lawyer and his or her clients to securely discuss legal matters online, download and upload documents for review, complete online legal forms, and handle other business transactions in a secure digital environment, including all of the backend management functions of a traditional law office. A VLO may be the sole software used by the virtual lawyer or may be used in conjunction with a traditional law office to deliver online legal services to clients.

virtual law practice—A professional law practice that exists online through a secure portal and is accessible to the client and the lawyer anywhere the parties may access the Internet.

web-based law practice management tools—Web-based software as a service (SaaS) applications used in conjunction with other law office software to conduct administrative and management tasks online, such as billing and time management.

virtual legal assistant—A professional legal assistant who accesses the virtual law office and assists the virtual lawyer remotely with administrative or other law practice management tasks.

virtual or online lawyer—A licensed professional providing legal services through a virtual law office to online clients.

virtual or online lawyer collaboration—Lawyers using technology to collaborate on legal cases or to network and share resources within the legal profession.

virtual paralegal—A certified paralegal who remotely accesses the virtual law office to work under the supervision of the virtual lawyer.

virtual reality law (also termed virtual law)—This refers to the development of law in virtual reality worlds, such as Second Life.

Sample Process for Legal Services Delivered Online

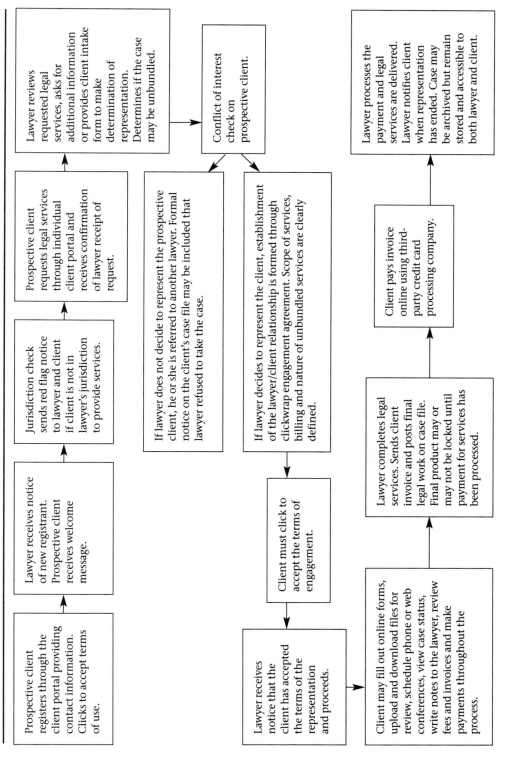

Prospective client registers through the client portal providing contact information. Clicks to accept terms of use.

Lawyer receives notice of new registrant. Prospective client receives welcome message.

Jurisdiction check sends red flag notice to lawyer and client if client is not in lawyer's jurisdiction to provide services.

Prospective client requests legal services through individual client portal and receives confirmation of lawyer receipt of request.

Lawyer reviews requested legal services, asks for additional information or provides client intake form to make determination of representation. Determines if the case may be unbundled.

Conflict of interest check on prospective client.

If lawyer does not decide to represent the prospective client, he or she is referred to another lawyer. Formal notice on the client's case file may be included that lawyer refused to take the case.

If lawyer decides to represent the client, establishment of the lawyer/client relationship is formed through clickwrap engagement agreement. Scope of services, billing and nature of unbundled services are clearly defined.

Client must click to accept the terms of engagement.

Lawyer receives notice that the client has accepted the terms of the representation and proceeds.

Client may fill out online forms, upload and download files for review, schedule phone or web conferences, view case status, write notes to the lawyer, review fees and invoices and make payments throughout the process.

Lawyer completes legal services. Sends client invoice and posts final legal work on case file. Final product may or may not be locked until payment for services has been processed.

Client pays invoice online using third-party credit card processing company.

Lawyer processes the payment and legal services are delivered. Lawyer notifies client when representation has ended. Case may be archived but remain stored and accessible to both lawyer and client.

Sample Virtual Law Practice Terms and Conditions for a Completely Web-Based Virtual Law Practice Providing Unbundled Legal Services Online

*(This limited services engagement agreement was modified from the terms and conditions drafted for Kimbro Legal Services, LLC, a completely Web-based virtual law office providing online unbundled legal services (**www.kimbrolaw.com**).*

The Terms and Conditions of Use ("Agreement") are provided by "Virtual Law Office," an online law practice providing legal services of the State of "Your Jurisdiction" and managed by "Your Name or Firm Name." The Agreement will govern your use of this Web site, including all content provided on the Web site and through access to all online services provided by "Virtual Law Office." The Agreement to provide legal services to you covers the time period from which you accept this Agreement and we have received your payment through our funds transfer service to the time we have provided you with the requested and purchased legal service.

You agree that it remains your responsibility to proceed as a pro se litigant by filing all legal documents and complying with "Your Jurisdiction" and local legal procedures. By providing you with limited legal services, "Virtual Law Office" has not agreed to attend a hearing or trial on your behalf or provide any legal services extending beyond those services that you have purchased and we have agreed to provide. We only provide limited legal assistance and document preparation and review. After performing the services purchased by you, we have no further obligation to you.

Limitation of Services
While authorities in some jurisdictions may deem this Web site and this law practice to be an advertisement for legal services in their jurisdiction, our Web site is not to be considered as a solicitation for legal services related to any other states' law. This Web site and this legal practice offer services related to "Your Jurisdiction" law only.

Unlike a geographically located law practice, "Virtual Law Office" will not provide physical legal representation or commence litigation on your behalf. The purpose of "Virtual Law Office" is to provide limited legal advice and general counseling on "Your Jurisdiction" legal matters with prompt service provided in a cost-effective manner. If we determine during our communication with you that your specific legal matter requires the engagement of a full-service law firm, such as in the event that your situation may require the commencement of a formal lawsuit, then we will promptly refer you to a full-service "Your Jurisdiction" law firm in your area or refer you to "Your Jurisdiction" Lawyer Referral Service.

Nature of Unbundled Legal Services

"Virtual Law Office" is not a prepaid legal service; it is an online legal practice where you are charged a fee for limited legal services related to "Your Jurisdiction" law. "Virtual Law Office" provides unbundled legal services. This means that the legal services provided by us only extend to those services of which you have requested and purchased and we have provided. After you have purchased a service and we have agreed to provide it and have completed the work, you cannot expect us to perform in any additional capacity. We will provide you with adequate notice of the scope of our relationship and what services will and will not be provided for you online.

For example, if we assist you in creating Estate Administration documents, it is not our responsibility to ensure that the forms are properly filed, to attend a hearing or trial on your behalf, or to provide any other legal services related to that matter beyond the original purchased and provided limited legal services. Likewise, after you have paid for the requested services and we have performed them, we will not expect any further payment from you other than payment for the original requested legal services performed by us.

As with any legal service, we cannot guarantee any legal outcome. By purchasing our services, you agree that it remains your responsibility to properly and timely file any legal documents and to comply with "Your Jurisdiction" law and local legal procedures.

If at any time we determine that the legal services you have requested require full-service legal representation, we will refer you to a full-service law firm providing "Your Jurisdiction" legal services.

Confidentiality—Security—Retainment of Records

"Virtual Law Office" provides limited legal services pertaining to "Your Jurisdiction" law only. The lawyer responsible for this site is licensed to practice law only in the State of "Your Jurisdiction."

In compliance with the professional rules and restrictions of the State Bar of "Your Jursidiction" and for reasons of personal integrity, this practice is bound by stringent professional standards of confidentiality. Any information received by us from our clients is held in strict confidence and is not released to anyone outside of this practice, unless agreed with by you, or as required under applicable law.

An attorney-client relationship with this practice is established only after a specific question has been posed to a lawyer at this practice through a prospective client's personal login page and that question has been confirmed as received through a reply communication from a lawyer at this practice. Prospective clients should be aware that our duties of confidentiality and the attorney-client privilege may not arise until a lawyer has expressly communicated the ability to respond to that prospective client. Once you have provided us with your personal information, we will first run a crosscheck for any possible conflict of interest before accepting representation of your matter. We may decline to provide our services to you if a conflict of interest is discovered.

All our records are securely retained in electronic files, along with secure backups, for the period of years required under "Your Jurisdiction" law.

Articles and Other General Public Information Provided on This Web Site

Any articles for general knowledge published on this Web site contain basic information on legal matters and are not meant to provide advice regarding a specific legal problem you may have. We remind you not to rely on this general information without first communicating with us or other legal representation regarding your specific legal situation.

Copyright

"Virtual Law Office" claims copyright protection on all of the content provided in this Web site. The content from this Web site may not be reproduced, copied, or redistributed in any form without the express permission of "Virtual Law Office." Furthermore, the content from this Web site cannot be modified nor can it be used for commercial purposes. Each document posted at this Web site shall contain the following copyright notice:

Copyright "Date" "Virtual Law Office Name." All rights reserved.

Client Funds

No fee will be charged or obligation incurred by registering on this Web site. In most situations, a client's funds will not be transferred to "Virtual Law Office" until the legal services requested by the client are ready to be accessed and received by the client on their personal login page. Some requested services may require the up-front payment of a retainer fee before "Virtual Law Office" will begin work. After the client's payment of the agreed upon price is confirmed through a Cardholder Information Security Program (CISP)–compliant credit card processor, the client will have complete access to the legal advice, documents, research, or other services provided by the lawyer. If further communication with the lawyer is required, the client may post a separate question regarding the received legal services or request a price quote for additional legal work. "Virtual Law Office" will not pay any court costs associated with your case that may be required as part of a lawsuit, filing fees, or service of process fees.

Technology—Security

"Virtual Law Office" does not rely on e-mail to communicate with clients. E-mail as it is commonly sent and received is unencrypted and does not provide a secure means of interacting with our clients. Primary communications are done through this Web site over secure HTTP, which provides you with the highest industry standard protection available on the Web. All payments are processed by CISP-compliant credit card processors, and no credit card or payment account numbers are stored on our servers.

Links and E-mail Addresses

Links posted on this Web site to other Web sites are provided only as a convenience to our clients. We assume no responsibility for the content, security, or reliability of any Web sites to which we have posted links.

Spamming, the unsolicited broadcasts of e-mail addresses or links in this Web site, is prohibited and unauthorized.

Web Tracking: Cookies, Information Collection, and Privacy Policy

1. *General Site*

To view the articles and public documents on this site you do not need to reveal any personal information. This site will present your browser with the option of accepting JavaScript and cookies in order to lay out the Web page correctly and to store customized settings for your next visit. These features may be disabled by your browser; however, this will limit the look and functionality of the Web site. All page requests are logged in order to properly maintain the service and security of this Web site.

2. *Virtual Law Office*

In order to use the virtual law office, you must first register a username and provide personal information about yourself. This information will be used during your transactions with "Virtual Law Office" to provide limited legal services in compliance with "Your Jurisdiction" law. Your information may be provided to a third party in order to provide the service you requested and/or as is required by law. All other use of your personal information will be limited to your attorney-client relationship with "Virtual Law Office." This site uses cookies to store a session ID. Therefore, in order to register on the Web site, cookies must be enabled so that we can provide you with a secure transaction.

Registration

In order to retain our services, you must register on our Web site. There will be no fee charged for registration on this Web site. By registering you will receive access to a personal information page where you may request our services in a secure manner. By registering on our Web site, you are representing that you are at least 18 years of age and able to enter into a binding contract with "Virtual Law Office." Furthermore, by registering you are representing that the information you provide to us is correct, accurate, and updated.

Reviewing and Updating Your Personal Content

"Virtual Law Office" requests that you keep your personal contact information current. After you have registered on our Web site, you may enter your personal information page at any time to review and update your personal information.

Contact Information

Because we are a virtual law practice, we would prefer that you provide your information to us using the technology provided for you on your personal client login page. However, if this is not possible and we require further information in order to review your legal matter, our mailing address is "Virtual Law Office Mailing Address."

Limitation of Liability—No Warranties

"Virtual Law Office" assumes no liability for any errors or omissions in the content of this Web site. We will not be responsible under any legal theory for damages, including direct, indirect, incidental, consequential, or special, arising as a result of your use of this Web site. As stated above, this Web site pertains to the practice of "Your Jurisdiction" law only. Therefore, the content of this Web site is not applicable in any other state other than "Your Jurisdiction."

The general information provided on this Web site is provided without warranty of any kind, express or implied. "Virtual Law Office" reserves the right to change, modify, add, and delete the content on this Web site.

Jurisdiction

The terms of this agreement will be governed by the laws of the State of "Your Jurisdiction." The state and federal courts located in "Your Jurisdiction" will have exclusive jurisdiction over any case or controversy arising from or relating to this agreement, the "Virtual Law Office" Web site, or any services provided by "Virtual Law Office." Each person who registers on this Web site consents irrevocably to personal jurisdiction in such courts with the respect to any matters and waives any defense of forum non conveniens. Furthermore, each person who registers on this Web site is deemed to have knowingly and voluntarily waived any right to a trial by jury in any case or controversy related to this agreement, the "Virtual Law Office" Web site, or any services provided by "Virtual Law Office."

Assignment

The rights and obligations created for you under this agreement may not be assigned to any other party.

Force Majeure

"Virtual Law Office" will not be deemed to be in breach of this agreement for any delay or failure in performance caused by reasons out of its reasonable control, including acts of God or a public enemy; natural calamities; failure of a third party to perform; changes in the laws or regulations; actions of any civil, military, or regulatory authority; power outage or other disruptions of communication methods; or any other cause that would be out of the reasonable control of "Virtual Law Office."

Severance

In the event that one or more of the provisions of this agreement shall be found unenforceable, illegal, or invalid, it shall not affect any other provisions of this agreement, and this agreement shall be construed as if the provision found to be unenforceable, illegal, or invalid had never been contained in the agreement, or the unenforceable, illegal, or invalid provision shall be construed, amended, and/or reformed to be made enforceable, legal, and valid.

IRS Circular 230 Disclosure

In compliance with the requirements of the IRS pertaining to the publication of Circular 230, we inform you that any advice contained on this Web site or in any communication originating from this Web site or this law practice that is related to U.S. federal tax advice is not intended or created to be used, and cannot be used, for the purpose of (1) either avoiding penalties under the Internal Revenue Code or (2) promoting, marketing, or recommending to another party any transaction or matter that is contained on this Web site or in any communication originating from this law practice.

Complete Understanding

This agreement supersedes any prior or contemporaneous communications, representations, or agreements between "Virtual Law Office" and the client and constitutes the complete and final agreement between the parties relating to this agreement, the "Virtual Law Office" Web site, or any services provided by "Virtual Law Office."

Sample Virtual Law Practice Terms and Conditions for a Virtual Law Practice Providing Unbundled Legal Services Online in Conjunction with a Physical Law Office

*(This limited services engagement agreement was modified from the terms and conditions drafted for Maryland Family Law Firm Virtual Law Office, a traditional law practice providing online unbundled legal services (**http://maryland familylawfirm.com**).*

LIMITED SERVICES ENGAGEMENT AGREEMENT

IF YOU ARE VIEWING THE FOLLOWING AGREEMENT PRIOR TO REGISTERING ON THE VIRTUAL LAW OFFICE WEB SITE OF _____ ("ATTORNEY"), PLEASE NOTE THAT THE FOLLOWING AGREEMENT IS FOR INFORMATIONAL PURPOSES ONLY AND WILL ONLY BECOME EFFECTIVE UPON YOUR REGISTRATION ON THIS WEB SITE, YOUR RECEIPT OF NOTICE FROM ATTORNEY THAT HE OR SHE IS WILLING TO PROVIDE LEGAL SERVICES TO YOU AND ENTER INTO THIS AGREEMENT, AND YOU ACCEPT THE TERMS AND CONDITIONS OF THIS AGREEMENT. IF YOU ARE VIEWING THIS AGREEMENT PRIOR TO REGISTERING ON THE WEB SITE, NO ATTORNEY-CLIENT RELATIONSHIP EXISTS BETWEEN ATTORNEY AND YOU AND ATTORNEY HAS NOT YET OFFERED THIS AGREEMENT FOR YOU TO ACCEPT.

THIS LIMITED SERVICES ENGAGEMENT AGREEMENT (hereafter, "Agreement") is made between __(attorney name/law firm name and address)_____ and Client, the person registering hereunder. It is intended to meet the lawful goals of Client and to state the respective parties' rights and obligations.

1. Importance of Review of this Agreement

It is crucial that Client carefully review all terms included in this Agreement. If Client is uncertain about the meaning of any aspect of this Agreement or wishes to discuss the Agreement, Client may contact Attorney by electronic message as provided on this Virtual Law Office Web site prior to registration.

2. Nature and Scope of the Services to Be Provided

Attorney's online services to unrepresented litigants do not purport to provide physical legal representation or commence litigation on behalf of limited service clients. The purpose of Attorney's limited representation under this Agreement is to provide for limited legal advice and counseling charged to Client with prompt service provided in a cost-effective manner. Limited services provided by Attorney pursuant to this Agreement are based entirely on information provided by Client to Attorney.

The Agreement to provide legal services to Client covers the time period from which both Client and Attorney accept this Agreement and Attorney receives Client's payment through Attorney's funds transfer service to the time Attorney has provided Client with the services provided for under the Agreement. After the provision of services provided for under this Agreement, Attorney will no longer act as Client's attorney and any attorney-client relationship will terminate.

While Attorney will provide information regarding proper filing and serving of documents provided for under this Agreement, Client agrees that it remains Client's full responsibility, unless Client retains counsel other than Attorney, to proceed as an unrepresented litigant by filing any and all legal documents in accordance with legal requirements, including court filing deadlines, statutes of limitation, and proper service of documents. Attorney has not agreed to confirm that Client has properly served, filed, or undertaken other necessary actions regarding the forms completed under this Agreement. Attorney has not agreed to attend a hearing or trial on Client's behalf or provide any legal services extending beyond those services which Client has purchased under this Agreement. After performing the services provided for under this Agreement, Attorney has no further obligation to Client unless mandated by the Rules of Professional Conduct provided by the State Bar in which the Attorney is licensed.

Limited services provided by Attorney under this Agreement neither obligates Attorney to note representation as "of record" orally or in writing in any Court nor to represent Client in any court or other legal proceeding whatsoever. Client acknowledges that Attorney is not obligated to sign any pleadings or papers nor communicate with any attorney who represents an opposing party in this matter, nor with an opposing party if that party is not represented by counsel in the matter.

If at any time limited legal services cannot reasonably or competently be undertaken in light of Client's specific legal needs and thus requires the engagement of a full-service law firm, Attorney will advise Client of the need for full-service representation. No fees will be due and owing for services as set forth in this Agreement as no services will have been provided.

As with any legal service, Attorney cannot guarantee any legal outcome.

3. Benefits of Full Representation
Client at any time has the alternative of seeking to retain full-service representation, which would provide Client with the benefit of a comprehensive range of legal services. While services to be provided under this Agreement are designed to be a cost-effective alternative to full-legal services, these services are no substitute for the benefits of full-service representation.

Client understands that at any time during the relationship provided for under this Agreement, Client may decide to retain full-service representation. If so, Client may seek the assistance of Attorney, any other private attorney, or any free legal services if available under such service's applicable income guidelines and other limitations. If Client elects to retain full-service representation from Attorney or any other attorney after Attorney has completed and Client has taken delivery of, legal services under this Agreement, Client expressly agrees to honor Client's payment obligations as set forth herein.

Attorney makes no representations that Attorney will agree to provide Client with full-service legal representation. In the event that Attorney and Client agree that Attorney will provide full-service representation, Attorney will provide Client with another agreement separate and apart from this Agreement, which separate agreement will detail the scope of Attorney's representation and the basis or rate of the fee and expenses for which client will be responsible.

Having been fully advised of the importance, benefits, and means of obtaining legal counsel for full-service representation and having specifically declined at this time to enter into an Agreement with Attorney or another attorney undertaking such full-service representation, Client hereby gives informed consent to the provision of the limited legal services provided for under this Agreement.

4. Fees

Services pursuant to this Agreement will be provided by Attorney at the rates set forth and agreed upon during the separate price quote process within the Virtual Law Office. After the legal services contracted for herein have been completed, but before Client takes delivery of the final legal services, Client will pay the agreed-upon price, which will be confirmed through a Cardholder Information Security Program (CISP)–compliant credit card processor. This Agreement constitutes Client's informed consent in writing that at the time of the payment of this fee, this fee has been earned by Attorney, is nonrefundable, and the fee is the property of Attorney at the time of its transfer to Attorney. Upon payment of the agreed-upon fee, Attorney will promptly make the agreed-upon legal services accessible to Client on Client's personal home page. Attorney will not pay any costs associated with Client's case that may be required as part of a lawsuit, including but not limited to, filing fees, or service of process fees. Upon Attorney's completion of services provided for under this Agreement, no further payment from Client will be due.

5. Services Solely Limited to _____—Content of Web Site

Attorney is only licensed to practice law in the State of _____. Attorney's Web site is not intended as an advertisement or solicitation by Attorney for legal services in any state or jurisdiction other than _____. Attorney maintains this Web site but links posted on this Web site to other Web sites are provided only as a convenience and Attorney assumes no responsibility for the content, security, or reliability of any Web sites to which Attorney has posted links.

Any articles for general knowledge published on this Web site do not constitute legal advice regarding a specific legal problem Client may have. Client must not rely on this general information without first communicating with Attorney or other counsel regarding Client's specific matter. Spamming, the unsolicited broadcasts of e-mail addresses or links in this Web site, is prohibited and unauthorized.

The individual responsible for the content of this Virtual Law Office (VLO) is <u>Attorney/Law Firm name</u>.

6. Confidentiality—Security—Retention of Records

In compliance with the professional rules and restrictions of the _____ State Bar and the _____ Rules of Professional

Conduct, Attorney is bound by stringent professional standards of confidentiality. Any information received by Attorney from Client is held in strict confidence and is not released to anyone outside of this practice, unless Client gives informed consent or as provided for under applicable law. All Client's records are securely retained in electronic files, along with secure backups, for the period of years required under _____ law.

Primary communications are done through this Web site over secure HTTP, which provides Client with the highest industry standard protection available on the Web. All payments are processed by CISP-compliant credit card processors, and no credit card or payment account numbers are stored on our servers. Those responsible for the maintenance of this site use secure programming techniques and best practices along with continual code auditing to ensure that this site is as secure as possible.

7. Copyright

Attorney claims copyright protection on all of the content provided in this Web site. The content from this Web site may not be reproduced, copied, or redistributed in any form without the express permission of Attorney. The content from this Web site cannot be modified nor can it be used for commercial purposes. Each document posted at this Web site and that has been authored by <u>Attorney/Law Firm Name</u> shall contain the following copyright notice:

© Copyright 2010. <u>Attorney/Law Firm Name</u>. All rights reserved.

8. Web Tracking: Cookies and Information Collection
A. *General Site*

To view articles and public documents on this virtual law office, a Potential Client does not need to reveal any personal information. This site will present Potential Client's browser with the option of accepting JavaScript and cookies in order to lay out the Web page correctly and to store customized settings for the next visit. These features may be disabled by a Potential Client's browser. However, this will limit the look and functionality of the virtual law office. All page requests are logged in order to properly maintain the service and security of this virtual law office.

B. *Virtual Law Office*

In order to use the virtual law office, a Potential Client must first register a username and provide personal information about him- or herself. This information may then be used during Client's transactions with Attorney solely to provide limited legal services under this Agreement and to assess whether Attorney can provide reasonably competent representation under the terms of this Agreement. This site uses cookies to store a session ID. Therefore, in order to register on the Web site, cookies must be enabled so that Attorney can provide a secure transaction

C. Registration

In order to retain the form completion services Attorney provides to clients, a Potential Client must register on Attorney's Web site. There will be no fee charged for registration on this Web site. By registering, Potential Clients receive access to a personal information page, where they may request our services in a secure manner. By registering on our Web site, Potential Client is representing that Potential Client is at least 18 years of age and able to enter into a binding contract with Attorney. Furthermore, by registering, Potential Clients represent that the information they provide is correct, accurate, and updated.

D. Reviewing and Updating Client's Personal Content

Attorney requests that Client keep personal contact information current. After registering on Attorney's Web site, Client may enter Client's personal information page at any time to review and update Client's personal information.

E. Contact Information

Attorney prefers that Client provide information using the technology provided for on Client's personal client login page. However, if this is not possible and Attorney requires further information in order to review Client's legal matter, Attorney's business mailing address is:

_____.

9. Extent of Liability

Attorney will not be responsible under any legal theory for damages, including direct, indirect, incidental, consequential, or special, arising as a result of Client's use of this Web site except insofar that nothing in this paragraph or Agreement shall in any way be construed as limiting Attorney's professional liability regarding any legal services rendered and/or contracted for under this Agreement.

The general information provided on this Web site is provided without warranty of any kind, express or implied. Attorney reserves the right to change, modify, add, and delete the content on this Web site.

10. Jurisdiction

The terms of this Agreement will be governed by the laws of the State of _____. The state and federal courts located in the State of _____ or such other binding arbitration entity as is otherwise agreed to between Attorney and Client will have exclusive jurisdiction over any case or controversy arising from or relating to this agreement, the Web site, blog, or any services provided by Attorney. Client consents irrevocably to personal jurisdiction in such courts with respect to any matters and waives any defense of forum non conveniens.

11. Assignment

The rights and obligations created for Client under this agreement may not be assigned to any other party.

12. Force Majeure

Attorney will not be deemed to be in breach of this Agreement for any delay or failure in performance caused by reasons out of its reasonable control, including acts of God or a public enemy; natural calamities; failure of a third party to perform; changes in the laws or regulations; actions of any civil, military, or regulatory authority; power outage or other disruptions of communication methods; or any other cause that would be out of the reasonable control of the Attorney.

13. Severance

In the event that one or more of the provisions of this Agreement shall be found unenforceable, illegal, or invalid, it shall not affect any other provisions of this Agreement, and this Agreement shall be construed as if the provision found to be unenforceable, illegal, or invalid had never been contained in the Agreement, or the unenforceable, illegal, or invalid provision shall be construed, amended, and/or reformed to be made enforceable, legal, and valid.

14. IRS Circular 230 Disclosure

In compliance with the requirements of the IRS pertaining to the publication of Circular 230, Attorney informs Client that any advice contained on this Web site, the blog, or in any communication originating from this Web site or this law practice that is related to U.S. federal tax advice is not intended or created to be used, and cannot be used, for the purpose of (1) either avoiding penalties under the Internal Revenue Code or (2) promoting, marketing, or recommending to another party any transaction or matter that is contained on this Web site or in any communication originating from this law practice.

15. Complete Understanding

This agreement supersedes any prior or contemporaneous communications, representations, or agreements between Attorney and Client and constitutes the complete and final agreement between the parties relating to this agreement, the Web site, blog, or any other services provided by Attorney.

This Agreement contains the entire Agreement of the parties. No other agreement, statement, or promises made on or before the effective date of this Agreement will be binding on the parties.

This Agreement, and all terms herein, may only be modified by subsequent written agreement of the parties, signed by both of them.

The effective date of this Agreement will be the date when both Attorney and Client have conveyed assent to it by indicating acceptance, verified with the time and date stamp of each party. This Agreement will not be fully executed until acceptance is confirmed by Attorney.

By clicking on "I accept" below, Client agrees to the Terms and Conditions set forth herein.

SaaS Providers and Products for Delivering Legal Services to Clients Online

Go online to **www.virtuallawpracticebook.com** to see an updated, categorized list of SaaS providers and products that may be used for eLawyering and to deliver legal services online.

Further Reading

Granat, Richard. "eLawyering for a Competitive Advantage—How to Earn Legal Fees While You Sleep," ABA eLawyering Task Force Web site, **http://meetings.abanet.org/webupload/commupload/EP024500/related resources/eLawyering_for_Competitive_Advantage.pdf** (accessed March 31, 2010).

Hornsby, William. "Improving the Delivery of Affordable Legal Services through the Internet: A Blueprint for the Shift to a Digital Paradigm," **http://www.abanet.org/legalservices/delivery/deltech.html** (accessed March 31, 2010).

Kennedy, Dennis, and Tom Mighell. *The Lawyer's Guide to Collaboration Tools and Technologies* (Chicago: ABA, 2009).

Lauritsen, Marc. *The Lawyer's Guide to Working Smarter with Knowledge Tools* (Chicago: ABA, 2010).

Mountain, Darryl, "Could New Technologies Cause Great Law Firms to Fail?" *Journal of Information, Law and Technology (JILT)* 1 (2001).

Susskind, Richard. *The End of Lawyers? Rethinking the Nature of Legal Services* (London: Oxford University Press, 2008).

State Bar Ethics and Advisory Opinions and Other Resources by Topic

The goal of this section is to provide resources for lawyers to review the ethics and advisory opinions of other state bars that relate to virtual law practice and other forms of eLawyering that relate to delivering legal services online. The following is by no means an exhaustive record of state bar ethics and advisory opinions related to aspects of eLawyering and virtual law practice. It is categorized by topic and listed in alphabetical order by state. Excerpts from several opinions have been included because they directly address virtual law practice and delivering legal services online. Other opinions are those relied upon for guidance because they relate to methods of eLawyering but do not specifically discuss virtual law practice. Opinions related to lawyer online advertising, online directories, and referral services were not included in this list unless they were mentioned in opinions related to Web site content. Other related ABA resources are also included.

This resource will be added to as new opinions and guidelines are issued and may be found at **http://www.virtuallawpracticebook.com**.

Advisory Opinions by Topic
A. *Delivering Legal Services Online*
"Suggested Minimum Requirements for Law Firms Delivering Legal Services Online," ABA LPM eLawyering Task Force (October 15, 2009),

http://meetings.abanet.org/webupload/commupload/EP024500/related resources/Minimum_Requirements_for_Lawyers_2009_10_24.pdf (accessed March 4, 2010).

"Draft Suggested Minimum Requirements for Law Firms Delivering Legal Services Online," published for the purpose of accepting comments by the ABA LPM eLawyering Task Force (October 2009), **http://meetings .abanet.org/webupload/commupload/EP024500/relatedresources/ Minimum_Requirements_for_Lawyers_2009_10_24.pdf** (accessed May 28, 2010).

Florida State Bar Opinion 00-4, FL Eth. Op. 00-4, 2000 WL 1505453, (Fla.St.Bar Assn.), (July 15, 2000):

> An attorney may provide legal services over the Internet, through the attorney's law firm, on matters not requiring in-person consultation or court appearances. All rules of professional conduct apply, including competence, communication, conflicts of interest, and confidentiality. An attorney may communicate with the client using unencrypted e-mail under most circumstances. If a matter cannot be handled over the Internet because of its complexity, the matter must be declined.
>
> **RPC:** 4-1.1, 4-1.6, 4-1.7 through 4-1.12, 4-5.3, 4-5.5(b), Subchapter 4-7, 4-7.6(b), 4-8.6(a)
>
> **Opinions:** 88-13; ABA Formal 99-413, Alaska 98-2, Illinois 96-10, New York 709, Ohio 99-2 and 99-9, South Carolina 94-27 and 97-08, Vermont 97-5
>
> **Cases:** *In re the Joint Petition of The Florida Bar and Raymond James and Associate*, 215 So. 2d 613 (Fla. 1968); *The Florida Bar v. Consolidated Business and Legal Forms*, 386 So. 2d 797 (Fla. 1980)
>
> A member of The Florida Bar has requested an advisory ethics opinion. The inquiring attorney would like to provide limited, on-line legal services to Florida residents on simple matters not requiring office visits or court appearances. The inquiring attorney contemplates that these services would include simple wills, incorporation papers, real estate contracts, residential leases and uncontested marital agreements. Documents would be generated at the client's option and the attorney would charge a fee less than the customary in-office charges. The documents would be reviewed by the inquiring attorney or another attorney authorized to provide legal services in Florida rather than by a paralegal or other nonlawyer. Charges would be made via credit card on a secure

server. The inquiring attorney will not charge for simple forms obtainable elsewhere without cost and anticipates providing links to other sites, including The Florida Bar and the Florida Secretary of State, where those forms may be accessed directly. The inquiring attorney asks if there are ethical limitations on offering such a legal service via the Internet.

There is no express provision in the Rules of Professional Conduct that prohibit the inquiring attorney from practicing law through the Internet. As noted by the New York State Bar Association Committee on Professional Ethics in its Opinion 709, it is permissible to practice over the Internet as long as the attorney complies with the ethics rules. See also Ohio Ethics Opinion 99-9 and South Carolina Ethics Opinion 94-27. In other words, the inquiring attorney would be held to the requirements of all of the Rules of Professional Conduct. For instance, the inquiring attorney must have a conflict screening process to avoid conflicts of interest under Rules 4-1.7 through 4-1.12. The name of the responsible attorney must also be identified. The inquiring attorney also must ensure client confidentiality under Rule 4-1.6. While the Professional Ethics Committee has yet to issue an opinion on the confidentiality implications of using e-mail to communicate with clients, almost all of the jurisdictions that have considered the issue have decided that an attorney does not violate the duty of confidentiality by sending unencrypted e-mail. However, these opinions also generally conclude that an attorney should consult with the client and follow the client's instructions before transmitting highly sensitive information by e-mail. See, e.g., ABA Formal Opinion 99-413, Alaska Ethics Opinion 98-2, Vermont Ethics Opinion 97-5, Illinois Ethics Opinion 96-10, South Carolina Ethics Opinion 97-08, and Ohio Ethics Opinion 99-2. Thus, sending the e-mail unencrypted would not be an ethical violation under normal circumstances.

Of course, the inquiring attorney is obligated to provide competent representation to these clients under Rule 4-1.1. Thus, if the client's situation is too complex to be easily handled over the Internet, the inquiring attorney must so inform the client. If the client is then unwilling to meet in person with the inquiring attorney, the inquiring attorney must decline the representation or, if representation has already begun, to withdraw.

Any work done by the inquiring attorney's nonlawyer employees must be supervised by the attorney as required by Rule 4-5.3 to ensure that the nonlawyer employee's conduct is compatible with the professional obligations of the inquiring attorney.

As the inquiring attorney's proposal involves the practice of law, the inquiring attorney can only perform the services through the attorney's law firm. Florida attorneys are not permitted to practice law through a corporate entity other than a professional service corporation, professional association or a professional limited liability company. See, Rule 4-8.6(a) and Florida Ethics Opinion 88-13. Practicing law through a regular corporation implicates the unlicensed practice of law and would result in the inquiring attorney violating Rule 4-5.5(b). See also, *In re the Joint Petition of The Florida Bar and Raymond James and Associate*, 215 So. 2d 613 (Fla. 1968) and *The Florida Bar v. Consolidated Business and Legal Forms*, 386 So. 2d 797 (Fla. 1980).

Regarding a related issue, the inquiring attorney, in order to avoid misleading appearances and to avoid any unlicensed practice of law in other jurisdictions, should indicate that the attorney can only answer questions limited to Florida law. If the inquiring attorney is admitted to practice in any other jurisdictions, the attorney should contact those jurisdictions to determine whether this proposal would meet the requirements of their rules.

Finally, the inquiring attorney's website must comply with the provisions of Rule 4-7.6(b). Any other advertising of the inquiring attorney's Internet practice must comply with the advertising rules found in subchapter 4-7 of the Rules Regulating The Florida Bar.

In conclusion, the inquiring attorney's proposal is permissible as part of the attorney's law practice through the attorney's law firm. As the proposal involves the practice of law, the inquiring attorney owes Internet clients all the ethical duties contained in the Rules of Professional Conduct.

[Revised: 06-23-2009]

New York State Bar Association Committee on Professional Ethics Opinion 709, NY Eth. Op. 709, 1998 WL 957924, (N.Y.St.Bar.Assn.Comm.Prof.Eth.) (September 16, 1998), **http://www.nysba.org/AM/Template.cfm?Section= Ethics_Opinions&CONTENTID=6317&TEMPLATE=/CM/ContentDisplay .cfm** (accessed on February 22, 2010)

North Carolina Bar 2010 Proposed Formal Ethics Opinion 7, "Subscribing to Software as a Service While Fulfilling the Duties of Confidentiality and Preservation of Client Property" (April 15, 2010), *North Carolina State Bar Journal*, Summer 2010, Volume 15, Number 2.

North Carolina Bar 2005 Formal Ethics Opinion 10, "Virtual Law Practice and Unbundled Legal Services," 2005 NC Eth. Op 10, 2006 WL 980309, (N.C.St.Bar.) (January 20, 2006) **http://www.ncbar.com/ethics/ethics .asp?page=3&from=1/2006&to=6/2006** (accessed February 22, 2010):

January 20, 2006

Virtual Law Practice and Unbundled Legal Services

Opinion addresses ethical concerns raised by an internet-based or virtual law practice and the provision of unbundled legal services.

Inquiry #1:

Virtual law Firm markets and provides legal services via the internet under the name virtual law Firm (VLF). VLF plans to offer and deliver its services exclusively over the internet. All communications in the virtual law practice are handled through email, regular mail, and the telephone. There would be no face-to-face consultation with the client and no office in which to meet.

May VLF lawyers maintain a virtual law practice?

Opinion #1:

Advertising and providing legal services through the internet is commonplace today. Most law firms post websites as a marketing tool; however, this opinion will not address passive use of the internet merely to advertise legal services. Instead, the opinion explores use of the internet as an exclusive means of promoting and delivering legal services. Many lawyers already use the internet to offer legal services, answer legal questions, and enter into client-lawyer relationships. While the Rules of Professional Conduct do not prohibit the use of the internet for these purposes, there are some key concerns for cyberlawyers who use the internet as the foundation of their law practice. Some common pitfalls include 1) engaging in unauthorized practice (UPL) in other jurisdictions, 2) violating advertising rules in other jurisdictions, 3) providing competent representation given the limited client contact, 4) creating a client-lawyer relationship with a person the lawyer does not intend to represent, and 5) protecting client confidences.

Advertising and UPL concerns are endemic to the virtual law practice. Cyberlawyers have no control over their target audience or where their marketing information will be viewed. Lawyers who appear to be soliciting clients from other states may be asking for trouble. *See* South Carolina Appellate Court Rule 418, "Advertising and Solicitation by Unlicensed lawyers" (May 12, 1999) (requiring lawyers who are not licensed to practice law in South Carolina but who seek potential clients there to comply with the advertising and solicitation rules that govern South Carolina lawyers). Advertising and UPL restrictions vary from state to state and the level of enforcement varies as well. At a minimum, VLF must comply with North Carolina's advertising rules by including a physical office address on its website pursuant to Rule 7.2(c). In addition, VLF should also include the name or names of lawyers primarily responsible for the website and the jurisdictional limitations of the practice. Likewise, virtual lawyers from other jurisdictions, who actively solicit North Carolina clients, must comply with North Carolina's unauthorized practice restrictions. *See* N.C. Gen. Stat. A7 84-4. 2.1. In addition, a prudent lawyer may want to research other jurisdictions' restrictions on advertising and cross-border practice to ensure compliance before aggressively marketing and providing legal services via the internet.

Cyberlawyers also tend to have more limited contact with both prospective and current clients. There will rarely be extended communications, and most correspondence occurs via email. The question becomes whether this limited contact with the client affects the quality of the information exchanged or the ability of the cyberlawyer to spot issues, such as conflicts of interest, or to provide competent representation. *See generally* Rule 1.1 (requiring competent representation); Rule 1.4 (requiring reasonable communication between lawyer and client). Will the cyberlawyer take the same precautions (i.e., ask the right questions, ask enough questions, run a thorough conflicts check, and sufficiently explain the nature and scope of the representation), when communications occur and information is exchanged through email?

While the internet is a tool of convenience and appears to respond to the consumer's need for fast solutions, the cyberlawyer must still deliver competent representation. To this end, he or she should make every effort to make the same inquiries, to engage in the same level of communication, and to take the same precautions as a competent lawyer does in a law office setting.

Next, a virtual lawyer must be mindful that unintended client-lawyer relationships may arise, even in the exchange of email, when specific legal advice is sought and given. A client-lawyer relationship may be formed if legal advice is given over the telephone, even though the lawyer has neither met with, nor signed a representation agreement with the client. Email removes a client one additional step from the lawyer, and it's easy to forget that an email exchange can lead to a client-lawyer relationship. A lawyer should not provide specific legal advice to a prospective client, thereby initiating a client-lawyer relationship, without first determining what jurisdiction's law applies (to avoid UPL) and running a comprehensive conflicts analysis.

Finally, cyberlawyers must take reasonable precautions to protect confidential information transmitted to and from the client. RPC 215.

Inquiry #2:

VLF offers its legal services to *pro se* litigants and small law firms seeking to outsource specific tasks. VLF aims to provide more affordable legal services by offering an array of "unbundled" or discrete task services. Unbundled services are legal services that are limited in scope and presented as a menu of legal service options from which the client may choose. In this way, the client, with assistance from the lawyer, decides the extent to which he or she will proceed *pro se*, and the extent to which he or she uses the services of a lawyer. Examples of unbundled services include, but are not limited to, document drafting assistance, document review, representation in dispute resolution, legal advice, case evaluation, negotiation counseling, and litigation coaching. Prior to representation, VLF will ask that the prospective client sign and return a limited scope of representation agreement. The agreement will inform the prospective client that VLF will not be monitoring the status of the client's case, will only handle those matters requested by the client, and will not enter an appearance on behalf of the client in his or her case.

May VLF lawyers offer unbundled services to clients?

Opinion #2:

Yes, if VLF lawyers obtain informed consent from the clients, provide competent representation, and follow Rule 1.2(c). The Rules of Professional Conduct permit the unbundling of legal services or limited scope representation. Rule 1.2, Comment 6 provides:

The scope of services to be provided by a lawyer may be limited by agreement with the client or by the terms under which the lawyer's services are made available to the client. A limited representation may be appropriate because the client has limited objectives for the representation. In addition the terms upon which representation is undertaken may exclude specific means that might otherwise be used to accomplish the client's objectives. Such limitations may exclude actions that the client thinks are too costly or that the lawyer regards as repugnant or imprudent.

Rule 1.2, comment [7], however, makes clear that any effort to limit the scope of representation must be reasonable, and still enable the lawyer to provide competent representation.

Although this Rule affords the lawyer and client substantial latitude to limit the representation, the limitation must be reasonable under the circumstances. If, for example, a client's objective is limited to securing general information about the law the client needs in order to handle a common and typically uncomplicated legal problem, the lawyer and client may agree that the lawyer's services will be limited to a brief telephone consultation. Such a limitation, however, would not be reasonable if the time allotted was not sufficient to yield advice upon which the client could rely.

VLF's website lists a menu of unbundled services from which prospective clients may choose. Before undertaking representation, lawyers with VLF must disclose exactly how the representation will be limited and what services will not be performed. VLF lawyers must also make an independent judgment as to what limited services ethically can be provided under the circumstances and should discuss with the client the risks and advantages of limited scope representation. If a client chooses a single service from the menu, e.g., litigation counseling, but the lawyer believes the limitation is unreasonable or additional services will be necessary to represent the client competently, the lawyer must so advise the client and decline to provide only the limited representation. The decision whether to offer limited services must be made on a case-by-case basis, making due inquiry into the facts, taking into account the nature and complexity of the matter, as well as the sophistication of the client.

New York State Bar Association Committee on Professional Ethics Opinion 709 (September 16, 1998), "Use of Internet to Advertise and to Conduct Law Practice Focusing on Trademarks; Use of Internet E-Mail; Use of Trade Names," NY Eth. Op. 709, 1998 WL 957924, (N.Y.St.Bar.Assn. Comm.Prof.Eth.) (September 16, 1998), **http://www.nysba.org/AM/ Template.cfm?Section=Ethics_Opinions&TEMPLATE=/CM/Content Display.cfm&CONTENTID=18862** (accessed February 24, 2010).

Ohio Supreme Court Opinion 99-9, "Lawyer-Client Relationship; Advice to Client; Initial Consultation; Internet," OH Adv. Op. 99-9, 1999 WL

1244454, (Ohio Bd.Com.Griev.Disp.) (December 02, 1999), **http://www .sconet.state.oh.us/Boards/BOC/Advisory_Opinions/1999/Op%2099- 009.doc** (accessed February 22, 2010):

> It is proper for an attorney to place an on-line intake form on the law firm world wide web site that enables web site visitors to e-mail legal questions to the law firm and receive responses by e-mail from an attorney for a fee. In providing such on-line legal representation, the attorney should comport with the Ohio Code of Professional Responsibility and the guidelines set forth in this opinion.

Oregon State Bar Ethics Opinion 2005-137 (August 2005), "Unauthorized Practice of Law: Joint Venture to Produce Interactive Legal Information System," OR Eth. Op. 2005-137, 2005 WL 5679561, (Or.St.Bar.Assn.), (August 2005), **http://www.osbar.org/_docs/ethics/2005-137.pdf** (accessed February 22, 2010):

> A lawyer may engage in a for-profit venture with a nonlawyer to offer a Web-based online legal information system to the public for a fee. The customers will be told that they are not communicating with or receiving information from an individual. They will be informed that they will be asked a series of questions previously stored on the Web site and will be provided with previously stored legal information or forms based on their responses to those questions. There is no human interaction; therefore by definition there is no "practice of law" involved. Opinions 2005-101, 2005-107, 2005-115; Or. Rev. Stat. §9.460; Rule 5.5(a).

Pennsylvania Ethics Opinion 2009-053, Pennsylvania Bar Association, (issued 2009) **http://www.philadelphiabar.org/page/EthicsOpinions** (accessed February 22, 2010)

Review published in the Pennsylvania Lawyer *Ethics Digest* (January/February, 2010):

2009-053

Utilization of Virtual Office

Inquirer sought guidance as to whether operation of a law practice through a "virtual office" would be permissible under the rules. Inquirer proposed to perform most of the work associated with the practice out of an office in inquirer's home. However, inquirer stated a preference not to meet with clients in inquirer's home or to identify inquirer's home address on legal stationery, advertising or other written communications. Inquirer proposed using available technologies and services to support a "virtual office" arrangement such as an answering service with a live receptionist to answer or transfer calls or to take a messages and a local mailbox service providing 24-hour access to mail, package delivery notification, full-service mail and package receiving, mail holding and forwarding, and postal services such as processing of return receipt requests. The address that would appear on inquirer's legal stationery, advertising and other communications would appear as follows:

Firm Name

123 Main Street (the street address of the local mailbox service location) Unit # 456 (the # would be that of the postal box within the mailbox service location)

City, Pa. 67890 (city, state and ZIP code of local mailbox service location).

The opinion concluded that the manner in which inquirer proposed to operate inquirer's law office would comply with the Pennsylvania Rules of Professional Conduct.

First, it was noted that the rules do not address the operation of a "virtual office." Second, Rule 7.5 (Firm Names and Letterheads) does not discuss what type of office/address information must be placed on letterhead or disclosed to clients and does not prohibit the use of a virtual office or private mailbox or similar service as a business address. Rather, the rules provide general guidance to lawyers concerning the manner in which their offices must operate.

Washington State Bar Informal Opinion 1916 (issued 2000), Washington State Bar Association, **http://mcle.mywsba.org/IO/print.aspx?ID=1156** (accessed February 22, 2010)

Regarding a Web site that allows clients to purchase estate planning online from the lawyer:

The inquiring lawyer has created a web site that allows clients to have estate planning documents produced via the Internet. The lawyer states that he has taken steps to protect client confidentiality, including individual client passwords, secure encryption and McFee [*sic*] Fortress encryption program that would run though the lawyer's office. The lawyer asks if these safeguards, in the context of online communications, comply with the confidentiality provisions of RPC 1.6.

The committee stated that it appears the lawyer has taken appropriate steps to protect client confidentiality under the circumstances. However, whether the particular software and methods used by the lawyer are adequate to provide the protections required under RPC 1.6 are questions of law that the committee is not permitted to answer.

The committee cannot analyze your forms for compliance with RPC 1.1, 1.3, and 1.4 since the committee does not interpret the standard of care for practice in any particular field of law.

Use of the Internet to represent clients in a jurisdiction other than Washington is an issue as yet unresolved under RPC 5.5 in Washington. Some jurisdictions are treating such representation as the unauthorized practice of law in their jurisdictions.

Informal opinions are provided for the education of the Bar and reflect the opinion of the Rules of Professional Conduct Committee. Informal opinions are provided pursuant to the authorization granted by the Board of Governors, but are not individually approved by the Board and do not reflect the official opinion of the Bar association. Laws other than the Washington State Rules of Professional Conduct may apply to the inquiry. The committee's answer does not include or opine about any other applicable law than the meaning of the Rules of Professional Conduct. Informal opinions are based upon facts of the inquiry as presented to the committee.

B. *Specifically Addressing Unbundled Legal Services*

ABA's Unbundling Resource Center: **http://www.abanet.org/legalservices/delivery/delunbundrules.html** (accessed May 28, 2010)

ABA Standing Committee on the Delivery of Legal Services white paper, "An Analysis of Rules That Enable Lawyers to Serve Pro Se Litigants," **http://www.abanet.org/legalservices/delivery/downloads/prose_white_paper.pdf** (accessed May 28, 2010)

Alaska Bar Association, Ethics Opinion No. 93-1, "Preparation of a Client's Legal Pleadings in a Civil Action without Filing an Entry of Appearance, AK Eth. Op. 93-1, 1993 WL 849636, (Alaska Bar.Assn.Eth.Comm.) (March 19, 1993), **https://www.alaskabar.org/servlet/content/indexes_aeot__93_1.html** (accessed February 22, 2010)

Arizona State Bar, Opinion 05-06, "Limited Scope Representation; Candor to Tribunal; Fees" (July 2005), **http://www.myazbar.org/Ethics/opinion view.cfm?id=525** (accessed February 22, 2010)

California State Bar, "Statement in Support of Limited Scope Legal Assistance (Unbundling)," (issued 2009), **http://calbar.ca.gov/calbar/pdfs/public-comment/2009/Limited-Scope-Statement.pdf** (accessed February 22, 2010)

Colorado State Bar, Opinion 101, "Unbundled Legal Services," (January 17, 1998; addendum added December 16, 2006), **http://www.cobar.org/ index.cfm/ID/386/subID/1822/CETH/Ethics-Opinion-101:-Unbundled-Legal-Services,-01/17/98;-Addendum-Issued-2006/** (accessed February 22, 2010)

District of Columbia Bar Opinion 330, "Unbundling Legal Services," (July 2005), **http://www.dcbar.org/for_lawyers/ethics/legal_ethics/opinions/ opinion330.cfm** (accessed February 23, 2010)

Massachusetts Bar Ethics Opinion No. 98-1 (May, 1998), **http://www .massbar.org/for-attorneys/publications/ethics-opinions/1990-1999/ 1998/opinion-no-98-1** (accessed May 30, 2010).

Michigan State Bar Ethics Opinion RI-347 (April 23, 2010), **http://www .michbar.org/opinions/ethics/numbered_opinions/ri-347.htm** (accessed June 8, 2010)

Montana State Bar Ethics Opinion No. 900409, regarding attorney sales of "do it yourself" divorce kits, **http://www.montanabar.org/displaycommon .cfm?an=1&subarticlenbr=103** (accessed February 24, 2010)

Montana State Bar Ethics Opinion No. 080711, regarding fixed fees for legal services, **http://www.montanabar.org/displaycommon.cfm?an=1& subarticlenbr=256** (accessed February 24, 2010)

New Hampshire Bar Association Ethics Committee Practice Ethics article, "Unbundled Services—Assisting the Pro Se Litigant" (May 12, 1999), **http://www.nhbar.org/pdfs/PEA5-99.pdf** (accessed February 24, 2010)

New Jersey Advisory Committee on Professional Ethics Opinion 713, "Duties of Attorneys Providing Limited Legal Assistance or 'Unbundled' Legal Services to Pro Se Litigants" (191 N.J.L.J. 302, January 28, 2008) (17 New Jersey Lawyer, N.J.L. 166, January 28, 2008), **http://lawlibrary.rutgers .edu/ethics/acpe/acp713_1.html** (accessed February 24, 2010)

New Jersey Committee on the Unauthorized Practice of Law Opinion 40 (13 New Jersey Lawyer, N.J.L 1311, June 21, 2004), **http://lawlibrary.rut-gers.edu/ethics/cuap/cua40_1.html** (accessed February 24, 2010)

North Carolina 2008 Formal Ethics Opinion 3, "Assisting a Pro Se Litigant" (January 23, 2009), **http://www.ncbar.com/ethics/ethics.asp? page=2&keywords=unbundled** (accessed February 24, 2010)

Utah State Bar Ethics Opinion No. 08-01 (April 8, 2008), UT Eth. Op. 08-01, 2008 WL 2110962, (Utah St.Bar.) (April 08, 2008) **http://www.utahbar .org/rules_ops_pols/ethics_opinions/op_08_01.html** (accessed February 28, 2010)

Virginia State Bar, LE Op. 1193, "Attorney/Client Relationship—Zealous Representation: Propriety of Placing Limitations on the Scope of Legal Services" (February 13, 1989), **http://www.vacle.org/opinions/1193.htm** (accessed June 8, 2010)

Washington State Bar Informal Opinion 1763 "Unbundled legal services; limited representation; subsequent representation of former client" (issued 1997), **http://mcle.mywsba.org/IO/print.aspx?ID=827** (accessed February 22, 2010)

C. *Addressing Electronic Storage of Law Office Data*

Arizona State Bar, Opinion 09-04, "Confidentiality; Maintaining Client Files; Electronic Storage; Internet" (December 2009), **http://www.myazbar .org/Ethics/opinionview.cfm?id=704** (accessed February 22, 2010)

Arizona State Bar Opinion 05-04, "Electronic Storage; Confidentiality" (July 2005)

Arizona State Bar Opinion 07-02, "Maintaining Client Files; Client's Papers and Documents; Electronic Storage" (June 2007)

Florida State Bar Opinion 06-1, FL Eth. Op. 06-1, 2006 WL 2502807, (Fla.St.Bar Assn.) (April 10, 2006), **http://www.floridabar.org/tfb/tfbetopin .nsf/SearchView/ETHICS,+OPINION+06-1?opendocument** (accessed May 30, 2010).

Maine Ethics Opinion 194 (December 11, 2007), **http://www.mebarover seers.org/Ethics%20Opinions/Opinion%20194.html** (accessed February 23, 2010)

Maine Ethics Opinion 183 (January 28, 2004), **http://www.mebarover seers.org/Ethics%20Opinions/Opinion%20183.htm** (accessed February 23, 2010)

Massachusetts Bar Ethics Opinion 05-04, **http://www.massbar.org/for-lawyers/publications/ethics-opinions/2000-2009/2005/opinion-05-04** (accessed February 23, 2010)

Missouri Advisory Committee of the Supreme Court of Missouri, Formal Opinion 127, "Scanning Client Files" (May 19, 2009), **http://www.mobar .org/formal/formal-127.doc** (accessed February 24, 2010)

Nevada State Bar Standing Committee on Ethics and Professional Responsibility Ethics Opinion No. 33 (February 9, 2006), **http://www.nvbar.org/Ethics/opinion_33.pdf** (accessed February 24, 2010)

New Jersey Advisory Committee on Professional Ethics Opinion 701, "Electronic Storage and Access of Client Files" (184 N.J.L.J. 171, April 10, 2006) (15 New Jersey Lawyer, N.J.L. 897, (April 24, 2006), **http://lawlibrary .rutgers.edu/ethics/acpe/acp701_1.html** (accessed February 24, 2010)

North Carolina 2008 Formal Ethics Opinion 5, "Web-Based Management of Client Records" (July 18, 2008), **http://www.ncbar.com/ethics/ethics.asp** (accessed February 24, 2010)

North Dakota State Bar Association Ethics Committee Opinion No. 99-03 (June 21, 1999), **http://www.sband.org/data/ethics/99-03.pdf** (accessed February 24, 2010).

Virginia State Bar Ethics Opinion No. ABA-398 (October 27, 1995). This is not specifically related to online storage but to the related issue of allowing a computer maintenance company to access lawyer's files on the computer and duty to protect client's confidential information in those files.

Virginia State Bar Ethics Opinion No. 1818 (September 30, 2005).

D. *Multijurisdictional Practice Issues*
Arizona Ethics Op. 97-04 (1997)

California Formal Ethics Op. 2001-155, 17 Law. Man. Prof. Conduct 456, CA Eth. Op. 2001-155, 2001 WL 34029609, (Cal.St.Bar.Comm.Prof.Resp.) (2001)

Iowa Ethics Op. 96-14 (1996)

West Virginia Ethics Op. 98-03 (1998)

E. *Web Sites and Domain Names in General*
Note: This does not cover lawyer online advertising, directories, or online referral sites unless they are mentioned in the discussion of Web sites.

ABA Formal Ethics Opinion 10-457, entitled "Lawyer Websites," issued August 5, 2010, **http://www.abanet.org/cpr/pdfs/10-457.pdf** (accessed September 30, 2010)

Arizona Ethics Op. 97-04 (1997)

Arizona Ethics Op. 2001-05, 17 Law. Man. Prof. Conduct 255 (2001)

California State Bar Formal Opinion Interim No. 03-0001 (2005), **http://calbar.ca.gov/calbar/pdfs/public-comment/2005/Prop-Opin-Web-Disclaim.pdf** (accessed May 30, 2010)

California State Bar Formal Opinion No. 2001-155 "What Aspects of Professional Responsibility and Conduct Must an Attorney Consider When Providing an Internet Web Site Containing Information for the Public About Her Availability for Professional Employment?," CA Eth. Op. 2001-155, 2001 WL 34029609, (Cal.St.Bar.Comm.Prof.Resp.), (2001), **http://www.calbar.ca.gov/calbar/html_unclassified/ca2001-155.html** (accessed February 22, 2010)

District of Columbia Bar Ethics Opinion 302, "Soliciting Plaintiffs for Class Action Lawsuits or Obtaining Legal Work Through Internet-based Web Pages" (November 21, 2000), **http://www.dcbar.org/for_lawyers/ethics/legal_ethics/opinions/opinion302.cfm** (accessed May 30, 2010)

Illinois Ethics Op. 96-10, IL Adv. Op. 96-10, 1997 WL 317367, (Ill.St.Bar.Assn.) (May 16, 1997)

Iowa Supreme Court Board of Professional Ethics and Conduct Opinion 00-01, "Internet—Web Site," (September 6, 2000), **http://www.iowabar.org/ethics.nsf/e61beed77a215f6686256497004ce492/5efce8b0ad7413258625695e0067ff37!OpenDocument** (accessed February 23, 2010)

Iowa Supreme Court Board of Professional Ethics and Conduct Opinion 00-07, "Internet—Web Site Links," (December 5, 2000), **http://www.iowabar.org/ethics.nsf/e61beed77a215f6686256497004ce492/09d823189cda5ebc862569b900556679!OpenDocument** (accessed February 23, 2010)

Iowa Supreme Court Board of Professional Ethics and Conduct Opinion 96-14, "Internet: Out of State-Home-Pages" (December 12, 1996), **http://www.iowabar.org/ethics.nsf/e61beed77a215f6686256497004ce492/51c336fb0e7f2f22862564970062c2d6!OpenDocument** (accessed May 30, 2010)

Kentucky Ethics Op. E-403 (March 1998), **http://www.kybar.org/30** (accessed May 30, 2010)

Kentucky Bar Association Ethics Opinion KBA E-427, "Lawyer and law firm domain names (web addresses)" (March 23, 2007), **http://www.kybar.org/30** (accessed May 30, 2010)

Maryland Ethics Op. 2002-18 (2002)

Maryland Ethics Op. 2004-15, "Domain Names" (2004)

Massachusetts Bar Ethics Opinion 07-01, (May 23, 2007), **http://www.mass bar.org/for-attorneys/publications/ethics-opinions/2000-2009/2007/ opinion-07-01** (accessed May 30, 2010)

Mississippi Bar Ethics Opinion 252 (April 22, 2005), **http://www.msbar .org/ethic_opinions.php?id=1391** (accessed February 24, 2010)

Missouri Bar Informal Advisory Opinions 980029 (1998), 20060005 (2006), **http://www.mobar.org/mobarforms/opinionResult.aspx** (accessed February 24, 2010)

New Jersey Committee on Attorney Advertising Opinion 32, "Lawyers' and Law Firms' Selection and Advertising of Internet Domain Names" (180 N.J.L.J. 654, May 23, 2005), (14 N.J.L. 1135, June 6, 2005), **http://law library.rutgers.edu/ethics/caa/caa32_1.html** (accessed February 24, 2010)

New York City Ethics Op. 1998-2," Law Firm Internet Websites," NYC Eth. Op. 1998-2, 1998 WL 1557151, (N.Y.C.Assn.B.Comm.Prof.Jud.Eth.), (December 21, 1998)

New York City Ethics Op. 2003-01, "Lawyers' and Law Firms' Selection and Advertising of Internet Domain Names," NYC Eth. Op. 2003-01, 2004 WL 837935, (N.Y.C.Assn.B.Comm.Prof.Jud.Eth.) (April 09, 2004)

Ohio Supreme Court Ethics Op. 99-4, 15 Law. Man. Prof. Conduct 284 (1999), OH Adv. Op. 99-4, 1999 WL 401676, (Ohio Bd.Com.Griev.Disp.) (June 04, 1999), **http://www.sconet.state.oh.us/Boards/BOC/Advisory_ Opinions/1999/Op%2099-004.doc** (accessed February 25, 2010)

Ohio Supreme Court Ethics Op. 2000-6 OH Adv. Op. 2000-6, 2000 WL 1872572, (Ohio Bd.Com.Griev.Disp.) (December 01, 2000), **http://www .sconet.state.oh.us/Boards/BOC/Advisory_Opinions/2000/Op%2000- 006.doc** (accessed February 25, 2010)

Pennsylvania Ethics Op. 96-17 (1996) PA Eth. Op. 96-17, 1996 WL 928126, (Pa.Bar.Assn.Comm.Leg.Eth.Prof.Resp.) (May 03, 1996)

Philadelphia Bar Association Ethics Opinion 2008-1 (February 2008), Phila. Eth. Op. 2008-1, 2008 WL 1849682 (Phila.Bar.Assn.Prof.Guid.Comm.), **http://www.philadelphiabar.org/page/EthicsOpinion2008-1?appNum=2** (accessed February 25, 2010)

South Carolina Bar Ethics Advisory Opinion 09-10 (issued 2009), **http:// www.scbar.org/member_resources/ethics_advisory_opinions/&id=678** (accessed February 28, 2010)

South Carolina Bar Ethics Advisory Opinion 04-06, "Unless the URL Is False or Misleading, It Is Permissible for a Law Firm to Use a Descriptive Web Address," SC Adv. Op. 04-06, 2004 WL 1520110, (S.C.Bar.Eth.Adv.Comm.) (issued 2004), **http://www.scbar.org/member_resources/ethics_advisory _opinions/&id=593** (accessed February 25, 2010)

Utah State Bar Ethics Opinion 97-10, UT Eth. Op. 97-10, 1997 WL 705482, (Utah St.Bar.) (October 24, 1997), **http://www.utahbar.org/rules_ops_ pols/ethics_opinions/op_97_10.html** (accessed February 28, 2010)

Utah State Bar Ethics Opinion 09-01 (February 23, 2009), **http://www .utahbar.org/rules_ops_pols/ethics_opinions/op_08_03.html** (accessed February 28, 2010)

Vermont Bar Association Advisory Ethics Opinion 2000-04 (issued 2000), (accessed February 28, 2010)

Virginia Bar Ethics Opinion 1842, "Obligations of a Lawyer Who Receives Confidential Information Via Law Firm Website or Telephone Voicemail" (September 30, 2008), **http://www.vacle.org/opinions/1842.htm** (accessed June 8, 2010)

Washington State Bar Informal Opinion 2080 (issued 2006), regarding the duty of confidentiality for inquiries through a law firm's website, **http://mcle.mywsba.org/IO/print.aspx?ID=1553** (accessed May 30, 2010)

West Virginia State Bar Ethics Opinion No. 98-03, "Attorney Advertising on the Internet," (October 16, 1998), **http://www.wvodc.org/pdf/lei/ Chronologic/LEI-98-03.pdf** (accessed February 28, 2010)

Regarding the Risk of Web Site Subjecting the Lawyer to Personal Jurisdiction in Each State

Snowney v. Harrah's Entm't Inc., 112 P.3d 28 (Cal. 2005)

Shamsuddin v. Vitamin Research Prods., 346 F. Supp.2d 804, 813 (D. Md. 2004)

Zippo Mfg. Co. v. Zippo Dot Com Inc., 952 F. Supp. 1119, 1124 (W.D. Pa. 1997)

F. Electronic Communications in General

ABA Formal Ethics Opinion No. 99-413, "Protecting the Confidentiality of Unencrypted E-Mail" (March 10, 1999)

Alaska Ethics Opinion No. 98-2, "Communication by Electronic Mail," AK Eth. Op. 98-2, 1998 WL 156443, (Alaska Bar.Assn.Eth.Comm.) (January 16, 1998), **https://www.alaskabar.org/servlet/content/98_2.html** (accessed February 22, 2010)

Arizona State Bar Opinion 97-04, "Computer Technology; Internet; Advertising and Solicitation; Confidentiality" (April 1997), **http://www.myazbar .org/Ethics/opinionview.cfm?id=480** (accessed February 22, 2010)

California State Bar Formal Opinion No. 2007-174, "Electronic Client Files," CA Eth. Op. 2007-174, 2007 WL 2461914, (Cal.St.Bar.Comm.Prof.Resp.) (2007), **http://calbar.ca.gov/calbar/pdfs/ethics/2007-174.pdf** (accessed February 22, 2010)

Delaware State Bar Ethics Opinion 2001-2 (issued 2001), **http://www.dsba .org/pdfs/2001-2.pdf** (accessed February 22, 2010)

District of Columbia Bar Opinion 281, "Transmission of Confidential Information by Electronic Mail" (February 18, 1998), **http://www.dcbar .org/for_lawyers/ethics/legal_ethics/opinions/opinion281.cfm** (accessed February 23, 2010)

Florida State Bar Opinion 06-2, FL Eth. Op. 06-2, 2006 WL 5865322, (Fla.St.Bar Assn.) (September 15, 2006), **http://www.floridabar.org/tfb/ tfbetopin.nsf/SearchView/ETHICS,+OPINION+06-2?opendocument** (accessed February 23, 2010)

Kentucky Bar Association Ethics Opinion KBA E-403 (March 1998), **http://www.kybar.org/30** (accessed May 30, 2010)

Massachusetts Bar Ethics Opinion No. 00-1 (issued 2000), **http://www .massbar.org/for-lawyers/publications/ethics-opinions/2000-2009/2000/ opinion-no-00-1** (accessed February 23, 2010)

Michigan State Bar Ethics Opinion RI-276 (July 11, 1996), **http://www .michbar.org/opinions/ethics/numbered_opinions/ri-276.htm** (accessed February 23, 2010)

Minnesota State Bar Lawyers Professional Responsibility Board Opinion No. 19, "Using Technology to Communicate Confidential Information to Clients" (January 22, 1999), **http://www.courts.state.mn.us/lprb/ opinions.html#o19** (accessed February 24, 2010)

Missouri Informal Advisory Opinions 990007 (issued 1999), 970230 (issued 1997), 970161, "Client-Lawyer Relationship, Confidentiality of Information" (issued 1997), **http://www.mobar.org/mobarforms/opinion Result.aspx** (accessed February 24, 2010)

Nevada State Bar Standing Committee on Ethics and Professional Responsibility Ethics Opinion No. 32 (March 25, 2005), **http://www.nvbar.org/Ethics/opinion_32.htm** (accessed February 24, 2010)

New York State Bar Association Committee on Professional Ethics Opinion 749, "Use of Computer Software to Surreptitiously Examine and Trace E-Mail and Other Electronic Documents," NY Eth. Op. 749, 2001 WL 1890308, (N.Y.St.Bar.Assn.Comm.Prof.Eth.) (December 14, 2001), **http://www.nysba.org/AM/Template.cfm?Section=Ethics_Opinions& CONTENTID=19004&TEMPLATE=/CM/ContentDisplay.cfm** (accessed February 24, 2010)

New York State Bar Association Committee on Professional Ethics Opinion 782, "E-Mailing Documents that May Contain Hidden Data Reflecting Client Confidences and Secrets," NY Eth. Op. 782, 2004 WL 3021157, (N.Y.St.Bar.Assn.Comm.Prof.Eth.) (December 08, 2004).

North Dakota State Bar Association Ethics Committee Opinion No. 97-09 (September 4, 1997), **http://www.sband.org/data/ethics/99-03.pdf** (accessed February 24, 2010)

Ohio, Supreme Court of Ohio Board of Commissioners on Grievances and Discipline Opinion 99-2, OH Adv. Op. 99-2, 1999 WL 231598, (Ohio Bd.Com.Griev.Disp.) (April 09, 1999), **http://www.sconet.state.oh.us/Boards/BOC/Advisory_Opinions/1999/Op%2099-002.doc** (accessed February 25, 2010)

South Carolina Bar Ethics Advisory Opinion 97-08 SC Adv. Op. 97-08, 1997 WL 582912 (S.C.Bar.Eth.Adv.Comm.) (issued June 1997), **http://www .scbar.org/member_resources/ethics_advisory_opinions/&id=469** (accessed February 25, 2010)

Utah State Bar Ethics Opinion 00-01, UT Eth. Op. 00-01, 2000 WL 543777, (Utah St.Bar.) (March 09, 2000), **http://www.utahbar.org/rules_ops_pols/ethics_opinions/op_00_01.html** (accessed February 28, 2010)

Virginia State Bar Ethics Opinion 1818, "Whether the Client's File May Contain Only Electronic With No Paper Retention" (September 30, 2005), **http://www.vacle.org/opinions/1818.htm** (accessed June 8, 2010)

Virginia State Bar Ethics Opinion 1791, "Is it Ethical Not To Meet Face-To-Face With Your Client if you Communicate by E-Mail or Telephone Instead?" (December 22, 2003), **http://www.vacle.org/opinions/1791.htm** (accessed June 8, 2010)

Washington State Bar Informal Opinion 2175 (issued 2008), **http://mcle .mywsba.org/IO/print.aspx?ID=1621** (accessed May 30, 2010)

West Virginia State Bar Ethics Opinion 2009-01 (June 10, 2005), regarding metadata in electronic documents, **http://www.wvodc.org/pdf/lei/LEI% 2009-01.pdf** (accessed February 28, 2010)

Wisconsin State Bar Ethics Opinion E-00-03, "Electronic files; client's demand for electronically stored documents" (issued 2000), **http://www .wisbar.org/AM/Template.cfm?Section=Wisconsin_ethics_opinions& CONTENTID=48462&TEMPLATE=/CM/ContentDisplay.cfm** (accessed February 28, 2010)

G. UPL over the Internet

New York City Ethics Op. 2000-1 "Duty to Preserve Confidences of a Prospective Client (Pre-Retention Communication); Conflict of Interest," NYC Eth. Op. 2001-1, 2001 WL 1870203, (N.Y.C.Assn.B.Comm.Prof.Jud. Eth.) (March 01, 2001), **http://www.abcny.org/Ethics/eth2000_1.htm** (accessed May 30, 2010)

Ohio Supreme Court Ethics Opinion 2001-2, OH Adv. Op. 2001-2, 2001 WL 417663, (Ohio Bd.Com.Griev.Disp.) (April 06, 2001), **http://www .sconet.state.oh.us/Boards/BOC/Advisory_Opinions/default.aspx** (accessed May 30, 2010)

How to Avoid UPL over the Internet

Arizona Ethics Opinion 99-10, "Directories; Legal Directories; Specialization; Biographical Data; Internet," (issued September1999), **http://www .myazbar.org/Ethics/opinionview.cfm?id=504** (accessed March 30, 2010)

California Formal Ethics Opinion 2001-155, 17 Law. Man. Prof. Conduct 456 (issued 2001), **http://calbar.ca.gov/calbar/pdfs/public-comment/ 2005/Prop-Opin-Web-Disclaim.pdf** (accessed March 30, 2010)

Massachusetts Ethics Opinion 98-2 (issued May 29, 1998), **http://www .massbar.org/for-attorneys/publications/ethics-opinions/1990-1999/ 1998/opinion-no-98-2** (accessed March 30, 2010)

North Carolina Ethics Opinion 2000-3 (July 21, 2000), **http://www.ncbar .gov/ethics/index.asp** (accessed March 30, 2010)

Philadelphia Ethics Opinion 98-6, 14 Law. Man. Prof. Conduct 130, Phila. Eth. Op. 98-6, 1998 WL 112691, (Phila.Bar.Assn.Prof.Guid.Comm.) (March 1998), **http://www.philadelphiabar.org/page/EthicsOpinion98-6? appNum=3** (accessed March 30, 2010)

H. Establishing the Attorney-Client Relationship Online

Arizona Ethics Opinion 02-04, 18 Law. Man. Prof. Conduct 714 "Confidentiality; E-mail; Internet; Initial Consultation; Disclaimers" (issued September 2002), **http://www.myazbar.org/Ethics/searchresult.cfm** (accessed March 30, 2010)

Nevada Ethics Opinion 32, 21 Law. Man. Prof. Conduct 299 (March 25, 2005), **http://www.nvbar.org/ethics/opinion_32.htm** (accessed March 30, 2010)

North Carolina Ethics Opinion 2000-3, "Responding to Inquiries Posted on a Message Board on the Web," (July 21, 2000), **http://www.ncbar.gov/ethics/** (accessed March 30, 2010)

Philadelphia Ethics Opinion 98-6, 14 Law. Man. Prof. Conduct 130, Phila. Eth. Op. 98-6, 1998 WL 112691, (Phila.Bar.Assn.Prof.Guid.Comm.) (March 1998), **http://www.philadelphiabar.org/page/EthicsOpinion98-6?appNum=3** (accessed March 30, 2010)

Vermont Ethics Opinion 2000-04 (issued 2000), (accessed March 30, 2010)

I. Duty to Prospective Clients Online

ABA Model Rule 1.18, "Client-Lawyer Relationship: Duties To Prospective Client" **http://www.abanet.org/cpr/mrpc/rule_1_18.html** (accessed March 30, 2010)

ABA Formal Ethics Op. 90-358, "Protection of Information Imparted by Prospective Client," (September 13, 1990)

Arizona Ethics Opinion 02-04, 18 Law. Man. Prof. Conduct 714, "Confidentiality; E-mail; Internet; Initial Consultation; Disclaimers" (issued September 2002), **http://www.myazbar.org/Ethics/opinionview.cfm?id=288** (accessed March 30, 2010)

California Formal Ethics Opinion 2005-168, CA Eth. Op. 2005-168, 2005 WL 3068090, (Cal.St.Bar.Comm.Prof.Resp.) (2005), **http://www.calbar.ca.gov/calbar/pdfs/ethics/2005-168.pdf** (accessed March 30, 2010)

New York City Ethics Opinion 2001-1, "Duty to Preserve Confidences of a Prospective Client (Pre-retention Communication); Conflict of Interest," NYC Eth. Op. 2001-1, 2001 WL 1870203, (N.Y.C.Assn.B.Comm.Prof.Jud. Eth.) (March 01, 2001), **http://www.abcny.org/Ethics/eth2001-01.html** (accessed March 30, 2010)

J. Accepting Credit Card Payments from a Client

California State Bar Formal Opinion 2007-172, CA Eth. Op. 2007-172, 2007 WL 1721961, (Cal.St.Bar.Comm.Prof.Resp.) (2007), **http://calbar.ca .gov/calbar/pdfs/ethics/2007-172.pdf** (accessed February 22, 2010)

New Mexico State Bar Advisory Opinion 2000-1, "Use of Credit Cards to Fund Trust Account Retainer Deposits" (2000), **http://www.nmbar.org/ legalresearch/eao/2000-2002/2000-1.doc** (accessed February 24, 2010)

Virginia Bar Association Advisory Ethics Opinion 89-10 (issued 1989), **http://www.vsb.org/site/regulation/ethics-opinions/** (accessed February 28, 2010)

Virginia State Bar, Opinion 186A, "Participation in Plan Providing for Use of Credit Cards for Payment of Legal Fees and Expenses" (June 18, 1981), **http://www.vacle.org/opinions/186A.htm** (accessed June 8, 2010)

Virginia State Bar, Opinion 999, "Law Firm—Credit Cards" (November 13, 1987), **http://www.vacle.org/opinions/999.htm** (accessed June 8, 2010)

Virginia State Bar, Opinion 1848, "Use of Credit Cards for Legal Services," a request to revisit Opinion 186A (April 14, 2009), **http://www.vacle.org/ opinions/1848.htm** (accessed June 8, 2010)

American Bar Association Formal Opinion Formal Opinion 00-419, "Use of Credit Cards for Payment of Legal Fees," (July 7, 2000), **http://www.aba net.org/media/youraba/200903/10A%2000-419.pdf** (accessed March 30, 2010)

K. Residency Requirements Affecting Virtual Law Practice

Missouri State Bar Informal Advisory Opinion 970098 (issued 1997), **http://www.mobar.org/mobarforms/opinionResult.aspx** (accessed March 30, 2010)

New Jersey Advisory Committee on Professional Ethics and the Committee on Attorney Advertising, Joint Opinion, ACPE 718/CAA 41 (March 2010), **http://www.judiciary.state.nj.us/notices/2010/n100326a.pdf** (accessed March 30, 2010)

Index

Selected Books from . . .
THE ABA LAW PRACTICE MANAGEMENT SECTION

The Lawyer's Guide to Collaboration Tools and Technologies: Smart Ways to Work Together
By Dennis Kennedy and Tom Mighell

This first-of-its-kind guide for the legal profession shows you how to use standard technology you already have and the latest "Web 2.0" resources and other tech tools, like Google Docs, Microsoft Office and Share-Point, and Adobe Acrobat, to work more effectively on projects with colleagues, clients, co-counsel and even opposing counsel. In *The Lawyer's Guide to Collaboration Tools and Technologies: Smart Ways to Work Together*, well-known legal technology authorities Dennis Kennedy and Tom Mighell provides a wealth of information useful to lawyers who are just beginning to try these tools, as well as tips and techniques for those lawyers with intermediate and advanced collaboration experience.

The Lawyer's Guide to Marketing on the Internet, Third Edition
By Gregory H. Siskind, Deborah McMurray, and Richard P. Klau

In today's competitive environment, it is critical to have a comprehensive online marketing strategy that uses all the tools possible to differentiate your firm and gain new clients. The Lawyer's Guide to Marketing on the Internet, in a completely updated and revised third edition, showcases practical online strategies and the latest innovations so that you can immediately participate in decisions about your firm's Web marketing effort. With advice that can be implemented by established and young practices alike, this comprehensive guide will be a crucial component to streamlining your marketing efforts.

The Lawyer's Guide to Adobe Acrobat, Third Edition
By David L. Masters

This book was written to help lawyers increase productivity, decrease costs, and improve client services by moving from paper-based files to digital records. This updated and revised edition focuses on the ways lawyers can benefit from using the most current software, Adobe® Acrobat 8, to create Portable Document Format (PDF) files.

PDF files are reliable, easy-to-use, electronic files for sharing, reviewing, filing, and archiving documents across diverse applications, business processes, and platforms. The format is so reliable that the federal courts' Case Management/Electronic Case Files (CM/ECF) program and state courts that use Lexis-Nexis File & Serve have settled on PDF as the standard.

You'll learn how to:

- Create PDF files from a number of programs, including Microsoft Office
- Use PDF files the smart way
- Markup text and add comments
- Digitally, and securely, sign documents
- Extract content from PDF files
- Create electronic briefs and forms

The Electronic Evidence and Discovery Handbook: Forms, Checklists, and Guidelines
By Sharon D. Nelson, Bruce A. Olson, and John W. Simek

The use of electronic evidence has increased dramatically over the past few years, but many lawyers still struggle with the complexities of electronic discovery. This substantial book provides lawyers with the templates they need to frame their discovery requests and provides helpful advice on what they can subpoena. In addition to the ready-made forms, the authors also supply explanations to bring you up to speed on the electronic discovery field. The accompanying CD-ROM features over 70 forms, including, Motions for Protective Orders, Preservation and Spoliation Documents, Motions to Compel, Electronic Evidence Protocol Agreements, Requests for Production, Internet Services Agreements, and more. Also included is a full electronic evidence case digest with over 300 cases detailed!

The 2010 Solo and Small Firm Legal Technology Guide
By Sharon D. Nelson, Esq., John W. Simek, and Michael C. Maschke

This annual guide is the only one of its kind written to help solo and small firm lawyers find the best technology for their dollar. You'll find the most current information and recommendations on computers, servers, networking equipment, legal software, printers, security products, smart phones, and anything else a law office might need. It's written in clear, easily understandable language to make implementation easier if you choose to do it yourself, or you can use it in conjunction with your IT consultant. Either way, you'll learn how to make technology work for you.

Social Media for Lawyers: The Next Frontier
By Carolyn Elefant and Nicole Black

The world of legal marketing has changed with the rise of social media sites such as Linkedin, Twitter, and Facebook. Law firms are seeking their companies attention with tweets, videos, blog posts, pictures, and online content. Social media is fast and delivers news at record pace. This book provides you with a practical, goal-centric approach to using social media in your law practice that will enable you to identify social media platforms and tools that fit your practice and implement them easily, efficiently, and ethically.

How to Start and Build a Law Practice, Fifth Edition
By Jay G Foonberg

This classic ABA bestseller has been used by tens of thousands of lawyers as the comprehensive guide to planning, launching, and growing a successful practice. It's packed with over 600 pages of guidance on identifying the right location, finding clients, setting fees, managing your office, maintaining an ethical and responsible practice, maximizing available resources, upholding your standards, and much more. If you're committed to starting your own practice, this book will give you the expert advice you need to make it succeed.

ABA LawPracticeManagementSection
MARKETING • MANAGEMENT • TECHNOLOGY • FINANCE

Google for Lawyers: Essential Search Tips and Productivity Tools
By Carole A. Levitt and Mark E. Rosch
This book introduces novice Internet searchers to the diverse collection of information locatable through Google. The book discusses the importance of including effective Google searching as part of a lawyer's due diligence, and cites case law that mandates that lawyers should use Google and other resources available on the Internet, where applicable. For intermediate and advanced users, the book unlocks the power of various advanced search strategies and hidden search features they might not be aware of.

The Lawyer's Guide to Working Smarter with Knowledge Tools
By Marc Lauritsen
This ground-breaking guide introduces lawyers and other professionals to a powerful class of software that supports core aspects of legal work. The author discusses how technologies like practice systems, work product retrieval, document assembly, and interactive checklists help people work smarter. If you are looking to work more effectively, this book provides a clear roadmap, with many concrete examples and thought-provoking ideas.

The Lawyer's Guide to Microsoft Outlook 2007
By Ben M. Schorr
Outlook is the most used application in Microsoft Office, but are you using it to your greatest advantage? *The Lawyer's Guide to Microsoft Outlook 2007* is the only guide written specifically for lawyers to help you be more productive, more efficient and more successful. More than just email, Outlook is also a powerful task, contact, and scheduling manager that will improve your practice. From helping you log and track phone calls, meetings, and correspondence to archiving closed case material in one easy-to-store location, this book unlocks the secrets of "underappreciated" features that you will use every day. Written in plain language by a twenty-year veteran of law office technology and ABA member, you'll find:

- Tips and tricks to effectively transfer information between all components of the software
- The eight new features in Outlook 2007 that lawyers will love
- A tour of major product features and how lawyers can best use them
- Mistakes lawyers should avoid when using Outlook
- What to do when you're away from the office

The Lawyer's Guide to Microsoft Word 2007
By Ben M. Schorr
Microsoft Word is one of the most used applications in the Microsoft Office suite—there are few applications more fundamental than putting words on paper. Most lawyers use Word and few of them get everything they can from it. Because the documents you create are complex and important—your law practice depends, to some degree, upon the quality of the documents you produce and the efficiency with which you can produce them. Focusing on the tools and features that are essential for lawyers in their everyday practice, *The Lawyer's Guide to Microsoft Word* explains in detail the key components to help make you more effective, more efficient and more successful.

The Lawyer's Guide to Microsoft Excel 2007
By John C. Tredennick
Did you know Excel can help you analyze and present your cases more effectively or help you better understand and manage complex business transactions? Designed as a hands-on manual for beginners as well as longtime spreadsheet users, you'll learn how to build spreadsheets from scratch, use them to analyze issues, and to create graphics presentation. Key lessons include:

- Spreadsheets 101: How to get started for beginners
- Advanced Spreadsheets: How to use formulas to calculate values for settlement offers, and damages, business deals
- Simple Graphics and Charts: How to make sophisticated charts for the court or to impress your clients
- Sorting and filtering data and more

Find Info Like a Pro, Volume 1: Mining the Internet's Publicly Available Resources for Investigative Research
By Carole A. Levitt and Mark E. Rosch
This complete hands-on guide shares the secrets, shortcuts, and realities of conducting investigative and background research using the sources of publicly available information available on the Internet. Written for legal professionals, this comprehensive desk book lists, categorizes, and describes hundreds of free and fee-based Internet sites. The resources and techniques in this book are useful for investigations; depositions; locating missing witnesses, clients, or heirs; and trial preparation, among other research challenges facing legal professionals. In addition, a CD-ROM is included, which features clickable links to all of the sites contained in the book.

30-Day Risk-Free Order Form
Call Today! 1-800-285-2221
Monday–Friday, 7:30 AM – 5:30 PM, Central Time

Qty	Title	LPM Price	Regular Price	Total
_____	The Lawyer's Guide to Collaboration Tools and Technologies: Smart Ways to Work Together (5110589)	$59.95	$ 89.95	$_____
_____	The Lawyer's Guide to Marketing on the Internet, Third Edition (5110585)	74.95	84.95	$_____
_____	The Lawyer's Guide to Adobe Acrobat, Third Edition (5110588)	49.95	79.95	$_____
_____	The Electronic Evidence and Discovery Handbook: Forms, Checklists, and Guidelines (5110569)	99.95	129.95	$_____
_____	The 2010 Solo and Small Firm Legal Technology Guide (5110701)	54.95	89.95	$_____
_____	Social Media for Lawyers: The Next Frontier (5110710)	47.95	79.95	$_____
_____	How to Start and Build a Law Practice, Fifth Edition (5110508)	57.95	69.95	$_____
_____	Google for Lawyers: Essential Search Tips and Productivity Tools (5110704)	47.95	79.95	$_____
_____	The Lawyer's Guide to Working Smarter with Knowledge Tools (5110706)	47.95	79.95	$_____
_____	The Lawyer's Guide to Microsoft Outlook 2007 (5110661)	49.99	69.99	$_____
_____	The Lawyer's Guide to Microsoft Word 2007 (5110697)	49.95	69.95	$_____
_____	The Lawyer's Guide to Microsoft Excel 2007 (5110665)	49.95	69.95	$_____
_____	Find Info Like a Pro, Volume 1: Mining the Internet's Publicly Available Resources for Investigative Research (5110708)	47.95	79.95	$_____

*Postage and Handling	
$10.00 to $49.99	$5.95
$50.00 to $99.99	$7.95
$100.00 to $199.99	$9.95
$200.00+	$12.95

Tax
DC residents add 5.75%
IL residents add 10.25%

*Postage and Handling	$_____
**Tax	$_____
TOTAL	$_____

PAYMENT

❏ Check enclosed (to the ABA)

❏ Visa ❏ MasterCard ❏ American Express

_____
Account Number   Exp. Date   Signature

Name _____ Firm _____
Address _____
City _____ State _____ Zip _____
Phone Number _____ E-Mail Address _____

Guarantee
If—for any reason—you are not satisfied with your purchase, you may return it within 30 days of receipt for a complete refund of the price of the book(s). No questions asked!

Mail: ABA Publication Orders, P.O. Box 10892, Chicago, Illinois 60610-0892
♦ Phone: 1-800-285-2221 ♦ FAX: 312-988-5568

E-Mail: abasvcctr@abanet.org ♦ Internet: http://www.lawpractice.org/catalog